Unless Recalled Ear

DATE DUE

Financing International Trade

Financing
International Trade

James C. Baker

Westport, Connecticut
London

Library of Congress Cataloging-in-Publication Data

Baker, James Calvin, 1935-
    Financing international trade / James C. Baker.
        p. cm.
    Includes bibliographical references and index.
    ISBN 1-56720-622-0 (alk. paper)
        1. International finance. 2. International trade. 3. Financial institutions,
    International. 4. Banks and banking, International. 5. Exports—United
    States—Finance. 6. Export credit—United States. 7. Insurance, Export
    credit—United States. 8. Export-Import Bank of the United States. 9. Foreign
    Credit Insurance Association I. Title.
HG3881.B2533 2003
332'.042—dc22   2003058002

British Library Cataloguing in Pubication Data is available.

Library of Congress Catalog Card Number: 2003058002
ISBN: 1-56720-622-0

First published in 2003

Praeger Publishers, 88 Post Road West, Westport, CT 06881
An imprint of Greenwood Publishing Group, Inc.
www.praeger.com

Printed in the United States of America

The paper used in this book complies with the
Permanent Paper Standard issued by the National
Information Standards Organization (Z39.48-1984).

10 9 8 7 6 5 4 3 2 1

To
David Felt,
my first real teacher

Contents

Illustrations

TABLES

FIGURES

Preface

For the past forty years, I have been a student of international financial institutions and markets. The banking system, and especially international banking, has been one of the focal points of my research. One of the major functions of any international bank is the financing of international trade. The international bank is the most instrumental institution in lending to exporters or importers or providing credits for transactions in international trade, whether that bank is a commercial bank in the United States, a merchant bank in Great Britain, or a universal bank in Germany. No matter what the bank is called, it is the key institution in granting trade credits to international traders.

International trade has been an accepted practice among the nations of the world for thousands of years. The Phoenicians carried on trade with faraway countries centuries before the age of Christ. East Africans plied their trade with India using primitive boats. Polynesians traded with neighboring islands hundreds of miles away in the Pacific Ocean. In the Germany of the Middle Ages, traders met at crossroads throughout the area and exchanged goods. Several of these trading locations emerged into today's cities with stock exchanges now organizing the trade of years ago. These were the so-called Börsen, where specie, foreign exchange, and securities were traded in addition to goods and services.

Discovery of precious metals and the desire for spices and other exotic agricultural products enticed the conquistadors from Spain and

Portugal to discover new lands. Trade has always been a means to integrate cultures and to satisfy desires for strange products not available locally. The early Dutch trading company, the East Asia Company, may have been the first multinational company, and its shares, listed on the Amsterdam Stock Exchange, may have been the first to be traded on a stock market.

As more and more trade took place, nations became closer culturally, politically, and economically. Regional groupings of countries emerged to facilitate more trade and to integrate political systems. Today, we have a United States of America, the most advanced of the economic and political systems. Europe has its European Union (EU), with political and economic integration and, for fifteen countries, a single currency: the makings of a United States of Europe. An additional ten countries have been invited to join EU. In Asia, the Association of South East Asian Nations (ASEAN) has brought national systems together to achieve common economic goals. The same is true for the Andean Pact countries and the Latin American Free Trade Association in Latin America. The North American Free Tree Agreement links Canada, Mexico, and the United States in a system of economic integration. The latter may be the forerunner of a common market comprised of North, Central, and South America.

All these modern day attempts at political or economic integration of national systems have resulted in record levels of world trade. The trillions of dollars of world trade must be financed by some method so that manufacturers have working capital means for further production. Such funding starts with the international financial system of banks and nonbank financial institutions.

The banking system has a dislike for risk. International trade is fraught with a variety of risks. The foreign purchaser may not be able to complete the payments for the goods and services shipped because of commercial problems. Political risk may cause defaults in payments. These political risks may arise from currency inconvertibility, expropriation of plant and equipment by the local government, interference or repudiation of a valid contract between the exporter and the importer, or loss because of violence resulting from civil war, political coup, insurrection, or riots. Public and private institutions are needed to insure transactions against these risks or to guarantee the trade credits granted by trade-financing entities.

This book is about this international trade finance system of financial institutions, public and private trade credit guarantee and insurance agencies, and other public and private associations and firms that facilitate international trade and its financing. The emphasis is on the U.S. system of commercial banks, U.S. Export-Import (Ex-Im) Bank, Foreign Credit Insurance Association (FCIA), Public Export Funding

Corporation (PEFCO), federal and state government agencies, and miscellaneous organizations and firms.

Coverage is also extended to a discussion of selected major export credit agencies from among the more than three dozen that operate around the world. A comparative analysis between the U.S. system, and the operations of representative examples of these foreign agencies is included.

The export credit agencies covered are representative of the several dozen operating around the world. The emphasis is on the U.S. system but the major agencies of the leading industrialized countries are also discussed. These include export-financing institutions in Australia, Canada, France, Germany, Great Britain, and Japan. Leading agencies in selected developing countries are also discussed, including those in India, Korea, Malaysia, and Thailand, as well as multilateral agencies whose business is devoted to regional areas. These include institutions that concentrate on Africa, the Islamic world, and a major part of South America.

The analysis and discussion of this important aspect of international business is intended to be an aid for potential exporters who perceive world trade to be too complex and esoteric an operation for them to participate. A very small percentage of U.S. firms making an exportable product actually enter the world of international trade. Perhaps the information about the U.S. international trade finance system centralized in this book will be useful for these potential world traders.

Finally, it must be stated that trade is the lubricant that breaks down cultural barriers and brings the world's countries closer together. Culture is "the combination of behavioral characteristics, habits, skills, arts, instruments, and institutions that have been developed, acquired, accumulated, or adapted by a certain people."[1] These factors are mixed together and the radical differences are reduced by the interaction of consumers acquiring goods and services globally from traders, who furnish these goods and services from a multitude of different nations. This is the activity that international trade finance is intended to facilitate. The institutions discussed in this work are designed to provide this service.

NOTE

1. James C. Baker, John K. Ryans, Jr., and Donald G. Howard, eds., *International Business Classics* (Lexington, MA: Lexington Books, 1988), p. 73.

Acknowledgments

This project was not achieved without the help of others. Those who assisted the author directly, as well as those who indirectly helped must be acknowledged. My research assistants during the past two years have mined the literature for relevant material. They are Gaurav Bansal and Amit Sinha from India and Frank Fofie and Peter Meso from West Africa. Their assistance was above and beyond the call of duty.

The subject of financing international trade has been one of the focal points in my international financial management courses as well as commercial banking classes I have taught. The stimulation from the discussions of many of my students during the past twenty-five years in these classrooms has given yeast to the project. Some of these students should be singled out. They include Ivan Azarov, John J. Badock, Jr., Margaret M. Bowers, Kathy Caric, Mike Griffith, Gayle L. Kangas, Brad Kauffman, Kyle Koenig, Yingjuan Li, Michael T. Likovetz, Morgan Lockard, Carolina Rubiano, Staci Savage, Julie Simpson, Laurie A. Skul, Ryan Stannert, Jarrod Tudor, Zhengjun Wang, Daniel Ward, Karen Wasiltschikow, and James W. Ziots, Jr. I must single out James Ebert for his assistance with the arcane topic of banker's acceptances, discussed in Chapter 3.

A number of agencies contributed material covering current operations and individuals from these institutions should be singled out for their assistance. Especially helpful were Joseph L. Butler of the U.S. Export-Import Bank and Lesley C. Weldon of the U.S. Department of Agriculture. The U.S. Small Business Administration also furnished valuable information. The assistance of these agencies was highly appreciated.

The editorial assistance I received from Greenwood Publishing Group was exceptionally good and decidedly improved the text, as was the case with my first two books published by them. The editorial staff at Publishing Synthesis, Ltd., especially the copyeditor Nicole Balant, were extremely helpful.

I trust that few, if any errors, have been included in this work. Nonetheless, I take full responsibility for any that were not eliminated.

Acronyms

ACI	American Credit Indemnity
Afreximbank	African Export-Import Bank
AIG	American International Group
ALADI	Latin American Integration Association
ANCOM	Andean Common Market
APEC	Asia-Pacific Economic Cooperation
ASEAN	Association of South East Asian Nations
ATPA	Andean Trade Preference Act
BAFT	Bankers Association of Finance and Trade
CAF	Corporación Andina de Fomento
CARICOM	Caribbean Community and Common Market
CARIFTA	Caribbean Free Trade Association
CBI	Caribbean Basin Initiative
CCC	Commodity Credit Corporation
CEFO	California Export Finance Office
Coface	Compagnie française d'assurance pour le commerce extérieur
CWTA	Cleveland World Trade Association
DEC	District Export Council
DISC	Domestic International Sales Company
ECA	export credit agency
ECGD	Export Credits Guarantee Division
ECOWAS	Economic Community of West African States
EDC	Export Development Corporation

EDCF	Economic Development Cooperation Fund
EFIC	Export Finance and Insurance Corporation
EIS	Export Insurance Services, Inc.
EMC	export management company
ETC	export trading company
Ex-Im	U.S. Export-Import Bank
Exim Korea	Export-Import Bank of Korea
FCI	Factors Chain International
FCIA	Foreign Credit Insurance Association
FEFC	Florida Export Finance Corporation
FSC	Foreign Sales Corporation
FTZ	foreign trade zone
GATT	General Agreement on Tariffs and Trade
GDP	gross domestic product
Gefco	Guaranteed Export Credit Corporation
GNP	gross national product
Hermes	Hermes Kreditversicherungs AG
ICIEC	Islamic Corporation for Insurance of Investments and Export Credit
IFO	international financial operations
India Ex-Im	Export-Import Bank of India
IRIS	International Remote Imaging Systems
JBIC	Japan Bank for International Cooperation
KEIC	Korea Export Insurance Corporation
LAFTA	Latin American Free Trade Association
L/C	letter of credit
LDC	less-developed country
LIBOR	London Interbank Offered Rate
MEI	Export-Import Bank of Malaysia Berhad
MIGA	Multilateral Investment Guarantee Agency
MNC	multinational corporation
NAFTA	North American Free Trade Agreement
NBFI	nonbank financial intermediary
NIST	National Institute of Standards and Technology
NPV	net present value
OAU	Organisation of African Unity
OECD	Organisation for Economic Cooperation and Development
OECO	Overseas Economic Cooperation Operations
OEFI	Ohio Export Finance Initiative
OPIC	Overseas Private Investment Corporation
PEFCO	Public Export Funding Corporation
SADC	Southern African Development Community
SBA	U.S. Small Business Administration

SNKC	South and North Korean Cooperation Fund
SWIFT	Society for Worldwide Interbank Financial Telecommunications
TDA	U.S. Trade and Development Agency
Thai Ex-Im	Export-Import Bank of Thailand
TIC	Trade Information Center
TPGN	Trade Point Global Network
UNCTAD	United Nations Conference on Trade and Development
USAID	U.S. Agency for International Development
USDA	U.S. Department of Agriculture
WTCA	World Trade Centers Association
WTO	World Trade Organization

Introduction to Export Trade Finance

This book is about international trade finance assistance to exporters and the evaluation of such aid. (It is not meant to be advisory about what government policy should do to improve trade flows and national economies; that is the subject of another book.) In the first two chapters, it examines the importance of global trade and the financing of that trade. Chapter 2 contains an examination of the importance of world trade from several viewpoints. Chapter 3 is devoted to the banking system as a major player in financing international trade, with the focus on U.S. financial institutions and methods for financing international trade, both conventional and nontraditional. The next three chapters focus on the major U.S. organizations whose objectives are to assist U.S. firms to export their goods and services: the U.S. Export-Import Bank, the Foreign Credit Insurance Association (FCIA), and the Public Export Funding Corporation (PEFCO). Chapter 7 covers other public and private sources of export assistance available in the United States, and an analysis of the cooperative efforts among U.S. agencies, banks, and specialized firms is covered in Chapter 8. A descriptive analysis of selected major foreign export credit agencies and their operations is the subject of Chapter 9, which also includes some comparative analysis presented. Finally, Chapter 10 presents an evaluation of the U.S. system of trade finance in relation to such operations performed in other countries. Appendixes and a selected bibliography conclude the book.

IMPORTANCE OF GLOBAL TRADE

Many centuries ago, early humanity found the benefits from trading with residents of other countries. The Phoenicians traded with African citizens. Someone stumbled on the theory of comparative advantage and found that specialization in the goods in which a comparative advantage existed followed by international trade with foreign residents who practiced the same economics could benefit all who engaged in this type of trade.

Trade Theories Other Than Comparative Advantage

Theories other than comparative advantage have been advanced to explain why nations trade. During the past twenty years, a new trade theory has been hypothesized by economists. The new position is referred to as the theory of increasing returns. This term is short for "increasing returns to scale" and is synonymous with "economies of scale."[1] This theory holds that trade happens in order to take advantage of economies of scale. Industries in two trading countries can achieve lower unit costs by producing large volume and spreading the high start-up expenses over the entire volume produced. If the countries did not trade with each other and relied on the domestic markets only, they might not be able to reach the highest level of scale economies. International trade will result in the volume, which will produce greater economies of scale.

Such a theory explains why nations trade the same product with each other. Location results in the higher economies of scale. For example, the Japanese and the United States trade automobiles with each other, but the Japanese locate their factories in the United States because of the larger market and better economies of scale. Similarly, car companies locate their production in Germany instead of France because the German automobile market is larger than the French market.

Other Reasons for International Trade

Kim and Kim discuss a number of reasons why such specialization increases production and, thus, national and personal income.[2] Among these are: (1) since natural skills among peoples are different, if each specialized in his or her natural skill, the total of their output would be greater than if both tried to do the other person's skill; (2) even if the skills of each person are identical, specialization is still better because it increases production and so each person's skills will improve from repetition; (3) specialization results in the simplification of tasks because it can lead to mechanization and the advent of large-scale machinery; (4) specialization by each person saves time because neither person loses time by shifting from one skill to another. Other motives for international trade include economies of scale from the synergistic effect when the whole becomes worth more than the individual parts. In addition, the differences in tastes among the citizens of different countries lead to trade that can satisfy these various tastes.[3]

International trade has become increasingly important to the world economy as well as the U.S. economy. Trade accounts for about 25 percent of U.S. and world gross domestic product (GDP). It is growing at twice the rate of any other economic sector. In terms of the United States, one-third of the small firms that make an exportable product and would like to export do not presently export what they manufacture. Of the small U.S. firms that do export, nearly two-thirds export to only one country.[4] The reasons for this paucity in U.S. exporting capability will become clear later in this book, especially in Chapter 3, when export procedures and documentation are discussed.

In short, the international flows of goods and capital that underlie international finance are critically important to the well-being of the world's nations. United Nations statistics show that the ratio of world exports to total gross domestic product has consistently increased since 1970.[5] Much of this growth in world trade can be attributed to the liberalization of trade and investment because of reductions in tariffs, quotas, currency controls, and other restrictions on the flow of international payments. In addition, the advances in communications and transportation facilities and their concomitant reductions in cost have also facilitated the growth in international trade.[6] Much of the trade liberalization has been accomplished by the implementation of several regional economic agreements and organizations.

Regional Economic Agreements

Several regional economic agreements or organizations have been established since the end of World War II for the purpose of facilitating an expansion of trade. The governments involved in these efforts have recognized the value of expanded trade. Some of these blocs have committed to the major objective of reducing or eliminating trade barriers such as tariffs and quotas. Others have gone further and have established political as well as economic institutions. The most representative of these are discussed in the following sections.

European Community. International trade has been the catalyst in the formation of regional economic agreements leading to trading blocs of nations. Six European nations signed the Treaty of Rome in 1957, which established the European Economic Community (EEC). The EEC's predecessors, Benelux, comprising Belgium, Netherlands, and Luxembourg, and the European Coal and Steel Community, comprising Benelux and France, Germany, and Italy, had sought a free trade bloc for coal and steel production in those countries. In the EEC, these six countries formed more than a trading bloc with the objective of free trade among the member countries. They also formed a political grouping with law-making, judicial, and administrative offices and further objectives of the free flow of labor and capital as well. Nine more countries have since been added to the European Community, including Denmark, Greece, Ireland, Portugal, Spain, and the United Kingdom. In addition, Austria, Finland, and Sweden of the European Free Trade Association have had the European Community single market benefits extended to them. Future expansion calls for the addition of ten new members, mostly East European countries.[7] These countries, to be admitted in 2004, are Cyprus, Czech Republic, Estonia, Hungary, Latvia, Lithuania, Malta, Poland, Slovakia, and Slovenia, according to www.eurunion.org/legislat/extrel/enlarge .htm, p. 3, accessed July 8, 2003. Turkey has been admitted as an associate member.

The European Community became more than a trading common market. In addition to the political structure and the free flow of labor and capital, it has also adopted a single currency, the euro, and a common central bank, the European Central Bank (a move initiated by the Treaty of Maastricht in 1992). On January 1, 2002, all member countries' currencies were replaced by the euro, except for Great Britain and Denmark, which voted against the new monetary system, and Greece, which was not ready for full membership. At any rate, this economic and political union has grown with the benefits from a single market for trade, labor, capital, and currency.

ASEAN. In Asia, a group of nations formed another association for the purpose of economic and political improvement. This is the Association of South East Asian Nations (ASEAN). Established in 1967, ASEAN's objectives established at its inception were to promote stability and economic growth in Southeast Asia. The organization has expanded trade with Japan and the United States, but its trade growth among member nations has grown even faster. Its members include Brunei, Cambodia, Indonesia, Laos, Malaysia, Myanmar (Burma), the Philippines, Singapore, Thailand, and Vietnam.

North American Free Trade Agreement. In 1992, representatives of Canada, Mexico, and the United States approved the North American Free Trade Agreement (NAFTA). Since 1994, NAFTA has become the world's largest trading bloc, with 365 million people and $7 trillion of purchasing power. A major objective of NAFTA was to eliminate tariffs among the three countries within fifteen years, or by 2009.

Caribbean Basin Initiative. The Caribbean Basin Initiative (CBI) was established during the U.S. Presidency of Ronald Reagan and is tied into the efforts to develop the nations of the Caribbean area. For example, American apparel manufacturers send precut pieces to the countries in the CBI, such as Haiti, the Dominican Republic, and Jamaica, where they are assembled and returned to the United States to be sold. The CBI format produces marginal exports for the United States, investments in the developing countries of that area, and low-priced clothing for U.S. consumers.

Andean Trade Preference Act. The Andean Trade Preference Act (ATPA) is a program similar to the Caribbean Basin Initiative. It promotes economic development in Bolivia, Colombia, Ecuador, and Peru. It was established under the George H. W. Bush administration (from 1989 to 1993). Its primary objective was to furnish these countries with an alternative to coca production by giving them more access to the U.S. market. (Coca is the plant from which cocaine is produced.)

World Trade Organization. The World Trade Organization (WTO) consists of 132 member nations dedicated to following rules that govern established world trade and economic policies. The WTO provides an arbitration mechanism that settles international trade disputes. A major objective of the WTO is to provide a level playing field for international exporters and importers.

A recent example of the work of the WTO involved a dispute between the United States and New Zealand with Canada over the subsidization of dairy products.[8] The WTO held that Canada unfairly subsidized dairy products sold to the United States and New Zealand. The organization ruled that Canada's Commercial Export Milk program amounted to a banned export subsidy. It further rules that sales by Canadian milk producers to milk processors were made below cost and that the Canadian government had set the domestic price of milk at above-market prices.

Asia-Pacific Economic Cooperation (APEC). In 1993, eighteen Asian nations formed a smaller version of the WTO to promote cooperation in trade and investment among Asian nations. Presently, APEC has twenty-one members, including People's Republic of China, Japan, South Korea, Hong Kong, Indonesia, the Philippines, Taiwan, and Thailand, as well as Canada, Mexico, Russia, and the United States.

Latin American Integration. Two original examples of regional economic cooperative integration were the Latin American Free Trade Association (LAFTA) and Caribbean Free Trade Association (CARIFTA). The names of these organizations were subsequently changed to Latin American Integration Association (ALADI) and the Caribbean Community and Common Market (CARICOM), respectively.[9]

CARICOM consists of sixteen Caribbean countries and Cuba, which formed this association of Caribbean States to develop stronger economic ties among the member countries. Members exporting to the United States give tariff concessions through the Caribbean Initiative, established by the United States.[10]

MERCOSUR was formed as a subregional group of ALADI in 1991. Its members are Argentina, Brazil, Paraguay, and Uruguay. These countries generate 70 percent of the gross national product of South America.[11] MERCOSUR abolished tariffs on merchadise goods traded among members, and a common external tariff was implemented in 1995.

ANCOM, the Andean Common Market, was formed in 1969. It is the second most important regional economic grouping in South America. Its current economic objective is to achieve openness in foreign trade and investment.

African Cooperative Integration. Three major organizations of African integration are the Economic Community of West African States (ECOWAS), the Organisation of African Unity (OAU), and the Southern African Development Community (SADC). Sixteen West African nations are members of ECOWAS, the oldest and strongest African regional group. The total population of the ECOWAS members is 203 million. However, the size and economic strength of Nigeria, one of its members with half the population of ECOWAS, makes it a group with unbalanced power. Expansion of the flow of goods and foreign capital into Africa is a major goal of OAU, an organization with 53 African nations as members. SADC's members number nearly 136 million. Its goal is to encourage foreign investment into South Africa.[12]

WORLD TRADE

Regional trading blocs have benefited world trade by making it less costly through the reduction in tariffs and nontariff barriers and by leading to further specialization and increased trade as well as increased foreign private investment into the respective regions. Several rounds of tariff cutting have been negotiated by the members of the General Agreement on Tariffs and Trade (GATT) since the end of World War II. The objective of this organization is to eliminate nontariff trade barriers and to reduce tariffs as much as possible.

Total world exports were estimated to be US$6.3 trillion in 2000, an increase of nearly 15 percent from 1999.[13] In 1999, they were estimated to be US$5.47 trillion, an increase of 3.5 percent from 1998.[14] The WTO, located in Geneva, Switzerland, pointed out that these regional trading integration agreements can result in faster trade growth, especially intraregional growth.[15]

For many countries, the combination of export and import trade can be a significant portion of their gross domestic product. This is true of nations such as Belgium, the Netherlands, and other European industrialized countries. For the United States, international trade has not been a large portion of the nation's output. However, U.S. exports of merchandise and services in absolute numbers are not insignificant. U.S. exports of merchandise goods and services grew from US$25.94 billion in 1960 to an estimated US$998 billion in 2001. The 2001 estimate includes exports of merchandise goods totaling US$718.8 billion.[16] According to the Federal Reserve Board, U.S. exports of goods and services declined to US$971.9 billion in 2002. Although U.S. exports and imports are not a large proportion of the nation's output, the United States is the leading country in the world in both exports and imports. The United States has not had a positive balance between merchandise goods and services exports and imports since 1975. For the years 2000 and 2001, the balance was negative between U.S. exports and imports of merchandise goods and services and more than US$350 billion each year. The United States has a relatively high propensity to import because of its high per capita income. See Table 1.1 for U.S. exports of goods and services for the 1960–2001 period. See Appendix 1 for a list of the ten leading exporters and importers by country for the year 2001. This table shows that 59.7 percent of world exports are made by the ten leading countries, as are 59.4 percent of world imports.

Importance of Exports

Several reasons can be advanced to explain why companies produce for the export market as well as for the domestic market.[17] These reasons may all be related to a desire to increase sales or profits and to protect them both from being eroded. A firm may desire to serve markets in which it has no production facilities or the local plant does not produce the firm's entire product line. The Japanese saw the United States as the largest automobile market in the world and began exporting in large quantities. These exports became so competitive against U.S. car production that the U.S. government placed import quotas on Japanese cars, thus forcing the Japanese to invest in production facilities in the United States.

TABLE 1.1   U.S. Exports of Goods and Services (US$millions), 1960–2001

Period	Total Exports	Total Imports
1960	25,940	22,432
1961	26,403	22,208
1962	27,722	24,352
1963	29,620	25,410
1964	33,341	27,319
1965	35,285	30,621
1966	38,926	35,987
1967	41,333	38,729
1968	45,543	45,293
1969	49,220	49,129
1970	56,640	54,386
1971	59,677	60,979
1972	67,222	72,665
1973	91,242	89,342
1974	120,897	125,190
1975	132,585	120,181
1976	142,716	148,798
1977	152,301	179,547
1978	178,428	208,191
1979	224,131	248,696
1980	271,834	291,241
1981	294,398	310,570
1982	275,236	299,391
1983	266,106	323,874
1984	291,094	400,166
1985	289,070	410,950
1986	310,033	448,572
1987	348,869	500,552
1988	431,149	545,715
1989	487,003	580,144
1990	535,233	616,093
1991	578,344	609,479
1992	616,547	653,004
1993	642,884	711,675
1994	703,890	800,568
1995	794,433	890,821
1996	852,120	953,963
1997	934,980	1,042,745
1998	932,679	1,099,612
1999	957,146	1,219,383
2000	1,064,239	1,442,920
2001	998,022	1,356,312

Source: U.S. Census Bureau, found at www.census.gov, September 6, 2002, pp. 1–3.

Other reasons to export include: to satisfy the host government's requirement that the local subsidiary should export; to remain competitive in the home market; to test foreign markets and foreign competition at a cost lower than direct investment in those markets; to meet actual or potential customers' requests for the firm's exports; to offset cyclical sales in the domestic market; to achieve additional sales, thus possibly reducing the firm's unit fixed costs; to extend the product life cycle by exporting to a country with a less advanced technology; to distract foreign competitors that have entered the firm's domestic market by countering them with exports to their home countries; to adopt the bandwagon effect, that is, to export because doing so has been successful for other firms; to remain competitive in the home market; to offset cyclical sales of the domestic market; to reduce unit fixed costs by using excess capacity to achieve additional sales; to extend the product life cycle by export to countries where technology is less advanced; to distract foreign competitors in the firm's home market by entering their home markets; and to provide materials for overseas subsidiaries.[18]

Other benefits of exporting can be cited. Of key importance from a country's exports of goods and services is the fact that they furnish the foreign exchange for imports of needed or desired merchandise goods and services. This is especially important to developing countries whose terms of trade are usually negative. Without foreign exchange, a country, no matter whether industrialized or less-developed, cannot purchase another country's merchandise goods or services.

Another important benefit of exports of goods and services is that they can reduce or eliminate current account deficits in a nation's balance of payments. Chronic deficits in the current and capital accounts of a nation's balance of payments will lead to the country's currency being overvalued and, sooner or later, the foreign exchange markets will depreciate that currency in the current global environment of a floating exchange rate international monetary system.

Thus, it is important for a country to expand its exports of merchandise goods and services to as much as its economy is capable of producing without a significant inflationary impact. For manufacturers of export goods, it is important that such sales are financed by some mechanism. Manufacturers must have the sales of their exported goods financed in order to recycle funds into future production. They cannot wait for the goods to be shipped to the importer (by whatever means) before they are compensated for such sales. A trade-financing mechanism must be established that can efficiently finance these sales, enabling the manufacturer to maintain the production cycle.

Almost any product is capable of eliciting a demand and capable of being exported. The exports of two firms in Cleveland, Ohio, are representative examples. One firm had the capability of producing bottle-washing equipment and was able to export large volumes of this machinery to Brazil, where milk and other products were still being sold in bottles. Another firm found a large market around the world for aquarium water because of the popularity in many cities for large aquarium exhibits. Only a special kind of water can be tolerated by fish, and this firm now has a large market for its product.

Less-developed countries. Exports are extremely important for less-developed countries (LDCs). Such sales result in foreign exchange for which the LDC can purchase needed imports. In addition, the production of manufactured or agricultural products that are exported results in tax revenues for the exporting country. For many of these countries, imports are very important. In subsequent sections of this book, case examples of the trade financing of such imports by export credit agencies will be discussed.

On the other hand, many firms manufacturing products that could be exported do not enter into international trade. Some of these firms are preoccupied with the domestic market and lack the resources to develop an international trade division. Some of these firms are reluctant to enter a new activity in which they do not have the expertise. The latter firms are unaware of foreign markets. They are unfamiliar with payment and financing procedures and the documentation required for such activities. In most cases, they simply lack the expertise to mount an export trade operation. Thus, many of them ignore queries from foreign purchasers about their product or service.

A very good treatment of the reasons for entering foreign markets can be found in an international business textbook by Donald A. Ball and Wendell H. McCulloch, Jr.[19] This same textbook is an excellent source of information on the subject of how foreign markets can be entered by exporters.[20]

IMPORTANCE OF TRADE FINANCE

The vast bulk of international trade finance is offered by the international banking system, through commercial banks. Financing international trade is one of the major functions performed by the global banking system. The mechanics of the international trade financing system are discussed in detail in Chapter 3.

More than US$6 trillion of merchandise goods are traded among the nations of the world annually. The vast bulk of this trade must be financed since up to three months or longer may elapse between the time the transaction is initiated and the time it is settled. The manufacturer of these goods must have payment so that the production cycle can be maintained. Without payment, the manufacturer cannot continue to produce the goods. A bank or its counterpart becomes engaged in the financing at nearly every stage. The stages of international trade finance and its mechanics are the major topics of Chapter 3.

Most international trade is made between exporters of one industrialized nation and importers of another. This trade generally requires only bank financing or an arrangement between the two trading parties. A letter of credit (L/C) may be used to facilitate the transaction. The L/C is issued by a bank on behalf of the importer, which promises to pay the exporter when the shipping documents have been presented. The bank essentially substitutes its credit for that of the importer, thus assuring the exporter of payment for the goods shipped. (The letter of credit will also be discussed in more detail in Chapter 3.) Thus, these transactions carry a minimum of financial risk, and such risk is usually the standard commercial risk, that is, credit risk.

A draft becomes part of the transaction and is an unconditional promise usually drawn by the exporter instructing the importer to pay its face amount when it is presented. If the exporter's bank stamps the draft as accepted—and the importer's bank may do this as well—a banker's acceptance is created. Thus, the accepted draft becomes a negotiable financial instrument and may be sold at a discount to an acceptance market dealer, who then sells it to investors specializing in banker's acceptances. The acceptance is held until maturity, when it is then returned to the accepting bank for payment with interest for the period to maturity of the accepted draft. The banker's acceptance will be discussed in more detail in Chapter 3.

Export Credit Agencies

However, some international trade must necessarily be made between parties where one, usually the importer, is located in a developing country or a country where political risk is encountered. Banks that offer international trade finance facilities do not like risk, and will avoid it if possible. In such cases, some type of export credit agency (ECA) or private insurer must be employed to lower the risk to the banking system. These parties may be government agencies or they may be privately owned parties.

More than thirty Organization for Economic Cooperation and Development (OECD) countries around the world have some type of public or private export-financing institution. More than three dozen ECAs do business in these countries. A list of these institutions is found in Appendix 2. Most facilitate export trade for companies in their respective countries only, but some, such as the Export-Import Bank of Korea, offer programs to companies in other countries. Some, such as the U.S. Export-Import Bank, only offer trade finance guarantees to U.S. exporters. Some, such as the Japan Bank for International Cooperation in Japan, offer trade-financing facilities to both Japanese exporters and Japanese importers. Japan cannot survive without imports, especially of raw materials, so the Japanese government must finance such import trade.

Role of Other Agencies

Various government agencies other than ECAs are instrumental in facilitating the financing of international trade. In the United States, for example, the U.S. Department of Agriculture and the U.S. Small Business Administration are involved in trade finance dealing with U.S. farm exports and the international trade of U.S. small business firms, respectively. The work of these and other U.S. governmental institutions operating in international trade finance will be discussed in Chapter 7.

Private Groups

Private groups and associations have been formed to facilitate various aspects of trade finance. In the United States, for example, the Foreign Credit Insurance Association (FCIA) and the Private Export Funding Company (PEFCO) operate to expand U.S. exports. FCIA works in conjunction with the U.S. Export-Import Bank to insure trade credits granted by the banking community for U.S. export transactions. PEFCO uses funds obtained from money and capital markets to make loans to foreign importers for the purpose of purchasing U.S. exports. The operations of FCIA will be discussed in Chapter 5. PEFCO's operations will be discussed in Chapter 6.

In Germany, Hermes Kreditversicherungs AG, a private insurer, acts as an agent for the German government to perform functions for the German exporter similar to those provided by the U.S. Export-Import Bank and most other nations' ECAs. In Great Britain, short-term export-financing activities, which were originally performed by the British Government's Export Credits Guarantee Division (ECGD), are now performed by private firms. These and other foreign ECAs will be discussed in Chapter 9.

Role of Trade Associations

Several trade associations are located in many countries, and these organizations promote and facilitate world trade in many ways. Some of these are city based and some are national associations. For example, many leading cities in the United States are home to world trade associations. Some of these groups are housed in a "world trade center," as in New Orleans. Other such organizations representative of these associations include the Baltimore World Trade Association, the San Francisco World Trade Association, and the Cleveland World Trade Association.

These organizations promote world trade in a variety of ways. They host annual world trade conferences, at which seminars and presentations on case studies about international trade are part of the program. Monthly luncheons or dinners are held at which speakers discuss world trade and the tools that may lead to increased trade. Some of the associations sponsor day-long executive seminars that discuss in detail world trade aspects. Their committees are dedicated to the study and improvement of various areas of international trade by local companies. They sponsor courses dealing with international trade mechanics such as documentation of international trade shipments. Some of these courses are designed to educate individuals who wish to become customs brokers, freight forwarders, and other trade officials.

Finally, national trade associations promote international trade in a variety of ways. These include the National Association of Manufacturers, the Bankers Association for Finance and Trade (BAFT), which is a grouping of commercial banks dealing in international trade finance, the American Film Marketing Association, for an industry that exports a high volume of American movies; and the National Tooling and Machinery Association.

SUMMARY AND CONCLUSIONS

International trade between nations is estimated to be more than US$6 trillion. This international trade occurs for several economic and behavioral reasons and offers a variety of benefits to the nations involved. Foreign exchange is earned with which imports can be purchased. Tax revenues are raised by the manufacture of merchandise exports. A country's economy and currency can be strengthened by international trade. Consumers' demand for products can be satisfied by international trade.

This trade must be financed by some organized institutional system. The vast bulk of it moves between industrialized countries and is financed by ordinary commercial banks, which either lend to the exporter or importer or provide trade credits. Sometimes the trade moves to countries with some political as well as commercial risk. Banks are reluctant to incur the entire risk of these transactions. Thus, export credit agencies sponsored by national governments and a handful of private institutions must step in and guarantee or insure some of the trade credits advanced by the banking system.

As we shall see in Chapter 3, international trade finance was the major function of international banking prior to 1960. In fact, this function was, perhaps, the only international operation of U.S. banks. Trade finance is still a primary source of revenue for many international banks.[21] Other international banking functions added in recent years include eurocurrency operations, investment banking, and global custody transactions.

The remainder of this book treats the entire international trade finance mechanism. The role of the commercial banking system will be discussed. The book then concentrates on the U.S. international trade system, including the U.S. Export-Import Bank, the Foreign Credit Insurance Association, and the Public Export Funding Corporation. Other federal and state government agencies involved in the trade finance process will be discussed, as will private firms, trade associations, and world trade centers, all of which facilitate international trade finance in some way. A comparative analysis of selected major ECAs around the world will follow. Finally, the U.S. system will be evaluated in the light of the major export-financing tools available in other countries.

NOTES

1. Douglas Clement, "Trading Places," *The Region* (Quarterly Publication of the Federal Reserve Bank of Minneapolis), 16 (December 2002): 11–13, 38–41.

2. Suk H. Kim and Seung H. Kim, *Global Corporate Finance: Text and Cases* (Oxford, England: Blackwell, 1999), p. 25.

3. Ibid., p. 29.

4. Donald L. Evans, "The Annual National Export Strategy Report of the Trade Promotion Coordinating Committee," statement before the Senate Committee on Banking, Housing, and Urban Affairs, Washington, D.C., May 14, 2002, p. 1; available on-line at www.state.gov/e/eb/rls/rm/2002/10161.htm., December 15, 2002.

5. Maurice D. Levi, *International Finance: The Markets and Financial Management of Multinational Business* (New York: McGraw-Hill, 1996), p. 3.

6. Ibid., p. 4.

7. Deborah Ball, "European Union Gets Ready to Grow," *Wall Street Journal*, October 10, 2002, pp. A12–13.

8. "WTO Rules against Canadian Dairy Subsidies," *Wall Street Journal*, December 23, 2002, p. A12.

9. John D. Daniels and Lee H. Radebaugh, *International Business: Environments and Operations* (Reading, MA: Addison-Wesley, 1998), p. 306.

10. Ibid.

11. Ibid., p. 307.

12. Daniels and Radebaugh, *International Business: Environments and Operations*, pp. 313–314.

13. Based on data from the Information Technology Section, United Nations; availabe on-line September 10, 2002, at www.un.org/reports/financing/profile.htm, p. 2.

14. WTO News; available on-line September 10, 2002, at www.wto.org/english/news_e/pres00_e/pr200_e.htm, p. 2.

15. Ibid., p. 4.

16. U.S. Census Bureau; available on-line September 6, at www.census.gov, pp. 1–3.

17. Donald A. Ball and Wendell H. McCulloch, Jr., *International Business: The Challenge of Global Competition* (Chicago, IL: Irwin, 1996), pp. 518–519.

18. Ibid., p. 519.

19. Ibid., pp. 41–58.

20. Ibid., pp. 58–67.

21. Jane E. Hughes and Scott B. MacDonald, *International Banking: Text and Cases* (Boston, MA: Addison-Wesley, 2002), p. 105.

2

How Financing
of International Trade
Is Perceived

As mentioned in Chapter 1, international trade occurs because of a number of reasons. The theories of comparative advantage, factor endowments, economies of scale, and product life cycle have been advanced as four major motives for international trade.[1]

THEORY OF COMPARATIVE ADVANTAGE

The theory of comparative advantage assumes that all countries will improve economically if each specializes in production of the good that it can produce more efficiently and buys other goods from a country that can produce more efficiently, assuming a comparative advantage exists between the countries.

THEORY OF ECONOMIES OF SCALE

The theory of increasing returns is a relatively new theory used to explain why international trade occurs. *Increasing returns* is shorthand for *increasing returns to scale,* which is synonymous with *economies of scale.* The theory holds that trade arises to take advantage of economies of scale. Companies in a country can gain lower unit costs by producing large volume and spreading start-up costs. By producing for both domestic and foreign markets, volume can be increased and costs can be reduced.[2]

THEORY OF FACTOR ENDOWMENTS

The theory of factor endowments assumes that countries are endowed differently in their economic resources. For example, Brazil has a favorable endowment in coffee because of its soil and weather, but the United States has favorable endowments in computer technology. Saudi Arabia is favorably endowed in petroleum, while Mexico has lower cost labor. This theory holds that countries are mutually benefited if they specialize in the production of those goods that use a large portion of the factor with which they are favorably endowed and then export those goods.

PRODUCT LIFE CYCLE THEORY

The product life cycle theory holds that all goods have a certain length of life. During this life cycle, the product goes through several steps beginning with production and ending with death of the product. These steps can begin with export of a product but, after the product matures, foreign investment by the producer may replace export trade.

OTHER MOTIVES FOR WORLD TRADE

Other motives for world trade in addition to these four theories have been identified. These include economies of scale and differences in tastes from one culture to another. Mass production and manufacturing techniques can result in increased production, some of which may be exported. Differences in taste from one country to another may lead to increased trade, as it did with the countertrade developed by PepsiCo when it traded Pepsi-Cola to Russia for Stolichnya vodka. Russians enjoyed the Pepsi-Cola and Americans enjoyed the vodka.

Trade may be initiated by the egos of top executives of domestic companies that are engaged in manufacturing a product that might have appeal for foreign purchasers.[3] For example, while I was a graduate student majoring in international business administration at Indiana University, officials of Arvin Industries, a Columbus, Indiana, manufacturer of replacement automobile mufflers, came to the Department of International Business at the university for advice. An Arvin top executive had traveled to Europe only eighteen years after the end of World War II and was surprised at the number of automobiles being driven by Europeans. Arvin had a large cash surplus available for new product development, and the executive thought Europe might be an excellent place to sell the company's replacement mufflers. In this way, some marginal trade in this product was initiated before competition from auto parts manufacturers in Europe caught up. Thus, some trade was initiated by a top executive based, in this case, on personal observation and a hunch.

Global trade has always been a tool for development. Multilateral international organizations have expended much energy in reducing regulations and restrictions on cross-border trade, especially trade between the industrialized and the developing countries. The World Trade Organization (WTO) is one of those organizations. Policy issues among nations concerning areas such as steel and agricultural products are fraught with restrictions, which confront these countries in their trade negotiations. For most developing nations, exports are essential in that they furnish the foreign exchange with which they can purchase technology and the necessities of life.

TRADE FROM THE MANUFACTURER'S VIEWPOINT

Most multinational corporations (MNCs) have significant foreign trade business. They export a huge amount of goods and services to their overseas affiliates. In fact, when MNCs expand their foreign direct investment in plant and equipment, some of this plant and equipment may be exported from the parent company. They may use overseas markets as a means of selling excess inventories. Many of these firms began international operations by exporting or licensing overseas firms to produce and market a product made according to patents or other intangible property rights. Such firms had neither the know-how nor the funds to resort to foreign direct investment. Some firms have exported their obsolete equipment to developing countries, where such machinery may still be usable. Domestic firms are encouraged by their governments to export because of the beneficial results to the country's balance of payments. Export trade furnishes foreign exchange, which can be used to import necessary goods and services or satisfy the demand and tastes of consumers.

Need for Trade Finance

The international trade generated from these operations must be financed. The export manufacturer must be paid for the products exported so that the manufacturing cycle can continue. If the manufacturer had to wait for full payment of the goods exported, it would not have the working capital funds for further manufacturing and would no longer have the goods that were already exported. Thus, some means of financing these transactions must be obtained with some immediacy.

Financing these transactions requires a great deal of capital. The banking system, covered in Chapter 3, is the financing mechanism that fuels the international trade system. In addition to the large amounts of funds needed, a variety of services must be provided to facilitate the trade financing, such as the issue of letters of credit and the creation of acceptances, and guarantees or insurance of trade credits.

Manufacturing firms usually do not have the funding or the expertise to facilitate the international trade finance. The special activities of banks and nonbank financial institutions have been available for centuries to furnish these services to the export manufacturer. A bank or its counterpart is engaged at nearly every stage of trade financing. The bank function of international trade financing has become very competitive. One of the important qualities of an international bank is the ability to provide some type of financial engineering to structure the form of trade finance needed by the customer.[4] These techniques include use of the letter of credit, the draft, the banker's acceptance, and forfaiting as well as the flotation of special instruments in capital markets to fund trade credits; these methods will be discussed in more detail in Chapter 3.

International trade and investment cannot be accomplished without foreign currency. The prices of the tremendous amount of foreign exchange needed to finance more than US$6 trillion of world trade annually is set by foreign exchange traders in these international banks. They trade the vast amounts of foreign exchange amounting to US$1.5 trillion or the equivalent every day. Without this international liquidity, the exporting manufacturers could not sell their goods and services in the international trading system.

TRADE FROM THE BANKER'S VIEWPOINT

The banking system has always financed the vast bulk of international trade. International trade finance is considered one of the five or six major functions performed by international banks. Such banks, especially those in the United States, however, did not consider international trade as significantly important to them until the late 1970s. Until then, trade finance to a U.S. bank was something carried out in the documentary department, and occasionally a bank division would arrange the insurance of trade credits, most often in conjunction with the Foreign Credit Insurance Association (FCIA), the subject of Chapter 5.

U.S. banks then saw the effects from the country defaults on sovereign loans. They recognized that sovereign credits might rise and fall but that international trade continued forever. Trade credits generated fee income for these banks. Thus, when the sovereign loan business collapsed in 1982, beginning with the default of the Mexican government on a jumbo loan, U.S. banks were able to fall back on a solid portfolio of trade finance.[5]

TRADE FROM A COUNTRY'S VIEWPOINT

World trade is extremely important to many countries and relatively unimportant to some, especially when measured against the country's gross domestic product (GDP). For a country such as the Netherlands, international trade is a large percentage of GDP. For the United States, it is a relatively small percentage. When total world merchandise exports are considered in terms of what a country exports as a share of the total, again trade is relatively important to a few countries. The United States exports are 12.48 percent of total world merchandise exports. Japan exports 7.73 percent of total world exports. For Germany the figure is 8.87 percent, for France it is 5.24 percent, for China it is 4.46 percent, and for the Netherlands it is 3.71 percent.[6] All the nations of the continent of Africa combined only export 2 percent of total world trade.[7] In the United States, the government has promoted exports as a national priority. The large trade deficits in the U.S. balance of payments in recent years have given U.S. companies opportunities to export.[8]

On the other hand, many countries have only a miniscule share of world exports, yet those exports are very significant in that they furnish the foreign exchange with which such countries can import necessities. Most of these countries are developing nations, with one or two major agrarian products that they can export. Ghana, for example, is a major producer of cacao beans, the major ingredient of chocolate. Ghana's share of total world exports is only .03 percent, but that portion is extremely important to Ghana's population. Kenya is a major exporter of coffee and tea, but its exports are only .04 percent of the world total. Chile is a major exporter of copper ore but has only a .30 percent of the world total. The twenty largest industrialized countries accounted for nearly 68 percent of total world merchandise exports in 2000.[9]

In short, trade matters to nearly every country in the world. It furnishes the foreign exchange with which countries can import the necessities of life as well as make foreign investments. The United Nations has ranked Canada as the best country in the world in which to live for the past six years. This country is inhabited by only 30 million people. What seems to be the secret at being chosen as a favorable country in which to live? The Canadian Government has cited world trade and international business as the most significant reasons for this perception of the country.[10]

On the other hand, some criticism has been leveled at international trade for its negative impact on job creation. *Trade and Globalization,* an on-line trade publications service, cited a report by economist Robert E. Scott published in the issue brief, *The Facts about Trade and Job Creation,*[11] in which the author states that the effect of trade on job growth during the recent economic expansion was negative, not positive as reported by public officials during the Bill Clinton administration. It was further reported in a citation by *Trade and Globalization* that the 1996 Farm Bill and unstable global markets for U.S. agricultural products hurt family farmers' incomes and the real prices of basic farm products.[12]

DevNews Media Center, an on-line service of the World Bank Group, cited a study relating global trade to development.[13] This report suggested five significant conclusions about trade and development at the present time. First, border restrictions on trade in merchandise goods may be important as national policy, but effective market access is more important, especially to developing countries that are limited in selling their products because of restrictions and regulations. Second, in order for developing countries to improve their access to foreign markets, reciprocal trade liberalization through the WTO is necessary. Third, trade liberalization is only a small part of the comprehensive domestic reforms needed in the developing countries for poverty-reducing economic growth. Fourth, rules governing global trade must be viewed from a developmental perspective if they are to reduce poverty. Finally, external assistance will be needed to integrate developing countries into the global economy and the WTO process.

Globalization

Globalization is a concept that should be considered because of its positive impact on world trade. Globalization is the process that results in an increasing flow of ideas, people, goods, services and capital leading to integration of economies and societies. Greater integration usually leads to the promotion of human freedom because of the spread of information and an increase in choices for consumers.[14]

Globalization is a movement that has different connotations. Globalization eminates from the act of international political, economic, and technological integration among the countries of the world. In terms of political integration, globalization can be measured by the number of state memberships in international organizations such as the World Bank. In terms of technology, globalization can be measured by the number of Internet users, Internet hosts, and secure servers. In terms of economic integration, globalization can be measured by international trade, foreign direct investment, portfolio capital flows, and international income payments and receipts. Personal contact by means of international travel and tourism, international telephone traffic, and cross-border transfers can also be used as a means to measure globalization.

The concept of globalization can be measured. The A.T. Kearney/ *Foreign Policy Magazine* Globalization Index was developed to measure the degree of globalization each country demonstrates.[15] This index includes rankings of sixty-two countries using thirteen variables involving economic integration, personal contact, technology, and political engagement. The 2002 ranking shows Ireland to be the highest ranked country among the sixty-two and Iran to be the lowest ranked. The United States is ranked eleventh.[16]

Other measurements can be derived from the results of globalization. For example, analysts have looked at the effects of globalization since the end of the nineteenth century, when the world had already become internationalized. Shipping costs declined and the resulting rapid increase in world trade caused the ratio of international trade to world output to reach a peak in 1913 that was not achieved again until the 1970s.[17] Other benefits from recent globalization include US$100 billion in savings resulting from the Uruguay Round trade agreement negotiated by the members of the General Agreement on Tariffs and Trade (GATT) in 1995. In addition, real incomes have doubled every 12 years in Korea since 1960, mostly as a result of the trade gains emanating from freer world trade. Spain, Mexico, and Chile have also increased their shares of world trade and per capita incomes since 1980 by participating in globalization.[18]

To some, globalization refers to international trade and investment and their positive effects on world development. Cultural barriers can be alleviated or eliminated, consumer needs can be satisfied, and political differences can be smoothed out. On the other hand, many view globalization as a movement designed to Westernize or Americanize the rest of the world. Global development agencies such as the World Bank and the International Monetary Fund[19] are viewed as enemies of the people. This occurs especially when they finance projects seen by some as dangerous to the environment or when financial support is given to dictator-run governments or despots who keep their populations underdeveloped while skimming the cream off the foreign economic assistance given by development agencies or industrialized nations. Some believe globalization is a means to permit international companies to control the scarce mineral resources found only in some developing countries.

These antiglobalization movements have focused on regional economic groups such as the North American Free Trade Area (NAFTA)

and the European Union (EU) in recent years.[20] Part of these criticisms
are based on self-interest. Labor unions in the United States have
opposed NAFTA because of the fear of losing jobs to Mexico. The
movement against the European Union stems from the loss of cultural
identity, dilution of individual national control as new members are
admitted, overcentralization of power as the EU expands its bureaucracy, and disappearance of national currencies as the euro replaced
them in twelve of the fifteen member nations at the beginning of 2002.
Both NAFTA and the EU are entities designed to eliminate tariff and
nontariff barriers in order to increase exports. Despite the efforts of
these regional groupings, exporters still find numerous restrictions and
roadblocks raised against their exports and NAFTA and EU find some
of the antiglobalization advocates railing against their efforts.

The antiglobalization movement gained more impetus during the
2001 Annual Meeting of the World Trade Organization in Seattle, Washington, when supporters of the movement against globalization rioted
in the streets. Multinational companies (MNCs) have been blamed for
fostering the problem which the antiglobalization movement attacks.
Some critics perceive that MNCs are promoted and protected by the
WTO and, thus, any annual meeting of this organization becomes an
anti-globalization event.

As inferred previously, globalization has been practiced for a long
time, perhaps more than a century. A better case can be made by
development economists that this movement has been more beneficial
for the countries of the world than that it has been detrimental. Trade
has increased significantly since the end of World War I. Global per
capita incomes have increased generally throughout the world. Consumer desires in much of the world have been satisfied by international
trade.

SUMMARY AND CONCLUSIONS

Why international trade occurs can be explained by a number of
theories. The most important of these are the theories of comparative
advantage, factor endowments, economies of scale or increasing returns, and the product life cycle. Other motives for world trade include
differences in taste from one culture to another and the desires of top
executives. Trade can be analyzed from different viewpoints. From the
manufacturer's viewpoint, trade can lead to increased profits. From the
nation's viewpoint, trade can generate the foreign exchange needed for
imports, which can result in economic development, satisfy the needs
of consumers, or alleviate deficits in the country's balance of payments.
In short, trade among the nations of the world can integrate cultural,

economic, political, social, and legal systems, and it has the potential to harmonize national differences. Thus, the positive impact of world trade can be facilitated and magnified by financing.

Although international trade can result in benefits for all parties concerned, it has been criticized for a number of reasons. Some studies have held that trade has had a negative impact on job growth in some countries. It has resulted in unstable markets for some products, especially agricultural goods. One large, well-organized, and vocal activist group has focused on globalization, holding that globalization has had a negative impact on most of the worlds' populations and has been implicated in global warming, harm to the environment, and much of the world's political instability. However, several studies since the beginning of the twentieth century have shown that the economic integration that results from globalization has increased world trade in general and international trade for many countries specifically, as well as increased per capita incomes in many countries that have participated in globalization efforts. Increased consumer choices in goods and services can, in many cases, be attributed to the process of globalization.

NOTES

1. Suk H. Kim and Seung H. Kim, *Global Corporate Finance: Text and Cases* (Oxford, England: Blackwell, 1999), pp. 25–29.

2. Douglas Clement, "Trading Places," *The Region* (Quarterly Publication of the Federal Reserve Bank of Minneapolis) 16 (December 2002): 11–13, 38–41.

3. Yair Aharoni, *The Foreign Investment Decision* (Boston: Harvard Business School, 1966).

4. Peter Montagnon, "Export Finance: A Time for Ingenuity," *Financial Times*, April 20, 1988, Section 3, p. I.

5. David Bowen, "Learning to Be Safe, Not Sorry," *Euromoney*, January 1985, pp. 133, 139.

6. "Trade and Economy: Data and Analysis," available on-line December 13, 2002 at www.ita.doc.gov/industry/otea/usfth/aggregate/h01t53.html, pp. 1–5.

7. Mohamed Daouas, "Africa Faces Challenges of Globalization," *Finance and Development* 38 (December 2001): 4.

8. Julie Brown, "Exports Fly High as Government Programs Offer Financing Aid," *Corporate Cashflow* 10 (July 1989): 34.

9. Ibid.

10. Department of Foreign Affairs and International Trade, "Why Trade Matters," available on-line December 13, 2002, at www.dfait-maeci.gc.ca/tna-nac/why-en.asp, 1–3.

11. Available on-line December 13, 2002, at www.epinet.org/sub-jectpages/trade.html, 3–4.

12. EPI Briefing Paper, "Exported to Death—The Failure of Agricultural Deregulation," available on-line December 13, 2002, at www.epinet.org/sub-jectpages/trade.html, 5.

13. World Bank Group DevNews Media Center, "Global Trade: A Tool for Development," available on-line December 13, 2002, at http://web.worldbank.org?WBSITE/EXTERNAL/NEWS/, 1–3.

14. Eduardo Aninat, "Surmounting the Challenges of Globalization," *Finance and Development* 39 (March 2002): 4.

15. A.T. Kearney, Inc., and the Carnegie Endowment for International Peace, "Measuring Globalization: Who's Up, Who's Down?" *Foreign Policy*, January/February 2003, pp. 60–72.

16. Ibid., p. 65.

17. Aninat, "Surmounting the Challenges of Globalization," *Finance and Development* 39 (March 2002): 5.

18. Ibid.

19. Kenneth Rogoff, "The IMF Strikes Back," *Foreign Policy*, January/February 2003, pp. 39–46.

20. Michael H. Moffett, Arthur I. Stonehill, and David K. Eiteman, *Fundamentals of Multinational Finance* (Boston: Addison-Wesley, 2003), p. 393.

3

Banking and Trade Finance

For all intents and purposes, international trade must be financed, for the reasons stated in Chapter 1. And most or all of international trade is financed by the banking system, whether that is the commercial bank in the United States, the merchant bank in Great Britain, or the universal bank in Germany. Other financial institutions, which specialize in other areas, may also occasionally finance international trade transactions. These include nonbank financial institutions such as savings and investment banks.

International trade transactions are fraught with documentation. Some transactions might have twenty or more different documents that must precede or accompany the shipment. The most important of these documents and their role will be discussed in subsequent sections of this chapter. They include the letter of credit (L/C), the draft, the bill of lading, marine insurance forms, and government approvals, and they include documents for both the shipping and financing part of the international trade transaction.

Five methods of payment are used in international trade: prepayment or cash in advance; letters of credit; drafts, including the use of a banker's acceptance; consignment; and open account. These will be discussed in more detail in this chapter.[1]

A number of methods are available for financing international trade. These include accounts receivable financing, factoring, letters of credit, banker's acceptances, working capital financing, medium-term capital goods financing (known as forfaiting), and countertrade. These methods will be discussed in this chapter.

Finally, banks dealing in international trade financing must, on occasion, work with government agencies known as export credit agencies (ECAs) and private groups that insure or guarantee part of the financing. These relationships usually occur when political risk is present in the transaction where the importer resides in a developing nation or transition economy such as a former communist country.

SHIPPING DOCUMENTATION

International trade transactions involve a number of documents for which the services of a freight forwarder are very valuable.[2] International trade documents differ from those needed for domestic transportation of goods. The most important of these documents are discussed in the following sections.

Bill of Lading

The bill of lading is a shipping document issued to an exporting company or its bank by a common carrier that transports the merchandise goods.[3] It is a receipt, contract, and title in one document. It can be either a straight bill of lading or an order bill of lading. The former requires that the carrier deliver the goods to the designated purchaser. It is used when the goods have been paid for in advance and does not represent title to the goods. The latter type provides that the carrier deliver the goods to the order of the exporter. Bills of lading can also be either clean or foul bills of lading. A clean bill of lading implies that the carrier has received the material to be shipped in good condition. A foul bill of lading includes documentation that the goods incurred some damage before the carrier received them for shipment.

Export License

The exporter needs to obtain an export license from any country through which its goods are transshipped to certain other countries. A country may be under a trade embargo in which trade to that country is prohibited, as is the case at present with the U.S. prohibition against shipments of certain goods from the United States to Iraq. The U.S. Department of Commerce must be contacted by U.S. exporters for such a license.

Pro Forma Invoice

A shipment may involve a pro forma invoice from the exporter to the importer. This document details the selling terms, price, and delivery if the goods have been shipped. The importer will send a purchase order to the exporter if the invoice is approved.

Commercial Invoice

The commercial invoice is a bill from the exporter to the importer for the goods shipped. In it, the goods are described and the payment terms are specified. This form may be used by governments to assess tariff duties.

Bill of Lading

A copy of the bill of lading is given by the exporter to the shipper. It is a receipt for the goods shipped and contains their description. It also is a contract for the shipper's services and shows what party holds title to the goods.

Consular Invoice

Some shipments of exports involve a consular invoice. Governments use this document to monitor imports. It is a means of raising revenue for the embassy that issues the invoice.

Certificate of Origin

The certificate of origin shows where the export goods originated. It is used by countries to implement a tariff schedule for imports.

Shipper's Export Declaration

The shipper's export declaration, when used, is a means of monitoring exports and compiling trade statistics. It is a tool with which nations gather data for balance of payments purposes.

Export Packing List

The export packing list documents each individual package in the shipment and details what is in the package. Shippers, freight forwarders, and customs officials use this document to determine what is in the shipment and whether it is the proper shipment.

Marine Insurance

Documents concerned with insurance of the goods shipped are a necessary item. This is insurance to compensate the owner of goods transported overseas in the event of loss that cannot be legally recovered from the carrier. Freight aircraft sometimes crash and ships sometime sink. Dock workers sometimes steal part of a shipment. In all these cases, the goods should have been insured while being shipped.

TRADE FINANCE DOCUMENTATION

When international trade is financed, the financing may be either traditional, that is, with the major documentation being the letter of credit, the draft, and, perhaps, a banker's acceptance, or nontraditional, that is, a longer dated structured transaction or a forfaiting transaction.

Traditional Trade Finance

Traditional trade finance is accomplished with letters of credit, drafts, and, in some cases, the use of a banker's acceptance. The letter of credit (L/C) is a guarantee of sorts that the importer or the importer's bank will pay for the trade transaction upon receipt by the bank of certain documents—especially the bill of lading, which shows that the goods have been loaded on a ship or airplane—about the trade to be shipped within a specified time. Such documents facilitate an export sale because they give the buyer credibility. In short, the L/C is an instrument issued by a bank or other party on the request of a customer who is the purchaser of the exported goods or service and is issued to benefit the exporter.

Letter of credit is the term most used in the English language. The rest of the world tends to use the term *documentary credit*, which is a literal translation of the French term *crédit documentaire*. The Paris-based International Chamber of Commerce prefers the French term or its literal translation.[4]

All L/Cs contain the following elements: (1) a payment undertaking given by the issuing bank; (2) issued on behalf of the buyer; (3) whose beneficiary is the seller; (4) a given amount of money for the goods shipped is shown; (5) the L/C is accompanied with specific documents representing the shipped goods; (6) the L/C has a specific time limit; (7) the shipping documents conform to terms and conditions set forth in the L/C; (8) the documents are presented at a specified place.[5]

Several types of L/Cs can be issued. These include irrevocable, revocable, confirmed, negotiable, back to back, transferable, revolving, clean, standby, sight bill, time bill, deferred payment, and red clause L/Cs.[6] The most significant of these types are discussed in the following sections. See Figure 3.1 for an example of a L/C, Figure

3rd National Bank of Idaho
Idaho Falls, Idaho

FOREIGN DEPARTMENT
Confirmed Irrevocable Straight Credit   Credit No. 0000
Jones & Company   Idaho Falls, Idaho, June 1, 20—
P.O. Box 888
Idaho Falls, Idaho xxxxx

DEAR SIRS:
    We are instructed by Banco Rosario, Mexico City, Mexico
To advise you that they have opened their irrevocable credit in your favor for account
of Compania Santo Domingo, Mexico City, Mexico
Under their credit number 300-456 for a sum or sums not exceeding a total of
$75,000.00 (Seventy-five thousand no/100 U.S. dollars)
Available by your drafts on us at sight For invoice
Value of 100%
To be accompanied by
1. Commercial Invoice: five copies signed by the beneficiaries with sworn statement
   regarding price and origin of merchandise
2. Air Waybill: three non-negotiable copies, cosigned to the order of: Air Mexico, Car-
   rera 10 Calle 50, Mexico City, Mexico, for notification of same
3. Consular Invoice: three copies
4. Certificate of Origin: three copies
5. Copy of the airmail letter addressed to: Air Mexico, Mexico City, Mexico, remitting
   original of shipping documents requested.
6. Packing List: three copies
7. Copy of the airmail letter addressed to: INA Insurance Company, Calle 20, No. 100-
   110, Mexico City, Mexico, covering details of shipment of merchandise, for insurance purposes Evidencing shipment of: "Widgets, registro de importacion No.
   5555 del 1 de Noviembre de 20—."
ALL DRAFTS SO DRAWN MUST BE MARKED DRAWN UNDER THE 3RD NATIONAL
BANK OF IDAHO FALLS CREDIT NO. XXXX, Banco Rosario No. L/C 333-555
    THE ABOVE MENTIONED CORRESPONDENT ENGAGES WITH YOU THAT ALL
DRAFTS DRAWN UNDER AND IN COMPLIANCE WITH TERMS OF THIS CREDIT
WILL BE DULY HONORED ON DELIVERY OF DOCUMENTS AS SPECIFIED IF PRE-
SENTED AT THIS OFFICE ON OR BEFORE August 25, 20—   : WE CONFIRM THE
CREDIT AND THEREBY UNDERTAKE THAT ALL DRAFTS DRAWN AND PRE-
SENTED AS ABOVE SPECIFIED WILL BE DULY HONORED BY US. UNLESS OTH-
ERWISE EXPRESSLY STATED, THIS CREDIT IS SUBJECT TO THE UNIFORM
CUSTOMS AND PRACTICE FOR COMMERCIAL DOCUMENTARY CREDITS FIXED
BY SEVENTH CONGRESS OF THE INTERNATIONAL CHAMBER OF COMMERCE
AND CERTAIN GUIDING PROVISIONS ALL AS ADOPTED BY CERTAIN BANKS
AND OTHER CONCERNS IN THE U.S.A.

              YOURS VERY TRULY,

        _____   _____
        ASSISTANT MANAGER   VICE-PRESIDENT, CASHIER
        William Smith, Vice President   John Jones, Vice President

cc: Banco Rosario, Mexico City, Mexico

Figure 3.1 Sample Letter of Credit

3.2 for an irrevocable L/C, and Figure 3.3 for the steps in a typical L/C transaction.

Irrevocable L/C. An L/C may be irrevocable when issued by the importer's bank and accepted irrevocably by the exporter's bank. It may also be issued by the exporter's bank at the request of the importer's bank. An irrevocable L/C can also be issued by a foreign bank without responsibility by the U.S. bank except to advise the exporter that an L/C has been issued.

Revocable L/C. A revocable L/C is seldom issued, especially when the parties to the transaction are from the United States and Europe, respectively. In fact, L/Cs are seldom exercised after being issued, although they do add credibility to the trade transaction. They also may have financial implications for the issuing bank since they are considered contingent liabilities (sometimes referred to as off–balance sheet items).

Other Types of L/Cs. Other types of L/Cs also can be issued.[7] The standby L/C signifies that the issuing bank will stand behind the borrower if payment cannot be made. Companies often issue standby L/Cs to back up commercial paper offerings. A performance L/C requires the bank to guarantee that the borrower will perform some prenegotiated service. The bank must make restitution if the borrower cannot perform the service.

Use of an L/C. The following is an example of the use of an L/C. Suppose the El Monte Motorcycle Company in Mexico City needs to import motorcycle brakes from Davis Bike Brake Company in Kansas City, Missouri. The latter company wants to be paid in advance but does not believe El Monte can pay by this method. Credit reports from the Mexico City area are unreliable. If the shipment were to be rejected by the purchaser, Davis would have to sell the brakes elsewhere in Mexico or have them shipped back to the home plant. Either alternative is unacceptable and would result in a loss on the shipment. El Monte is unwilling to pay in advance because the manufacturer might become insolvent or fail to ship the brakes for some other reason.

El Monte gets its bank to issue an L/C stating that the bank will honor a draft drawn against it if the appropriate shipping documents accompany the draft. Thus, Davis Bike Brakes can ship the brakes with minimal risk. El Monte does not have to pay until the brakes have been shipped and are out of the seller's control. The risk borne by the bank can be hedged in a number of ways without recourse to either the exporter or the importer.[8]

Multinational Bank N.A.
P.O. Box 4444, Chicago, Illinois
CABLE ADDRESS: MultiB
TELEX NO. 2468135
SWIFT NO. PQRSTU 80

OUR ADVICE NUMBER: FQ0000062
ADVICE DATE: 10APR98
ISSUE BANK REF: 4424/STU/33682
EXPIRY DATE: 25JUL98

****AMOUNT****
USD****30,000.00

BENEFICIARY:
THE BURNED BRICK CO.
4612 SOUTH STREET
CHICAGO, ILLINOIS

APPLICANT:
SUK KIM CO.
555 DUK SOO ST.
SEOUL, KOREA

WE HAVE BEEN REQUESTED TO ADVISE TO YOU OF THE FOLLOWING LETTER
OF CREDIT AS ISSUED BY:
SEOUL NATIONAL BANK
2 BANK TOWER
SEOUL, KOREA

PLEASE BE GUIDED BY ITS TERMS AND CONDITIONS AND BY THE FOLLOWING:
CREDIT IS AVAILABLE BY NEGOTIATION OF YOUR DRAFT(S) IN DUPLICATE AT
SIGHT FOR 100 PERCENT OF INVOICE VALUE DRAWN ON US ACCOMPANIED BY
THE FOLLOWING DOCUMENTS:

1. SIGNED COMMERCIAL INVOICE IN 1 ORIGINAL AND 3 COPIES.

2. FULL SET 3/3 OCEAN BILLS OF LADING CONSIGNED TO THE ORDER OF
SEOUL NATIONAL BANK, SEOUL, KOREA NOTIFY APPLICANT AND MARKED
FREIGHT COLLECT.

3. PACKING LIST IN 2 COPIES

EVIDENCING SHIPMENT OF: 20,000 SPECIAL GLAZED BRICKS
                        FOB CHICAGO, ILLINOIS

SHIPMENT FROM: CHICAGO, ILLINOIS   TO: SEOUL, KOREA
LATEST SHIPPING DATE: 25JUN98

PARTIAL SHIPMENTS NOT ALLOWED   TRANSHIPMENT NOT ALLOWED

ALL BANKING CHARGES OUTSIDE SEOUL ARE FOR BENEFICIARYS ACCOUNT.
DOCUMENTS MUST BE PRESENTED WITHIN 21 DAYS FROM B/L DATE.

AT THE REQUEST OF OUR CORRESPONDENT, WE CONFIRM THIS CREDIT AND
ALSO ENGAGE WITH YOU THAT ALL DRAFTS DRAWN UNDER AND IN COMPLI-
ANCE WITH THE TERMS OF THIS CREDIT WILL BE DULY HONORED BY US.

PLEASE EXAMINE THIS INSTRUMENT CAREFULLY. IF YOU ARE UNABLE TO COM-
PLY WITH THE TERMS OR CONDITIONS, PLEASE COMMUNICATE WITH YOUR
BUYER TO ARRANGE FOR AN AMENDMENT.

Figure 3.2 An Irrevocable Letter of Credit

1) Buyer and seller agree to terms including means of transport, period of credit offered (if any), and latest date of shipment acceptable.
2) Buyer applies to bank for issue of letter of credit. Bank will evaluate buyer's credit standing, and may require cash cover and/or reduction of other lending limits.
3) Issuing bank issues letter of credit, sending it to the Advising bank by air-mail or electronic means such as telex or SWIFT.
4) Advising bank establishes authenticity of the letter of credit using signature books or test codes, then informs seller (beneficiary).
5) Seller should now check that letter of credit matches commercial agreement and that all its terms and conditions can be satisfied.
6) Seller ships the goods, then assembles the documents called for in the letter of credit (invoice, transport document, etc.).
7) The Advising bank checks the documents against the letter of credit. If the documents are compliant, the bank pays the seller and forwards the documents to the issuing bank.
8) The Issuing bank now checks the documents itself. If they are in order, it reimburses the seller's bank immediately.
9) The Issuing bank debits the buyer and releases the documents (including transport document), so the buyer can claim the goods from the carrier.

Source: ec-Finance.com, "The Letter of Credit Process," available on-line at www.ec-finance.com/site/about_lcs/letter_of_credit_process.htm, January 31, 2003, p. 1; reproduced with permission from ec-Finance.com.

Figure 3.3 The Letter of Credit Process

Draft. An export draft is an unconditional order drawn by a seller on the buyer that instructs the buyer to pay the amount of the shipment when the draft is presented. This is a sight draft. A representation of a sight draft is shown in Figure 3.4. If the payment is to be made on some future date agreed to by the parties, the draft is a time draft. In a typical trade transaction, the exporter requests that the draft and supporting documents be sent by its bank to the importer's bank in the foreign country and collection will be made according to the L/C transaction.[9] A draft can be denominated in either the exporter's or the importer's currency.

Banker's Acceptance. A banker's acceptance is created when the exporter's bank stamps "Accepted" on the face of the draft. This act turns the draft into a negotiable instrument, which can be sold at a discount to an acceptance market dealer. The dealer, in turn, sells it to a banker's acceptance market investor, who specializes in such financial instruments whose face value is usually more than US$1 million. The investor will hold the acceptance until it matures and then return it to the accepting bank for the principal and accrued interest. A banker's

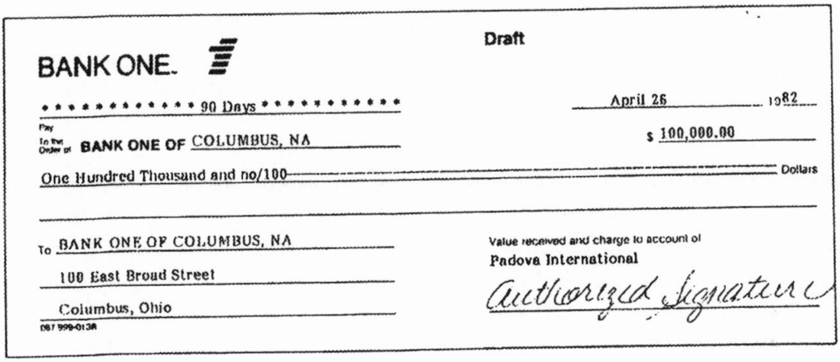
Draft

BANK ONE.

************ 90 Days ************ April 26 1982

Pay to the Order of BANK ONE OF COLUMBUS, NA $ 100,000.00

One Hundred Thousand and no/100 Dollars

To BANK ONE OF COLUMBUS, NA
100 East Broad Street
Columbus, Ohio

Value received and charge to account of
Padova International
Authorized Signature

087 999-0138

Figure 3.4 Example of a Draft

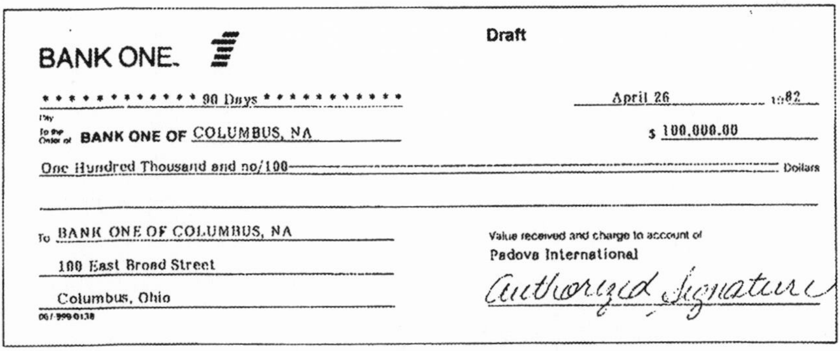
Draft

BANK ONE.

************ 90 Days ************ April 26 1982

Pay to the Order of BANK ONE OF COLUMBUS, NA $ 100,000.00

One Hundred Thousand and no/100 Dollars

To BANK ONE OF COLUMBUS, NA
100 East Broad Street
Columbus, Ohio

Value received and charge to account of
Padova International
Authorized Signature

087 999-0138

In this example, Padova International completes a draft for $100,000 drawn on BANK ONE to finance imported inventory from Italy. BANK ONE accepts the draft and creates a Bankers Acceptance which will mature 90 days after the acceptance date, on July 24, 1982.

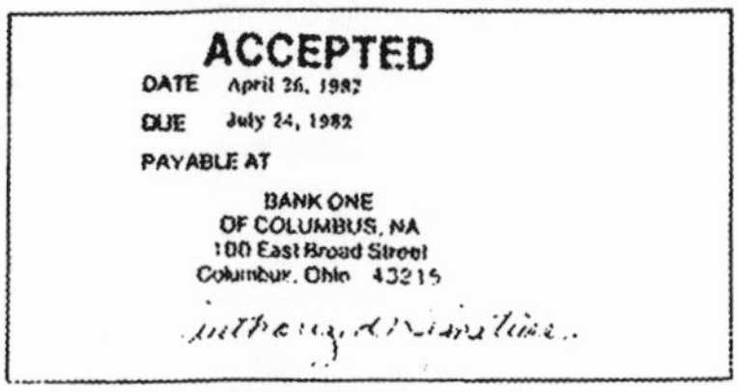
ACCEPTED
DATE April 26, 1982
DUE July 24, 1982
PAYABLE AT
BANK ONE
OF COLUMBUS, NA
100 East Broad Street
Columbus, Ohio 43215
Authorized Signature

To create a Bankers Acceptance, BANK ONE affixes an acceptance stamp to the draft, indicates the acceptance and maturity dates, and adds an authorized signature.

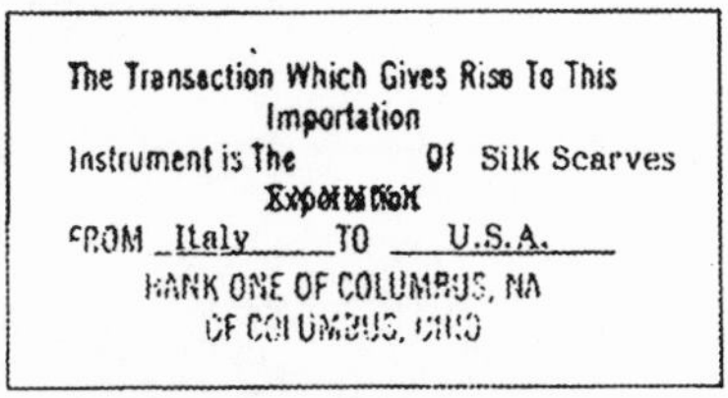
The Transaction Which Gives Rise To This Instrument is The Importation / Exportation Of Silk Scarves
FROM Italy TO U.S.A.
BANK ONE OF COLUMBUS, NA
OF COLUMBUS, OHIO

An eligibility stamp is used to describe the type of transaction, the merchandise and the countries of the importer and exporter.

Figure 3.5 Example of a Banker's Acceptance

acceptance is shown in Figure 3.5. Figure 3.6 diagrams the various steps in the creation of a banker's acceptance.

Some of these steps occur simultaneously. As Figure 3.6 shows, the exporter's bank may be short a payment on the transaction at various times. After all the documentation has been received by the exporter, its bank will finance the transaction by advancing funds as in Step 6, so that the exporter can get the funds back into the stream of production. However, the exporter's bank receives funds, less a discount, from the acceptance dealer after the draft has been accepted, as in Step 10. The exporter's bank again is short of funds when it pays off the principal and interest to the acceptance investor when the acceptance is presented

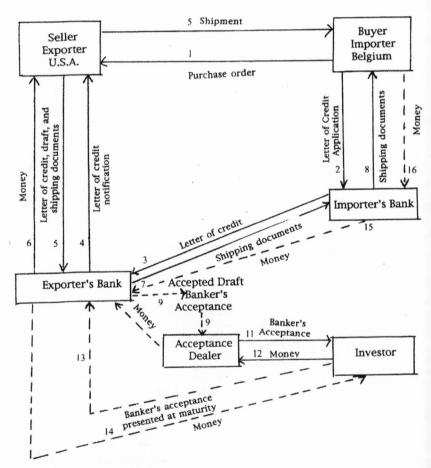

Source: Northern Trust Company, Chicago, Illinois.

Figure 3.6 Creation of a Banker's Acceptance

at maturity, as in Step 14. However, by this time, the importer's bank has probably advanced funds to the exporter's bank, as in Step 15. The final transaction, then, is in Step 16, when the importer arranges to pay for the import loan granted by the importer's bank.

The market for banker's acceptances was created in 1913 when the instrument was authorized by Section 13 of the Federal Reserve Act. Section 13 permitted the Federal Reserve Banks to rediscount, purchase, and sell eligible acceptances. The market for such instruments had already been established in Europe, and the Federal Reserve thought such an instrument could reduce the cost of financing exports and imports for U.S. firms.

The success of the banker's acceptance has been mixed. It was created in the United States in the midst of the liquidity crisis of the 1907 depression, which led to the Federal Reserve Act and the establishment of the Federal Reserve system. During the 1920s, one-third of U.S. trade was financed by acceptances. During the Great Depression in the 1930s, very little world trade was carried out and the banker's acceptance was used only sparingly. After World War II and until the mid-1980s, the use of banker's acceptances surged. The volume of acceptances amounted to US$74 billion in 1984, but by 2001, the volume had declined to US$4.8 billion. Other, less costly methods of financing trade are available, including commercial paper, Euro-commercial paper, and bank loans.

Such instruments compete well against the banker's acceptance. Commercial paper is less costly for borrowers and is unsecured for those borrowers with good credit. In addition, more information is usually available for investors in commercial paper than for banker's acceptances. Euro-commercial paper gives U.S. firms accessibility to an alternative capital market because of its conversion to a common currency. Spreads on Euro-paper and banker's acceptances have declined in recent years.[10]

Banker's acceptances are subject to a number of risks. These include transactions, compliance, credit, liquidity, foreign exchange, and reputation risks. Transactions risk arises from fraud, error, and the inability to deliver goods and services purchased. Compliance risk arises from the creation of an acceptance that is ineligible because it does not conform to Federal Reserve Board regulations. Credit risk is caused by the inability of the importer to pay for the imported goods or services, thus placing the payment obligation on the accepting bank. Liquidity risk arises from few investors in the secondary market willing to purchase banker's acceptances. Exchange risk is caused by adverse fluctuations in the foreign exchange market and can be hedged by acceptable techniques. Reputation risk emanates from the consumer's opinion of the accepting bank. If the bank makes a practice of accepting drafts drawn on unstable companies, it will be considered negatively by consumers and the secondary market for these acceptances will be adversely affected.

The secondary market. The exporter can hold a banker's acceptance or the exporter or exporter's bank can sell the instrument at a discount into a secondary market. These instruments are not traded on any organized exchange, but a market for them is made by a handful of acceptance dealers who discount the instruments to individual investors, mutual funds, or pension funds. The market is tiered in that larger, better known banks with higher credit ratings carry a lower discount rate than those with lower credit ratings. The banks in the large money centers generally offer the lowest discount rates.[11]

Nontraditional Trade Finance

Nontraditional trade finance consists of either a longer-dated structured transaction or a forfaiting transaction. These types of finance will be discussed in the following sections.

Longer-dated Structured Transaction. Banks do not desire to carry the risk of export financing to which they commit because they may be unwilling to increase risk on their balance sheets.[12] Thus, they essentially construct longer-dated structured transactions by placing their trade finance paper and project-related notes with institutional investors through securitizing the loans. The short- and medium-term export loans can thus be converted into longer-term funding.

An example of such a deal involved US$310 million in financing for the Angolan oil industry. A three-year contract was negotiated between Sonangol, the Angolan oil producer, and BP, the multinational petroleum company. UBS, a Swiss bank, arranged the prepayment deal with Angola. The Angolans had to lift the oil, and BP had to pay for it. The transaction contained both delivery and payment risk. UBS issued a letter of credit to cover the oil shipments. The trade transaction appears to be a project loan, but with a letter of credit and syndicate arrangement for the funding. The three-year contract was to be repaid for twenty-nine months but could be paid within a year.

Forfaiting. Forfaiting involves the purchasing, without recourse, of an accounts receivable whose credit terms are longer than 90 to 180 days, the normal length to maturity in factoring of receivables.[13] Political and transfer risks are assumed by another bank referred to as the forfaiter. The term is derived from the French term, *à forfait*, meaning to surrender a right. Forfaiting is designed for medium-term trade financing in which the medium-term risk is converted into a series of short-term loans. For example, a company may manufacture and export a large boiler whose cost is in the millions of dollars and financing might be arranged for five years. The five-year note may be broken up into a series of 10 six-month notes, each priced for its specific time to maturity.

Forfaiting has been practiced since the 1950s and was pioneered by European banks, primarily in Switzerland, Germany, and Austria, to finance trade to the Eastern bloc countries. It has succeeded because the method has been highly profitable for international banks and relatively more secure than other types of lending. Few American banks use this method. The financing, known as à forfait, consists of a purchase of claims arising from merchandise exports and due at some clearly stated future date and has no recourse for the seller of the claims, that is, the exporter. The seller of the claims is called the forfaitiste, and the purchaser of such claims is the forfaiteur. Short- and medium-term financing is shifted to long-term financing, and the transaction risk is shifted to a third party. It thus is a hybrid form of export financing. Forfaiting is generally used to finance capital goods, meaning that transactions usually exceed US$500,000 in value. The technique is diagrammed in Figure 3.7.

Figure 3.7 shows that after the exporter (X) and the importer (M) agree on payment, delivery, and the other terms, the importer's bank avalizes the importer's note or notes, that is, the bank guarantees their payment and sends them to the exporter's bank. The exporter can hold the notes to maturity or sell them to a forfaiteur for immediate cash. If the latter course is chosen, the notes can be discounted into the à forfait market and subsequently held by more than one investor. Thus, the credit risk of the transaction can be shifted to other parties.

Several advantages stem from the use of forfaiting to finance some types of international trade. First, quick funding is facilitated. Forfaiteurs usually work more rapidly than government agencies that handle export trade financing. Forfait houses recognize the value of foreign receivables and work with guarantees issued by banks and government agencies. They give the exporter money up front before collecting, in many cases, from the buyer. They can even convert receivables into commercial paper that is marketable.[14]

Second, forfaiting reduces the risk to which the exporter is exposed. Third, forfaiting requires less documentation than a traditional trade-financing deal. Fourth, problems of collection are eliminated since they now become the problem for the forfaiteur. Fifth, currency, political, and credit risks are borne by the forfaiteur. Sixth, it makes no difference from where the goods originated. Seventh, a contract can be financed 100 percent. Finally, the exporter can involve the forfaiteur at an early stage of pricing the contract so that determination of the potential profit from the transaction can be made earlier.

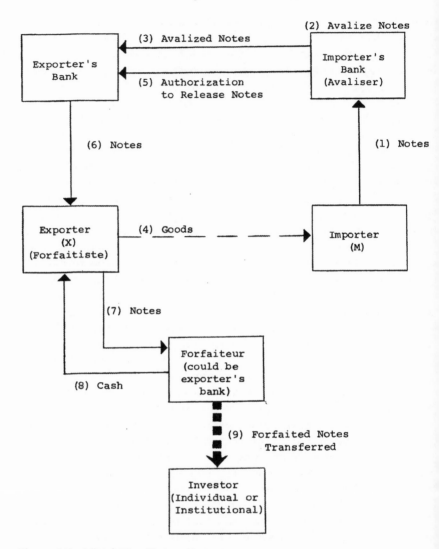

Figure 3.7 A Forfaiting Transaction

However, forfaiting does encounter some disadvantages. High interest rates are usually built into the discount rates that are set for the notes. Forfaiting costs are generally higher than Eurocurrency rates, but the method may not be more expensive than funding by other methods since, for example, no export credit insurance fees are incurred. Forfaiting may encounter litigation costs. These arise from making sure the paper forfaited is unconditional, irrevocable, and unrelated to any performance of commercial goods. Different nations have different definitions of terms such as unconditional and irrevocable. When things go wrong with a forfaited deal, it may be difficult to determine what law is applicable, whether the exporter's or the importer's national law. Funding may also present a problem. Most forfaiting agreements are small and in amounts that mature at different intervals. Notes involving funding for five years may cause funding problems for small banks, which are the typical forfaiteurs. Large banks may not fund the longer-term notes for fear their reputation might be damaged by going after small amounts in the forfaiting market.[15]

When the advantages and disadvantages of forfaiting are weighed together, the handwriting on the wall shows a market facing uncertainty.[16] Part of this problem can be found in the relatively high interest rates charged to convert medium- and long-term risk to a shorter-term risk. Part of the problem lies in the fact that the traditional markets for forfaiting, Russia and East Europe, have declined in recent years. Among the financial institutions offering this service, several have reduced or eliminated their forfaiting operations. Among these are the United Kingdom Commercial Bank consortium, AI Trade Finance, and Lloyds of London's Trade and Project Finance Division. In addition, Chase Manhattan left the market, Crédit Commercial de France closed its United Kingdom operation, and the Hungarian International Bank, once a strong forfait bank, has downsized its operations in the market. On the other hand, London Forfaiting has become an important player. Liquidity in the forfaiting market has declined drastically and, thus, a secondary market for this paper is much thinner.

Although the Russians and East Europeans have become less important in the forfaiting business, other areas of the world are subject to increased use of this type of trade finance. The emerging markets of the developing world need the type of equipment and goods that lend themselves to medium-term or longer financing. Forfaiting can be an important means of financing such business and reducing of nonpayment risk to the exporters and original lending institutions.

A Case Example of a Forfaited Transaction. International Remote Imaging Systems Inc. (IRIS) presents a good example of a case of forfaiting.[17] IRIS wanted to finance exports totaling US$850,000 in 2001 to Turkey, a country with a high degree of political and economic instability. Inflation in Turkey in 2001 reached an annual rate of 90 percent. This was coupled with the fact that the Turkish bureaucracy was heavy-handed in its treatment of trade in the absence of constitutional property rights. Because of these problems, no customer in Turkey could obtain trade finance from a Turkish bank, and the Turkish legal system kept foreign companies from doing business there.

IRIS's Turkish customer was a distributor of medical equipment and wanted to pay IRIS's invoice over two years. The Turkish company did not qualify for credit insurance or for the U.S. Export-Import Bank (Ex-Im) guarantees of trade credits. However, the Turkish distributor could get a Turkish bank to guarantee repayment, the aval needed for a forfait transaction. The aval is a guarantee of the importer's note or bill by a bank in the importer's country. IRIS shipped the equipment to Turkey and received a series of promissory notes from the Turkish distributor, which had been guaranteed by the Turkish bank. IRIS sold the notes at a discount to a European bank in a classic forfaiting deal, thus securing immediate cash. IRIS then factored the forfaiter's discount into the sales price and also charged the Turkish distributor interest of 12 percent for the two-year term. All parties to the transaction benefited from this non-traditional method of trade finance.

TRADE FINANCE WHERE COUNTRY RISK IS INVOLVED

ECA-Assisted Trade Finance

More than thirty nations have some three dozen export credit agencies (ECAs), which facilitate the financing of international trade. These agencies guarantee or insure the trade credits granted by commercial banks to exporters from the respective country or, in some cases such as Japan, to importers. In the United States, the U.S. Export-Import Bank performs this function. The ECA for Great Britain is the Export Credit Guarantee Department (ECGD). In France, Coface performs such operations. In Germany, a private insurer, Hermes, guarantees trade credits as an agent for the government. The Export Development Corporation is the ECA in Canada. Japan has two institutions that perform these functions: the Export-Import Insurance Department and the Japan Bank for International Cooperation. Korea also has two organizations involved in this business: the Korea Export Insurance Corporation and the Export-Import Bank of Korea. These and other ECAs will be discussed in more detail and evaluated in Chapter 9.

Private Insurers

Several private groups or firms also facilitate international trade by insuring international trade credits or assisting in financing international trade transactions. In the United States, two private firms are involved: the Foreign Credit Insurance Association (FCIA) and the Private Export Funding Company (PEFCO). FCIA is a consortium of private U.S. insurance companies that insures trade credits granted by the banking system and supplements the work of the U.S. Export-Import Bank. PEFCO borrows funds on money and capital markets and uses these funds to make loans to foreign importers for the purpose of purchasing U.S. exports. FCIA and PEFCO usually become involved when the U.S. trade being financed is a transaction with an importer in a country with some degree of political risk. These organizations will be discussed in detail in Chapters 5 and 6.

Some commercial banks assist exporters whose goods do not meet the Ex-Im criterion of 51 percent or more U.S. content to become eligible for trade credit insurance. Several insurance firms have been elicited by commercial banks making export loans to provide commercial and political risk insurance to U.S. exporters. These firms include the FCIA, American International Group (AIG), American Credit Indemnity (ACI), and Lloyds of London.

PAYMENT PROCEDURES

Payment terms that exporters make available to importers include cash in advance, open account, consignment, letters of credit, and documentary drafts. The choice of method may be a primary determinant in whether the exporter obtains the order.[18]

Cash in Advance

If the exporter does not know the credit standing of the importer, terms involving cash in advance or prepayment are usually desirable. Very often, banks will not advance trade credits in such cases unless an ECA or other, similar institution insures or guarantees the trade credits. The buyer is at a disadvantage under such terms because some of its working capital may be tied up until the transaction is finalized. Moreover, the buyer has no guarantee that what was ordered will be delivered. On the other hand, prepayment presents no risk to the exporter. Thus, few buyers will pay in advance unless their side of the transaction is financed.

Open Account

The seller assumes all the risk if the sale is made on open account. Such terms are generally only offered to the most reliable customers in a politically stable country. Under such terms, the exporter's capital is tied up until payment has been received. Usually the goods are available to the buyer before payment. The importer has little or no risk in an open account transaction. One advantage of open account financing is the absence of bank fees and the much simpler documentation involved. The disadvantage is that if a problem occurs, the exporter has little or no recourse to cover its money.

Consignment

Under consignment terms, goods are shipped to the buyer and no payment is made until they have been sold. Whether title to the goods passes from the exporter to the importer is a legal question. Usually possession passes to the importer while title remains with the exporter. The exporter assumes all the risk and, thus, a detailed credit check of the importer should be made before such terms are offered. The goods are available to the importer before payment, which means that the importer incurs little or no risk.

Letter of Credit

A letter of credit (L/C) gives nearly as much protection to the exporter as cash in advance terms. The L/C is requested by the exporter and drafted by the importer's bank. It essentially implies that the importer's bank will stand behind the transaction and guarantee payment. As with the previously discussed financing types, it is usually used when the transaction is between buyers and sellers from industrialized, politically stable countries. The L/C is normally treated by the issuing bank as a contingent liability since the possibility exists that that bank will have to pay for the transaction if the buyer fails to do so for some reason. This, however, is a remote possibility and seldom happens.

Payment in an L/C transaction is generally made at shipment time, and the goods are available after payment. The exporter has little or no risk, depending on payment terms, but the importer must rely on the exporter to ship the goods described in the shipping documents.

L/C financing of export trade does have drawbacks.[19] American companies that are required to obtain an L/C may be put at a competitive disadvantage. European companies usually use open credit terms in their international dealings, and therefore do not require L/Cs. Thus, foreign buyers may move their business to sellers that offer open credit terms. European companies have a long history of buying credit insurance to hedge their open credit terms. In addition, the cost of LCs may be relatively higher than other methods of financing export trade.[20] From a bank's viewpoint, many money center banks do not want to spend the time it takes to draft an L/C, especially with the thin profit margin the instrument offers the bank. Most local banks do not have the know-how when international markets are considered.[21] Rates generally are .4 to .6 percent of the value of the merchandise being insured. British banks charge 1.5 to 2.0 percent a month on the face value of the credit extended, and banks in Brazil may charge as much as 6 percent. Finally, L/Cs may have another disadvantage for the buyer. It has been estimated that 40 percent of L/Cs have documentary discrepancies or other errors that have to be resolved. The exporter may have to incur the cost of dealing with these discrepancies. In other words, L/Cs are paper and compliance intensive and tie up capital. Some believe that certain events, such as the delivery of goods, should determine when payment is made.[22]

The typical L/C includes items that are obsolete terms used decades ago yet are still being used in some L/Cs being issued today. For example, telexes of some document or another may be referred to, when telex machines are rarely found. Some L/Cs mention a certificate that certifies another certificate, which is a redundancy. Some L/Cs mention more than one courier in the same company, especially for bills of lading, yet one courier per company is sufficient. Other language may be inserted in L/Cs that is outmoded, redundant, or simply incorrect.[23]

Asian companies in countries such as Taiwan, Hong Kong, and Singapore reduced their usage of L/Cs drastically between 1998 and 2001. In 1998, 50 to 60 percent of total trade transactions in these countries used L/Cs, but by 2001, the usage had dropped below 30 percent. The major reason cited included the long processing time required for L/Cs. The negotiations for their L/Cs from the time of shipment to the time of presentation by the issuing bank generally took more than twenty days.[24] Large U.S. retailers driving trade with Asian suppliers have increased trading on open account or cash on delivery. This contract manufacturing concept has reduced the need for L/Cs.[25] Time is money to an exporter.

Because of these disadvantages of the L/C, credit insurance has been used more and more by exporters.[26] The cost of credit insurance is usually a fraction of 1 percent of sales. Credit insurance can eliminate the paperwork and handling of L/Cs and, thus, reduce the number of discrepancies found in many of them. The cost of credit insurance has the advantage of being tax deductible.

With the decline in the use of L/Cs for the reasons already mentioned, some trade analysts believe that they might be replaced by what are known as *electronic deferred payment certificates*.[27] These documents stem from the electronic trade (e-trade) finance systems that have recently emerged from the world of technology, and are transmitted through electronic communications networks.

Electronic doumentation has a number of advantages.[28] Trade documented in this manner has quicker turnaround times, is more efficient, and results in cost benefits. However, these advantages will probably come at the cost of more standardization of documentation and offerings by financial service providers.

Payment by Drafts

The method of payment by draft depends on the type of draft used. If a sight draft is employed, payment is made when the shipment is carried out and the goods are available after payment has been made. The risk to the exporter is that the goods must be disposed of if the importer fails to pay. The risk to the importer is that the exporter may not ship the goods listed in the documentation, although it is possible that the importer may inspect the goods before payment. If a time draft is used, payment is made after the draft has reached maturity and goods are available before payment is made. The exporter's risk is that it must rely on the buyer to pay the draft. Again, the risk to the importer is that the goods ordered may not be what the exporter ships, although the importer may inspect the goods before payment is made.

TRADE FINANCE METHODS

The most frequently used methods to finance international trade include accounts receivable financing, factoring, letters of credit, banker's acceptances, working capital financing, medium-term capital goods financing (forfaiting), and countertrade. Letters of credit and forfaiting were described earlier in this chapter. The remaining five methods will be discussed in the following sections.

Accounts Receivable Financing

The financing of international trade transactions by accounts receivable assumes that the exporter is willing to advance credit to the importer because a complete credit check was conducted before the transaction was begun and that the importer was found to be creditworthy. If the exporter needs funds immediately, its bank will provide a loan to the exporter secured by an assignment of the accounts receivable. In the case of a default by the importer, the exporter will be liable to the bank for repayment of the loan. Length to maturity of accounts receivable financing is from one to six months, and the loan rate is often higher than for a domestic accounts receivable transaction because of the risk that the importer's government may restrict payment as a result of exchange controls. Export credit insurance advanced, for example, by an ECA is often required when accounts receivable financing is used.

Factoring

When accounts receivable are generated by an international trade transaction, the risk of nonpayment by the importer may arise. In such a case, the receivables may be sold by the exporter to a bank known as a factor. Factoring of accounts receivable has been used on domestic transactions in the United States for many years. Factoring of international trade accounts is a relatively young activity. A few banks have specialized in international factoring. First Bank of Boston is an example. Factors Chain International presents another example of the growth in factoring. This is a firm that coordinates a network of 150 member institutions in fifty-three countries that are involved in international factoring. It will be discussed in more detail in Chapter 7.

The benefits to the exporter, other than obtaining funds earlier than payment of receivables by the importer and improving its cash flow, include the lack of administrative cost in maintaining and monitoring the accounts receivable. The factor will assume the risk of nonpayment by the importer, administration of the account, and collection of the funds, thus assuming the credit exposure to the importer. Factors usually use export credit insurance to reduce or eliminate the risks involved. Since the risk passed on to the factor is higher, the interest rate charged on this type of financing will be higher as well.[29]

Factoring in Jamaica. A good case study of a factoring operation in which a government agency and private banks are involved can be demonstrated by the facility provided by the National Export-Import Bank of Jamaica Limited.[30] This program is a cooperative effort between the Jamaica agency and Sun Bank, for markets in the United States and Canada, and the Hong Kong Shanghai Bank, for markets in Asia. It is a factoring program that involves the purchase of a company's export receivables with or without recourse. Major clients of this program include companies exporting to the United States, Canada, and the United Kingdom. Advances are provided for up to 80 percent of the invoice value for a maximum period of 120 days and at an annual interest rate of 10 to 12 percent. The factoring in this program does not require a commercial bank guarantee. The Jamaica factoring program offers three benefits to the exporter: (1) provision of working capital, (2) relief from the administration of receivables collections, and (3) credit risk protection against nonpayment.

Working Capital Financing

Working capital financing involves a bank that makes short-term loans to an importer, thus allowing it to make a payment on the international trade at some future date. The maturity on these loans is beyond that of a banker's acceptance period. An importer's purchase is usually the acquisition of inventory. The loan finances the working capital cycle, beginning with the purchase of the inventory, and ends with the production of goods that are sold, the creation of accounts receivable, and its conversion to cash. Such a loan might be made to the exporter to finance the manufacture of the merchandise to be exported.

Countertrade

Countertrade is a quasi-form of international trade finance. It is the act of linking the sale of goods to one country with the purchase or exchange of goods from that same country. Barter is one form of countertrade that has been practiced for thousands of years. In recent years, countertrade has become popular because of balance of payments problems incurred by some countries, lack of foreign exchange or currency inconvertibility, debt problems in developing countries, and lack of demand in some parts of the world. In addition, countertrade has been used because of poor demand for some countries' basic commodities or a desire to comply with trade regulations of importing countries.

A number of multinational corporations (MNCs) have employed some type of countertrade with companies in Asia, Latin America, and Eastern Europe. A well-publicized countertrade transaction mentioned earlier was that between PepsiCo in the United States and Stolichnya, the Russian vodka producer. As a result, Pepsi-Cola was exported to Russia and vodka was exported to the United States.

Problems can be incurred in countertrade transactions. They are usually complex and may involve several contracts or protocols. They often require parties other than the exporter and importer to execute the transaction. They may require additional payment or financial terms to complete the transaction. They are difficult to price in that each side of the transaction should be equal essentially in value.

Wave of the Future: E-Trade

The wave of the future in export trade transactions and financing may have emanated from the on-line technology of e-commerce. International trade transactions are complex in their execution and fraught with many types of difficulties of documentation and financing. Some firms have initiated operations using e-commerce technology, and some success has been achieved by these experiments. Banks involved with export financing have been working with e-platforms to solve some of the complex problems in financing international trade. A platform is the computer configuration to handle a certain task. Three such platforms working in conjunction with commercial banks are Bolero, CCEWeb, and TradeCard. In addition, international banks such as ABN AMRO in the Netherlands, Bank of America, JP Morgan Chase, and Wells Fargo have developed e-trade systems. These will be discussed in the following sections.

Bolero.net. Bolero seems to be at the forefront of e-trade finance with its bolero.net electronic trading platform.[31] This system, launched in 1999 and jointly owned by the Society for Worldwide Interbank Financial Telecommunications (SWIFT) and the Through Transport Club, permits importers to verify that terms of the settlement have been met before releasing payment.[32] SWIFT is a secure global communications network that connects more than 6,600 financial institutions in 189 countries. An electronic bill of lading is offered when the ownership of the goods is transferred. A bill of lading is a trade document providing the terms of the contract between the shipper and the transportation company to move freight between stated points at a specified charge. In a typical case, Bolero.net expedited a coffee export transaction through its platform for the Colombian coffee industry. The deal was executed in 2000 through a Colombian national growers' association representing half a million Colombian coffee growers. The transaction involved a consignment of 17.5 tons of arabica coffee shipped from Colombia to the United Kingdom. NatWest Bank acted as banker for the importer, and Chase Manhattan Bank acted for the Colombian growers' association, the exporter. The e-commerce transaction was carried out and financed in much less time than traditional export trade financing generally demanded.

Bolero also launched its boleroSURF program in 2002. JP Morgan Treasury Services was the first financial institution to adopt this program, which had been developed by the Brussels-based Bolero consortium for automated handling of open account transactions. BoleroSURF insures that both parties to a cross-border trade have fulfilled their obligation, thus allowing payment to take place.[33]

CCEWeb. CCEWeb is an e-trade system supporting documentary credits, standby L/Cs, collections, and open accounts. Payment guarantees are provided by banks.[34]

ABN AMRO. The Amsterdam-located bank uses its MaxTrade system for L/C initiation and collection.[35] It offers a solution for cross-border trade management solutions, conducts risk and order management, and settles transactions.

Bank of America. Bank of America offers a system including L/C initiation, management, and collection.[36] It supports amendments to commercial and standby L/Cs as well as collection of documents.

JP Morgan Chase. The TradeDoc system of JP Morgan Chase offers automated preparation of trade documents by integrating its system with the exporter's system.[37]

TradeCard. TradeCard's system verifies that the settlement terms have been satisfied.[38] Payment is guaranteed with Coface credit insurance.

Coface is the major French government export credit agency; it will be discussed in more detail in Chapter 9.

LCconnect. LCconnect is an on-line system for L/C applications. It works with existing bank L/C-processing systems.[39] The system assists the exporter or importer with the selection of banks that will issue or confirm L/Cs.

Wells Fargo. Wells Fargo's commercial electronic office can automate the preparation and receipt of export L/Cs.[40] It can also facilitate export trade finance by permitting exporters to sell accounts receivable to Wells Fargo for quick payment, a form of international factoring.

As more electronic trading platforms are developed, international trade financing will be facilitated by less documentation and speedier transactions. The case of Siemens Capital Corporations is an example in point.[41] Previous to the company's use of e-trade facilities, the application for an L/C was a lengthy paper transaction. An application was typed by Chase using a Word document. It was then printed, signed by two Siemens officers, and faxed back and forth until the language was agreeable, the text was sufficiently specific, and all errors were removed. The L/C then took a week on average to clear. The e-trade version now takes 24 to 48 hours. The benefits to the international trade community will be expanded sales and lower cost transactions.

THE FUTURE OF TRADE FINANCE FOR BANKS

The market for trade finance has become extremely competitive for banks in the last twenty years. Banks have recognized that they must turn to capital market techniques to meet this competition. They have had to structure their trade financing deals to give the borrower what is needed. Securities markets have become more sophisticated, and debt swap markets have grown significantly during this period. Thus, financial engineering has become an important tool for export finance.[42] For example, National Westminster Bank and Banque Paribas provided a US$50 million loan facility to Wardair, a Canadian airline, to finance the purchase of twelve Airbus A-310/300 airliners. These banks used a system of letter of credit guarantees coupled with long-term funding from the borrower's local bond market. Similarly, First Chicago Bank financed the purchase of a new blast furnace by South Korea's Pohang Iron and Steel Company. The deal was worth £100 million and incorporated the conversion of conventional sterling export credits into low interest dollar and Swiss franc debt through the swap market. Finally, Morgan Grenfell Bank of Great Britain also used the swap market to arrange a £33 million, 11 1/2 year, fixed-term credit to the Soviet Union to support the Yugoslav content of a factory automation plant order.

THE BEST TRADE FINANCE BANKS

After the preceding discussion about the role of banks in the international trade finance process and the concomitant documentation such trade requires, a final note is necessary about the world's best trade finance banks. Each year, the trade publication, *Global Finance*, publishes an annual survey entitled, "The World's Best Trade Finance Banks." One of the banks in the survey is awarded the title of winner of the survey. For 2003, a U.S. institution, Citigroup, was named the top trade finance bank.[43] Citigroup was cited as having specialized knowledge of local markets in reducing the riskiness of overseas transactions in its financing operations and is the lead arranger of trade transactions guaranteed by the U.S. Export-Import Bank. Citigroup not only was named the best trade finance bank globally but also was named best in the Americas. The best trade finance bank selected for Europe was ABN AMRO in the Netherlands. HSBC Holdings was named best for Asia. Bank Austria Creditanstalt was selected as best in Central and Eastern Europe. The best trade finance banks selected by *Global Finance,* including those that are headquartered in the countries whose ECAs are discussed in Chapter 9, are listed in Figure 3.8.

ECAs of the following countries are examined in Chapter 9: Australia, Canada, France, Germany, India, Japan, South Korea, and the United Kingdom. ECAs from Malaysia and Thailand, as well as three multilateral ECAs representing South American, Moslem, and African countries, are also included in the discussion in Chapter 9, but no banks were selected in the global survey from these countries. Westpac Banking of Australia was selected as best trade finance bank in that country because of its on-line banking system, known as ImpEx, and its use of the bolero.net platform, which facilitates paperless international trade. (Bolero was discussed in more detail earlier in this chapter.) The best trade finance bank selected in Canada is the Royal Bank of Canada. It was cited for its 3,500 correspondent banking relationships. BNP Paribas was selected in France because of its international network of interconnected trade centers. WestB was named the best trade finance bank in Germany because of its lending operations, which are guaranteed by the U.S. Export-Import Bank. ICICI Bank is India's best in this industry and the first Indian bank to provide resident foreign currency accounts. Mitsubishi Tokyo Financial Group was selected in Japan since the bank controls a large share of Japanese companies' overseas business. The Korea Exchange Bank is a specialist bank in trade finance and foreign

Global	Citigroup
Americas	Citigroup
Europe	ABN AMRO
Central & Eastern Europe	Bank Austria Creditanstalt
Asia	HSBC Holding
Argentina	Citigroup
Australia	Westpac Banking
Austria	Bank Austria Creditanstalt
Belgium	Fortis Bank
Brazil	Banco do Brasil
Canada	Royal Bank of Canada
China	Bank of China
Colombia	Bancolombia
Finland	Nordea
France	BNP Paribas
Germany	WestB
Hong Kong	HSBC Holdings
India	ICICI Bank
Indonesia	Bank Mandiri
Italy	IntesaBci
Japan	Mitsubishi Tokyo Financial Group
Mexico	Grupo Financiero Banamex Accival
Netherlands	ABN AMRO
Nigeria	United Bank for Africa
Norway	Den norske Bank
Russia	Alfa Bank
Saudi Arabia	Saudi American Bank
Singapore	DBS Group
South Africa	Standard Bank
South Korea	Korea Exchange Bank
Spain	Banco Bilbao Vizcaya
Sweden	Nordea
Switzerland	Credit Suisse Group
Taiwan	International Commercial Bank of China
Turkey	Garanti Bank
United Kingdom	Barclays Bank

Source: Gordon Platt, "World's Best Trade Finance Banks 2003," *Global Finance*, Vol. 17, February 2003, pp. 33–38.

Figure 3.8 Best Trade Finance Banks for 2003 (as selected by *Global Finance*)

exchange. Barclays Bank was selected as best trade finance bank in the United Kingdom because it leads all non-U.S. banks in arranging transactions for the U.S. Export-Import Bank.

SUMMARY AND CONCLUSIONS

International trade financing is primarily implemented by the banking system. The process is fraught with documentation. Freight forwarders and customs brokers facilitate the documentation process. Banks make loans to exporters or importers because trade must be processed; the loans are made without recourse for the exporter. Few manufacturers would export their products if they had to do so with recourse to them in the case of nonpayment by the importer. In the case of nonpayment, they could lose both the goods exported and the payments.

Banks convert the draft (the document that orders payment for the goods by the person who owes the money or agrees to make the payment to the creditor to whom the money is owed) into a banker's acceptance, thus essentially securitizing the document and enabling it to be discounted into a negotiable instruments market in which a dealer makes a market for investors who specialize in banker's acceptances. The instrument has facilitated international trade in the past, although the emergence of other means of trade finance have caused a decline in its use.

Banks still engage in nontraditional methods of trade finance. Although European banks have deemphasized forfaiting, many U.S. banks have adapted the method for certain types of merchandise goods. Forfaiting has become an accepted mode of getting payment into the exporter's hands much faster than a more traditional means of trade finance.

Finally, the use of L/Cs has declined drastically in recent years for a number of reasons. L/Cs involve a lengthy process to administer and issue, and they often contain costly errors in their language. Several services have become available that offer exporters electronic means for trade documentation. These systems are based on e-commerce platforms and can both speed up the pre-shipment process and reduce the cost of international trade transactions.

Regardless of the method of finance used to facilitate international trade transactions, the banking system is still the initiating force in financing the trade. Whether the transactions are traditional, that is, via letters of credit, sight drafts, and other documentation involved, or whether they are nontraditional, that is, a forfaiting transaction or countertrade, the banking system is all important in the financing of international trade. However, banks are averse to risk. Many international trade transactions are exposed to commercial or political risk, and banks would prefer to reduce or eliminate any risks of these types. Therefore, they prefer to have the trade credits they grant to exporters either guaranteed or insured by some third party. The next three chapters will cover the U.S. institutions that guarantee or insure trade credits: the U.S. Export-Import (Ex-Im) Bank, the Foreign Credit Insurance Association (FCIA), and the Public Export Funding Corporation (PEFCO).

NOTES

1. Jeff Madura, *International Financial Management* (Mason, OH: South-Western, 2003), pp. 560–563.

2. John D. Daniels and Lee H. Radebaugh, *International Business: Environments and Operations* (Reading, MA: Addison-Wesley, 1998), pp. 725–726.

3. Suk H. Kim and Seung H. Kim, *Global Corporate Finance: Text and Cases* (Oxford, England: Blackwell, 1999), pp. 315–316.

4. Ray August, *International Business Law: Text, Cases, and Readings* (Englewood Cliffs, NJ: Prentice-Hall, 1993), p. 565.

5. "Letter of Credit," available on-line January 23, 2003, at www.credit-to-cash.com/export_import/letter_of_credit.shtml, p. 1.

6. August, *International Business Law*, p. 567.

7. Jane E. Hughes and Scott B. MacDonald, *International Banking: Text and Cases* (Boston: Pearson Education, 2002), p. 105.

8. This example is based on www.law.utk.edu/cle/letcred/1-VB.HTM, p. 1., accessed January 31, 2003.

9. Donald A. Ball and Wendell H. McCulloch, Jr., *International Business: The Challenge of Global Competition* (Chicago: Irwin, 1996), pp. 529–530.

10. James Ebert, "International Trade Finance: The Banker's Acceptance," unpublished paper, Kent State University College of Business Administration, August 2002, pp. 15–16.

11. Ibid., p. 16.

12. James C. Baker, *International Finance: Management, Markets, and Institutions* (Upper Saddle River, NJ: Prentice-Hall, 1998), pp. 233–234.

13. James C. Baker and Richard J. Wayman, "Forfaiting: A Little-Known Method of International Trade Financing," in William W. Sihler, ed., *Classics in Commercial Bank Lending* (Philadelphia: Robert Morris Associates, 1985), pp. 497–509.

14. Bill Holstein, "Congratulations, Exporter! Now About Getting Paid. . .," *Business Week*, January 17, 1994, p. 98.

15. Baker and Wayman, "Forfaiting," pp. 505–506.

16. David Rudnik, "The Great Leap Forward," *Euromoney*, May 1991, p. 120.

17. Juan Hovey, "Process Shields Exports from Foreign Crises," *Los Angeles Times*, available December 26, 2002, at www.meridianfinance.com/forfaiting-art.shtml, pp. 1–3.

18. Madura, *International Financial Management*, p. 561.

19. Russ Banham, "Letters of Credit Losing Favor with U.S. Exporters; Credit Insurance Seen as More Viable Hedge," *Journal of Commerce* 415 (February 18, 1998): 4A.

20. Ibid.

21. Holstein, "Congratulations, Exporter!" p. 98.

22. Gordon Platt, "The Incredible Shrinking Letter of Credit," *Global Finance* 16 (September 2002): 52.

23. Musson International Freight Forwarders Inc., "Letter of Credit," available on-line January 31, 2003, at www.mussonfreight.com/letter.htm

24. Michael H. Moffett, Arthur I. Stonehill, and David K. Eiteman, *Fundamentals of Multinational Finance* (Boston: Addison-Wesley, 2003), p. 549.

25. Platt, "The Incredible Shrinking Letter of Credit," p. 98.

26. Gordon Platt, "U.S. Risk Managers Discover Export Credit Insurance," *Journal of Commerce*, April 26, 2000, p. 11.

27. Jonathan Bell, "E-Trade Finance: The Race Is On," *Euromoney*, December 2000, p. 57.

28. Ibid.

29. Julie Brown, "Exports Fly High as Government Programs Offer Financing Aid," *Corporate Cashflow* 10 (July 1989): 32; Holstein, "Congratulations, Exporter! Now About Getting Paid. . .," p. 98.

30. Available on-line September 23, 2002, at www.eximbankja.com/export_factoring.html, pp. 1–2.

31. Jonathan Bell, "E-Trade Finance: The Race Is On," *Euromoney*, December 2000, pp. 56–57.

32. Russ Banham, "Maiden Voyage," *CFO*, 18 (November 2002): 75.

33. Platt, "The Incredible Shrinking Letter of Credit," p. 52.

34. Banham, "Maiden Voyage," p. 75.

35. Ibid.

36. Ibid.

37. Ibid.

38. Ibid.

39. Ibid.

40. Ibid.

41. Ibid., p. 76.

42. Peter Montagnon, "Export Finance," *Financial Times*, April 30, 1988, Section 3, p. I.

43. Gordon Platt, "World's Best Trade Finance Banks 2003," *Global Finance* 17 (February 2003): 33–38.

4

The U.S. Export-Import Bank

More than three dozen export credit agencies (ECAs) have been established by the governments of more than thirty countries around the world.[1] An ECA that is a focal point of this book is the agency established by the U.S. government: the U.S. Export-Import Bank (Ex-Im). This chapter is devoted to the Ex-Im's history, evolution, and operations of this agency.

Ex-Im has nothing to do with imports. The name is a misnomer. Ex-Im is only involved in transactions that result in the export of U.S. merchandise. In addition, Ex-Im has never done what its original charter mandated it to do. The institution was established in 1934 by an act of the U.S. Congress to facilitate the financing of trade with the Union of Soviet Socialist Republics (USSR), to which the U.S. government, under President Franklin Roosevelt, had just given official recognition. The Great Depression had already begun at that time, and little or no international trade was carried out during the 1930s. The institution was not used during World War II and, after the end of the war, the Cold War between the United States and the USSR began. Thus, trade between the two governments was never financed in a method requiring the guarantees of Ex-Im during those years.

In 1945, the Export-Import Bank Act was passed by the U.S. Congress and signed into law, creating the U.S. Export-Import Bank as we know it today. The agency was established to supplement, but not compete with, private export financing. It is not an aid or development agency, but its operations sometimes seem to be in the form of assistance to developing nations due to the nature of the trade it facilitates.

Ex-Im offers a number of services. It provides guarantees of working capital loans for U.S. exporters. It guarantees the repayment of loans or makes loans to foreign purchasers of U.S. merchandise goods and services. It provides credit insurance against nonpayment by foreign buyers as a result of either political or commercial risk or both. Ex-Im offers these services only if exports of goods or services from the United States result and a reasonable assurance of repayment is present. (These and other programs offered by Ex-Im will be discussed in more detail in subsequent sections of this chapter.)

Although Ex-Im is not a foreign aid agency, it does place emphasis on assisting exports to developing countries. Another mission of the agency is to counter trade subsidies granted by other governments. In addition, it has placed more emphasis on export transactions by U.S. small businesses, promotion of the export of environmentally beneficial goods and services, and the expansion of project finance capabilities.

The management of Ex-Im is centered in a board of directors, which consists of a chair, vice-chair, and three additional board members. No more than three of these members may be of the same political party. They are appointed by the president of the United States and serve at the president's discretion and for staggered terms.

The Ex-Im has had a checkered history. In addition to being established for a role it has never performed, the agency has had its share of controversy. In 1953, U.S. President Dwight D. Eisenhower nearly abolished the institution for budgetary reasons and because of a perception that it was in competition with the World Bank. Some historians believe that President Ronald Reagan wanted to end the agency's operations. In recent times, President George W. Bush announced a planned 25 percent cut in the budget of Ex-Im because of deficit spending by the government. Other questions have been raised about the conflict between its stated missions and the types of business that it promotes by its operations. These controversies will be discussed in detail later in this chapter.

EX-IM PROGRAMS

Ex-Im administers a number of financing, guarantee, and insurance programs. These operations are designed to assist the financing of the exports of US goods and services. Ex-Im operations have supported more than US $400 billion of U.S. exports during its years of operations The major programs include: guarantee of working capital, guarantee of medium- and long-term trade credits, credit guarantee facilities, assistance of environmental and nuclear exports, insurance of export credits, medium- and long-term loans, project finance, and aircraft finance. These will be discussed in more detail in the following sections.

Working Capital Guarantee Program

The Working Capital Guarantee Program enables exporters to obtain the working capital needed to bid, construct, or enhance production and to complete foreign contract awards, all prior to the actual exports necessary for the project. By guaranteeing the working capital credits obtained from a bank, the commercial lender is encouraged to make such a loan when it is related to an export activity. The Ex-Im guarantee covers 90 percent of the principal and interest of the loan and is backed by the full faith and credit of the U.S. government.[2]

Certain criteria have been developed by Ex-Im that the lender and the exporter must follow to be eligible for this program. The lender can be any bank, provider of commercial credit, or other public or private lender with at least three years of operating experience. The exporter must be a commercial firm with a revenue-producing operating history and be domiciled in the United States. The firm must have a tangible net worth.

Loans guaranteed under this program may be used to acquire inventory for export, to pay for direct and indirect costs of production or purchase of export-related goods, to support letters of credit that are to be used as bid or performance bonds or payment guarantees, and by an indirect exporter acting as an agent of the exporter. Ex-Im works with the Private Export Funding Corporation (PEFCO) in an alternate funding program for lenders and exporters. This relationship will be discussed in more detail in Chapter 6.

Medium- and Long-Term Programs

Medium- and long-term export transactions can be supported by either loans or guarantees under this Ex-Im program. This program will be discussed in this section.

Guarantee Program. Ex-Im guarantees private sector loans made to buyers of U.S. exports when the buyers have good credit. The guarantee covers the repayment risk. Some of the up-front risk is borne by the importer, who must pay down at least 15 percent of the transaction. The Ex-Im guarantee covers 100 percent of the remaining 85 percent of both commercial and political risk, although guarantee of political risk only is also offered by Ex-Im. All U.S. capital equipment, projects, and services that are exported are eligible for the guarantee. Repayment terms range from one to ten years depending on the value of the transaction, the characteristics of the project or products being exported, the importer's country, and the competitive terms offered by other official credit institutions.

Ex-Im offers a credit guarantee facility under this program. This facility is a medium-term line of credit extended to a foreign bank or company by a funding bank guaranteed by Ex-Im. Of course, the objective of this facility is to finance exports of U.S. goods and services. Two funding options are available under this facility. One option evidences each individual disbursement with a promissory note from the foreign bank. The other option consolidates multiple disbursements into a single promissory note from the foreign bank.

Direct Loan Program. Under this program, Ex-Im makes fixed-rate loans directly to foreign importers of U.S. goods and services. These loans are made with the objective of assisting the U.S. exporter faced with competition from other foreign suppliers supported by their export credit agencies or banks. Ex-Im can lend up to 85 percent of the value of the goods in the contract and offers the option of a guarantee or loan. The same type of goods and services eligible under the guarantee program are eligible for these medium- or long-term loans. Repayment of direct loans ranges from five to ten years and is generally made in semiannual payments.

Export Credit Insurance Program

Ex-Im's Export Credit Insurance Program assists U.S. exporters in the development and expansion of their export sales. This program protects U.S. exporters against nonpayment by foreign importers or debtors as a result of political or commercial conditions. Policies under this program can cover shipments to one importer or to many importers. They may be comprehensive in their coverage of both political and commercial risks or cover political risk only. They can cover both short- and medium-term sales. The program includes three policies aimed at small business firms in the beginning stages of an export business: the Small Business Policy, the Small Business Environmental Policy, and the Umbrella Policy. These policies will be discussed in the following sections.

Small Business Policy

Ex-Im has formulated and implemented a comprehensive set of programs designed to assist small U.S. firms in the exporting process. As mentioned in Chapter 1, 30 percent of small U.S. firms would like to export their product or products, but for one or more reasons, they do not export. Two-thirds of those that do export only ship goods to one country. In recent years, as much as 80 percent of Ex-Im's transactions have assisted small- and medium-sized U.S. firms.

Ex-Im coordinates its operations with the U.S. Small Business Administration (SBA), especially with its Working Capital Guarantee Program. Under this program, Ex-Im extends repayment guarantees to lenders on secured, short-term working-capital loans made to qualified exporters. The major objective is twofold: to increase U.S. exports and to help smaller U.S. firms.

One representative example of Ex-Im assistance to small businesses is demonstrated by the case of MWI Corporation of Deerfield Beach, Florida.[3] This company has grown over the years by using Ex-Im's facilities. The company was established in 1926 and manufactures pumps and other water-related equipment sold worldwide. Its sales have quadrupled and its workforce tripled since its first Ex-Im commitment in 1983. MWI was selected by Ex-Im for the Small Business Exporter of the Year award in 1997.

Small Business Environmental Policy

Ex-Im provides two programs for small- and medium-sized business firms designed to cover environmental risks. These are the umbrella policy and trade guarantees, insurance, and direct loans to small- and medium-sized firms.

Umbrella Policy. This is a policy of special assistance to small exporters. It provides assistance to the exporter by paying premiums and reporting shipments to the underwriter. Ex-Im uses specialty brokers such as Export Insurance Services in Atlanta, Georgia, to deliver its umbrella policy activity.[4]

Ex-Im and Large U.S. Companies. In recent years, Ex-Im has concentrated on assistance to small- and medium-sized U.S. exporters. However, the agency does work with large U.S. companies with trade guarantees and insurance and direct loans. If the transaction does not involve a dangerous shipment, the parties are relatively good credit risks, and the deal is advantageous to U.S. trade, Ex-Im will assist large U.S. companies.

One example of this support is the case of an extension granted by the Brazilian Government in 1995 to Raytheon Company to build a US$1.4 billion radar system. The system will do environmental surveillance in the Amazon region over a period of eight years. Ex-Im financed US$1.3 billion of the project.[5]

Another Ex-Im transaction with a large U.S. firm involved a loan to a Russian concern to purchase equipment from Caterpillar Company. Ex-Im loaned US$86.2 million to Gazprom, Russia's leading natural gas producer, to purchase 295 tractors from Caterpillar. Had Ex-Im not made the loan, Caterpillar would have lost the sale to Komatsu of Japan. The loan was made although Russia was US$367.7 million in arrears on U.S.-guaranteed grain credits. Gazprom's repayment to Ex-Im was guaranteed by the Bank for Foreign Trade of the Russian Federation. The order represented eight months of production for Caterpillar.[6]

Credit Guarantee Facility

The Credit Guarantee Facility expands the leverage of Ex-Im operations.[7] Under this program, financial institutions can group trade-financed exports, make collections, and have the transactions underwritten as a group. This system is much more efficient than dealing with each transaction by itself. The characteristics of the Credit Guarantee Facility includes: a line of credit guarantee between a U.S. lender and a foreign importer, coverage of multiple sales of U.S. capital goods and services, a minimum facility amount of US$10 million, and coverage for a one-year period.

Project Finance Program

The Project Finance Program allows Ex-Im to support projects developed by U.S. exporters when they compete in international growth industries. This is a specialized program, which includes limited recourse project financing for new or expansion projects where repayment is from the project's cash flows. This program extends only to those projects that rely on the successful completion of several contractual arrangements in compliance with the legal framework and investment regulations of the countries in which they are located.

Aircraft Finance Program

Under the Aircraft Finance Program, Ex-Im assists the export of new or used aircraft manufactured in the United States. These aircraft may include helicopters. Ex-Im also can finance asset-based commercial aircraft.

Nuclear Program

The Nuclear Program is designed to assist exporters of commercial nuclear power plants in generating electricity and in supplying nuclear fuel and fuel reloads, nuclear research reactors, and reactors manufactured for medical radio-isotope uses. This program applies only for exporters that are environmentally responsible and includes measures to protect health and safety. Some of the projects assisted by Ex-Im under this program have been criticized by environmental groups. This issue will be discussed subsequently in this chapter.

Specialty Programs

Ex-Im has developed a number of specialty programs, including the Engineering Multiplier Program, the Operations and Maintenance Contracts Program, the Lease Coverage Program, and the Tied Aid Program.[8] These will be discussed in the following sections.

Engineering Multiplier Program. The Engineering Multiplier Program was developed to assist the stimulation of exports of U.S. architectural, industrial design, and engineering services. Expansion of these types of exports will increase the potential for future U.S. exports. The program covers 85 percent of the export value and the obligor is the foreign buyer.

Operations and Maintenance Contracts Program. The Operations and Maintenance Contracts Program provides Ex-Im loans and guarantees for start-up costs, testing and control expenses, repairs, preventive maintenance, and on-site salaries.

Lease Coverage Program. Ex-Im guarantees financing for leases to foreign entities to assist U.S. exporters and foreign lessors of U.S.-manufactured equipment and related services under the Lease Coverage Program.

Tied Aid Program. The Tied Aid Program is a U.S. trade policy tool that provides trade financing to match identified foreign competitive finance offerings.

CASE STUDIES OF EX-IM OPERATIONS

A number of cases involving Ex-Im operations are discussed in this section. These cases are representative of the programs outlined previously in this chapter.

Shin Satellite

Shin Satellite Corporation of Thailand applied for a loan of US$140 million from the Ex-Im in 2001 to be used to establish a new company, iPSTAR, an Internet service provider. The new company issued an initial public offering in September to furnish the equity for this start-up.[9]

Reforming Business Practices in Asia

Ex-Im launched a program to foster corporate reform in Asia as part of its role of being one of the few major lenders to Asian importers.[10] Ex-Im assists Asian importers in three ways: (1) it lends directly to the importer or guarantees a foreign commercial bank loan to the importer; (2) it lends to the importer's local bank or guarantees a foreign commercial bank loan to the local bank; (3) it insures a letter of credit from the importer's local bank. Since Ex-Im has more than US$13 billion in outstanding credit in Asia, the agency has sufficient leverage to encourage corporate reform.

Ex-Im uses Korea as a model and has extended a large amount of financial assistance to that country, mostly in the form of insuring short-term letters of credit. See Table 4.1 for Ex-Im financial assistance to Asian countries.

Russian Banking Partnerships

Ex-Im recently developed a program of partnerships with fifteen Russian banks. Most of these banks are private and will guarantee payment for purchases by Russian companies of U.S.-made equipment.

TABLE 4.1   U.S. Export-Import Bank Assistance (US$millions) to Asian Countries (as of April 30, 1999)

Recipient Country	Medium-term loans and guarantees	Short-term Insurance	Total Outstanding
China	1,673	14	5,893
Singapore	101	0	111
South Korea	88	1,700	1,493
Taiwan	86	3	84
Philippines	61	9	1,480
Indonesia	27	0.1	2,858
Malaysia	0.4	16	257
Thailand	0	16	612
Total	2,307	1,758	12,788

Source: Bruce Gilley, "Reforming Zeal," *Far Eastern Economic Review,* 162 (May 27, 1999): 51.

This program was developed at a time when Russia's largely unregulated banking system had not yet been revamped after the Russian financial collapse of 1998.[11]

Ex-Im and Nonbank Financial Intermediaries

Non-bank financial intermediaries (NBFIs) often target small- to medium-size exporters for international financing assistance.[12] NBFIs can take advantage of the Ex-Im multibuyer policy by offering open-account payment terms to foreign buyers that are small- and medium-sized. The title to the shipment is taken by the NBFI, which essentially becomes the exporter of record and, thus, assumes the direct foreign payment risk. The Ex-Im multibuyer policy permits the NBFI to commit Ex-Im insurance coverage for a foreign buyer trading for the first time without the administrative problems of applying to Washington, D.C., for approval.

One example of this relationship between Ex-Im and an NBFI involved a newspaper company in northern Mexico. The firm needed extended payment terms to purchase U.S. newsprint and equipment. The U.S. exporter was unwilling to extend payment terms. An NBFI signed a purchase agreement that permitted it to export US$400,000 of newsprint and equipment monthly with terms of up to 180 days. The agreement was insured by Ex-Im for a five-year period and resulted in US$4.8 million of annual exports made by the NBFI and the U.S. exporter.

Small Business Assistance

MWI Corporation. An example of Ex-Im's Working Capital Guarantee Program and a small business operation can be found in the case of MWI Corporation of Deerfield Beach, Florida.[13] MWI is a family-owned manufacturer of pumps and other water-related equipment, which it sells worldwide. Since its first commitment from Ex-Im in 1983, MWI sales have quadrupled and its workforce has tripled to 250 employees.

Poof Products. Another case of Ex-Im assistance of small business firms is demonstrated by the case of Poof Products of Plymouth, Michigan.[14] This small exporter of foam toys operates with forty-five employees. Poof has increased its export sales with the use of Ex-Im's export credit insurance. Its sales expansion was especially significant to Canada, Mexico, and New Zealand. Recently, the company utilized Ex-Im's short-term multibuyer insurance to cover nonpayment risks.

Taylor Machine Works International. Taylor Machine Works International, Inc., of Annandale, New Jersey, is a small exporter of heavy-duty forklift trucks.[15] It used Ex-Im's export credit insurance and met foreign competition by taking advantage of the multibuyer insurance policy. Between 1990 and 1996, Taylor's export sales increased from approximately US$3 to 4 million to US$18.5 million. Its overseas sales rose 500 percent in only six years.

TDT Inc. TDT Inc., Prosperity, West Virginia, manufactures coal-washing equipment, which removes excess material from the coal so that it burns more cleanly. TDT faced competition from larger foreign companies, which could offer better terms to purchasers even though, from an environmental standpoint, TDT manufactured a superior product. Ex-Im guaranteed a US$295,000 loan to a TDT buyer, Semirara Coal Corporation in Manila, the Philippines, thus opening up business in the Philippines and giving TDT a competitive position in the Asian market.[16]

Assistance to Other Nations

Ex-Im is not an agency whose objective is foreign economic assistance, that is, foreign aid. However, if assistance granted to a country will enhance U.S. exports, assistance may be given which, on the surface, appears to be economic aid. The following are examples of this seeming conflict in the objectives of Ex-Im.

Assistance to Korea. During the Asian economic crisis in which Korea was involved, Ex-Im extended short- and medium-term credit to that nation. The credit extended amounted to US$2.25 billion. At the same time, Ex-Im authorized US$750 million of short-term export credit insurance for Korean banks. More aid in the form of credit insurance and medium-term credit was authorized at that time to banking exports of U.S. capital goods and services.[17]

Assistance to Thailand. Ex-Im also assisted Thailand in 1998. Thailand was also one of the countries involved in the Asian economic crisis. Ex-Im provided US$1 billion in trade financing to Thai exporters for their imports of raw materials needed for production. This assistance by Ex-Im was in cooperation with a consortium of private banks, the Asian Development Bank, and the Japanese export credit agency.[18]

Assistance to India. In 2000, Ex-Im extended US$2 billion of credit lines to Indian exporters. This assistance was divided between US$1 billion in Indian rupee-denominated trade finance and US$1 billion in loan guarantees for small- and medium-sized Indian importers. This package supported the sale of ten Boeing 737-800 commercial airliners to Jet Airways. The United States is considered India's largest trading partner and largest source of foreign direct investment.[19]

Assistance to People's Republic of China. Ex-Im has assisted China's energy projects. The assistance was in the form of a US$50 million export credit facility for the Chinese to finance the development of small- to medium-size projects using geothermal, wind, photovoltaic, biomass, and cogeneration technologies. The financial terms are favorable, and the Chinese must import goods and services from the United States under this facility.[20] In addition, Ex-Im has assisted small- and medium-sized Chinese firms such as Chindex International, a Bethesda, Maryland, firm that derives US$22 million in sales from the Chinese market. Chindex exports equipment and supplies to the medical sector and, in 1998, it opened its own hospital in Beijing in a joint venture with local firms. During the 1996–1999 period, Chindex committed to three transactions with the assistance of Ex-Im. In one, Ex-Im provided a tied aid loan to match subsidized competition from the Austrian ECA. In another transaction, Ex-Im provided a guarantee on credit issued by ABN AMRO Bank of the Netherlands.[21]

Assistance to Ghana. Ex-Im has assisted the nation of Ghana by financing a project for the Ghana National Petroleum Corporation.[22] Ex-Im guaranteed a US$300 million loan made by Standard Chartered Bank (U.S.) and funded by PEFCO to finance the development of the Tano oil and gas fields offshore of western Ghana. This case is an example of a number of public and private, U.S. and foreign banks and agencies in a cooperative effort to finance a project in a developing country. In addition to the Ex-Im, Standard Chartered Bank, PEFCO relationship, the U.S. Maritime Administration provided a guarantee for US$65 million worth of bonds placed by Lazard Freres to finance a barge-mounted natural gas-fired power plant being constructed by Westinghouse Electric Corporation and designed for the Ghana project. In addition, the Japan Overseas Economic Co-operation Fund provided the equivalent of US$110 million in yen for an increase in capacity of the power plant being constructed.

Assistance to Mexico. The U.S. government made a significant effort to assist Mexico in the reduction of its sovereign debt after the 1982 default on its jumbo loan. Incentives to attract foreign manufacturing to Mexico were offered by U.S. government agencies. A five-year window was offered by the United States to Mexico during which Mexican exports to the United States would not be subject to some tariffs or quotas.

Ex-Im financing incentives were made a part of this package.[23] These incentives included guarantees on trade credits made by banks to U.S. exporters to ship goods to foreign investment projects located in Mexico by U.S. manufacturers.

Ex-Im Assistance to Industrial Sectors

Ex-Im provides assistance to specific industries whose products make very good prospects for export to other countries. The forest products industry is a good example of this focus by Ex-Im.

Ex-Im Assistance for the U.S. Forest Products Sector. The U.S. forest products sector has received a large amount of assistance from U.S. banks and export credit insurers.[24] For example, wood products are now 60 percent of the export finance business of AmSouth Bank, a regional lender located in Alabama. Exports to Japan, Korea, and Taiwan have been especially large in recent years. The financing has been arranged by banks such as AmSouth and First National Bank of Maryland. These banks and others have used Ex-Im services such as the Working Capital Program and the multibuyer policy to underwrite their export credit financing. They also obtain credit insurance from Ex-Im. These banks also work with the Commodity Credit Corporation of the U.S. Department of Agriculture in the arrangement of export credit guarantees on logs and lumber shipments. The work of this agency will be discussed further in Chapter 7.

FINANCIAL ANALYSIS OF EX-IM OPERATIONS

Ex-Im has been operating for sixty-seven years. During that time, the agency has supported more than US$400 billion of U.S. exports. In fiscal year (FY) 2001, Ex-Im supported US$12.5 billion in U.S. export sales, assisting 2,358 U.S export transactions. According to the Ex-Im annual report, the agency supports US$18 for each dollar appropriated by the U.S. Congress.[25] Operations for FY2001 by Ex-Im programs are broken down in the following sections. The operations for FY2001 are representative of Ex-Im's operations for much of its history.

Small Business

Nearly 18 percent of Ex-Im's total authorizations for FY2001 supported small U.S. exporters. This amounted to US$1.6 billion. In fact, 90 percent of transactions assisted by Ex-Im's programs were aimed at small U.S. firms.[26]

Working Capital

Ex-Im guaranteed US$600 million in transactions under the Working Capital Guarantee Program for pre-export financing in FY2001. More than US$500 million of this amount guaranteed financing for small U.S. exporters.

Export Credit Insurance

Ex-Im issued US$2.2 billion in export credit insurance in FY2001. Some 98 percent of the policies issued under this program were made to small U.S. exporters.

Project and Structured Finance

In FY2001, Ex-Im financed US$1 billion for limited recourse projects in the energy and petrochemical industries. More than US$1.1 billion was authorized by Ex-Im for structured finance transactions for telecommunications and energy sector exports to Latin America and Asia.

Aircraft

In FY2001, Ex-Im financed exports totaling US$2.5 billion for exports of U.S.-manufactured aircraft. This financing was made to export fifty-three large commercial aircraft to twelve airlines located in eleven countries.

Environmental

Ex-Im financed the exports of US$394 million worth of U.S. goods and services deemed environmentally beneficial to the importing countries during FY2001. Guarantees for environmentally sound exports were made totaling US$68 million.

Energy

Ex-Im supported twenty-three transactions for U.S. exports to energy production and transmission projects in foreign countries during FY2001. The value of these exports totaled US$2 billion. In addition, Ex-Im assisted U.S. exports of US$1.37 billion in the petroleum industry.

High Technology

Ex-Im financed US$900 million of U.S. high technology exports in FY2001. These sales included electronics, telecommunications, and medical equipment.

Services

Ex-Im financed the U.S. export of US$695 million of services in FY2001. These included engineering, design, consulting, and training services.

Agriculture

In FY2001, Ex-Im assisted the U.S. export of US$117 million of goods, services and equipment in the agricultural sector. These goods and services included agricultural commodities, livestock, and foodstuffs.

EVALUATION OF EX-IM OPERATIONS

This concluding section is devoted to an evaluation of Ex-Im's operations as though it were working in a vacuum. However, a more in-depth evaluation will be made of the Ex-Im in Chapter 10 after the discussion of other ECAs in Chapter 9. A comparative analysis and evaluation will be discussed in Chapter 10.

Positive Operations

However Ex-Im operates, its specific mission is to increase U.S. exports. The agency has recently entered into a stage in which it encourages reforms with corporate and government restructurings in other countries. This reform movement is not altogether altruistic in that the underlying motive is to open more doors to U.S. exporters and give banks in industrialized countries a greater opportunity to finance more U.S. export trade in more regions of the world.[27]

Ex-Im has made an impact worldwide with its standards dealing with environmental and reform concerns. The agency has encouraged U.S. export sales and this has resulted in the creation of thousands of American jobs. The mere presence of an official export credit agency of the U.S. Government offers advantages that go beyond its day-to-day operations of guaranteeing export trade credits.

Ex-Im is not an aid agency such as the U.S. Agency for International Development (AID). However, the organization has recently used its mission to finance medical supplies and equipment to countries ravaged with HIV/AIDS, especially those in Africa.[28] To accomplish this, Ex-Im directed US$1 billion financing for health care across sub-Saharan Africa during 1999. The financing was aimed at medical equipment, adviser services to hospitals, and pharmaceuticals. Financing for this area was extended to five years instead of the traditional six months for medicines.

Some Problems

During the past five decades Ex-Im has fulfilled its mission of assisting U.S. exporters to obtain financing for their exports. However, some complaints have been leveled at the agency. Critics have found fault with Ex-Im since 1967.[29] At that time, the research of these critics suggested that Ex-Im had a competitive disadvantage vis-à-vis ECAs in Japan and Europe. These early problems involved internal problems and U.S. congressional curbs against the U.S. system of foreign credit insurance. Many of these problems have been alleviated by changes in Ex-Im operations since then. Other problems have been eliminated by the adoption of new and less competitive methods of operation by some of the major foreign ECAs. These changes will be discussed in more detail in Chapter 9.

Other charges have been made against Ex-Im in recent years. One of the strongest of these charges has been made by the environmental community, whose representatives have accused U.S. business with polluting the environment and fueling global warming. Since the Ex-Im provides financing to U.S. corporations to export many products that may harm the environment, it has become a magnet for complaints from this area.[30]

The focus of the charge advanced by groups such as Friends of the Earth International, is that Ex-Im has facilitated the construction of billions of dollars in fossil fuel and mining projects since 1992, which can harm the environment and cause global warming. Cited projects with which Ex-Im has assisted include the Paiton coal-fired power plant in Indonesia; an oil-drilling and pipeline project in Chad and Cameroon built by ExxonMobil, Chevron, and other companies, and a proposed power plant in Thailand to be built by California's Edison Mission.

The Friends of the Earth group is not partial in its criticism of assistance it deems to be destructive of parts of the environment. At the same time this organization criticized Ex-Im for financing what was believed to be a destructive pulp mill in Indonesia, it attacked the Overseas Private Investment Corporation for its investment analysis of a planned pipeline through the Amazon basin and the World Bank for considering plans to assist the construction of a pipeline in Africa.[31]

In addition to Friends of the Earth, other groups have criticized Ex-Im operations for not being environmentally sound. Some of these groups attempted to block Ex-Im's US$317 million loan guarantee for the sale of an instrumentation and control system and advanced design nuclear fuel to the Temelin nuclear reactor in the Czech Republic.[32] This reactor is located forty miles from the Austrian border. Among the groups that have criticized this financing by Ex-Im was an Austrian delegation. Ex-Im was convinced that the project was safe and furnished the guarantee.

Ex-Im has been criticized by some U.S. industries because of its loans to foreign companies. For example, the U.S. steel industry has charged that Ex-Im loans to foreign steel makers have harmed the U.S. steel industry. An example of this issue can be demonstrated by the guarantee of an US$18 million loan to Benxi Iron and Steel Company of China. The reasoning for this assistance of the foreign steel maker was that at least three U.S. companies, including General Electric, would benefit from this transaction because of the exports of machinery they would make to the project. The result was that American jobs would not be lost due to the guaranteed loan.[33]

Another charge often made against Ex-Im operations is that the agency is slow relative to other ECAs in investigating the credit risk of importers and foreign banks making trade loans that Ex-Im is considering to guarantee or to extend insurance. On the other hand, this slowness in the credit analysis by Ex-Im may be countered by the belief of some that the U.S. agency is more aggressive than other ECAs, particularly ECGD, the British agency. Ex-Im spends more time looking at foreign borrowers in detail, while agencies such as ECGD may focus more on the major banks with which they deal when underwriting trade credits.

A Cato Institute study recommended the abolition of Ex-Im.[34] (Cato Institute is a think tank based in Washington) The authors of this report refute the Ex-Im's supposition that it benefits the United States by assisting U.S. exporters in their attempt to compete against foreign companies that receive subsidies from their governments, that Ex-Im creates jobs for Americans, and that its work improves the U.S. balance of payments. The Cato study holds that U.S. exporters have done much better than their counterparts in Germany, Japan, the United Kingdom, and France and that they have not suffered much from subsidized competition. They suggest that only Canada surpassed the United States in relative export growth. They show that a U.S. General Accounting Office study in 1997 found that both the United States and Canada subsidized a far smaller amount of exports than did their previously mentioned counterparts.

The Cato study also refutes the claim that U.S. employment benefits from the work of Ex-Im. The authors claim that the cumulative impact on employment from exports is "indeterminate and weak" and, in fact, suggest that in recent years, the U.S. dollar has been bid up, causing exports to be more difficult to make and imports to be more attractive to U.S. consumers.

In addition, the Cato authors suggest that export credit subsidized by Ex-Im is too small to have much of an impact on the trade balance. Only about 1 percent of U.S. exports in 2001 were backed by Ex-Im. The authors found that private credit markets are much deeper and more accessible than they were in the period when Ex-Im was established. Finally, they hold that it may be unconstitutional or, at least, unfair for Ex-Im to use taxpayers' money to assist particular businesses, such as the now-defunct Enron, General Electric, and other large firms that do not need assistance from taxpayers in the form of export credit guarantees or insurance. See Table 4.2 for a listing of the top ten U.S. companies in terms of Ex-Im assistance in FY2000.

Finally, another charge made by the Cato study is that Ex-Im provides financing for exports to countries that do not have trouble obtaining export credits. Furthermore, some of this financial aid displaces private investment by funding projects that otherwise might not have been undertaken.[35] The authors of this report argue that Ex-Im could immediately reduce its lending procedures without hindering its mission to face competition from foreign subsidies since only a fraction of Ex-Im financing requests are in reply to subsidized foreign competition.

Whether these charges are well founded or not, Ex-Im's record of operations for the past fifty years points to a tremendous amount of U.S. exports assisted and a concomitant benefit to the gross national product

TABLE 4.2   Top Ten U.S. Companies in Assistance from the Export-Import Bank (FY2000)

U.S. Company	Revenues*	Total (Loans & Guarantees)**	Percentage of Total
1. Boeing	$ 51,321	$3,384	43.1
2. Bechtel Int'l	14,300	1,475	18.8
3. Varian Assoc.	704	674	8.6
4. United Technologies	26,583	334	4.3
5. Willbros Engineers	314	200	2.5
6. Halliburton	11,944	172	2.2
7. Raytheon	16,895	150	1.9
8. Enron	100,789	132	1.7
9. General Electric	129,853	127	1.6
10. Schlumberger	10,034	87	1.1
TOTAL TOP 10 COMPANIES		$6,735	
GRAND TOTAL		$7,844	

Source: Annual Report FY2000 of the Export-Import Bank of the United States (Washington: Export-Import Bank of the United States, 2000), and various annual reports of the companies listed.
*In millions of US dollars
**In thousands of US dollars

of the United States. Nevertheless, the administration of George W. Bush has proposed deep budget cuts for Ex-Im. The proposed cut of 24.5 percent reduces U.S. funding of Ex-Im to US$698 million.[36] James Harmon, outgoing chairman of Ex-Im, warned the administration that U.S. companies were losing markets to foreign competition because of inadequate trade finance.

Finally, Ex-Im has encountered severe competition from other ECAs as well as private insurers. The work of foreign ECAs will be covered in more detail in Chapter 9. Ex-Im is also facing competition from foreign insurers in its own U.S. market.[37] For example, Swiss insurers have entered the top ranks of trade credit and political risk insurance. Zurich Insurance Group and Swiss Reinsurance have put together networks of both products in the last few years. Zurich Insurance acquired all of Baltimore, Maryland-based Fidelity & Deposit over several years. Fidelity & Deposit was founded in 1890 and has been quite active in surety operations with the construction industry and with fidelity bonds for financial institutions. The company entered into a joint venture in credit insurance with the NCM Group, a leading European trade credit insurer. After the takeover by Zurich Insurance, the latter company formed Zurich-American Political Risk, based in Washington. The new affiliate has adopted a strategy of co-insurance and reinsurance with official political risk agencies such as Overseas Private Investment Corporation (OPIC) and the Multilateral Investment Guarantee Agency (MIGA). Swiss Reinsurance (Swiss Re) acquired NCM, the group with which Zurich Insurance had formed a joint venture. Swiss Re also is a shareholder of the Euler Group in Paris. The latter is one of the private companies which took over the short-term credit work of ECGD in Great Britain. Euler bought 50 percent of American Credit Indemnity in Baltimore. The latter has increased its business in export credit insurance significantly. Thus, Ex-Im is facing competition from both abroad and at home.

SUMMARY AND CONCLUSIONS

Ex-Im was established in the early 1930s to finance trade between the United States and the newly recognized Union of Soviet Socialist Republics. For economic and political reasons, this objective was never initiated. Instead the agency became the U.S. government export credit agency to facilitate the financing of U.S. exports in the 1950s. Since then it has assisted U.S. firms with US$400 billion of export insurance, guarantees, and loans. Its activities include a Working Capital Guarantee Program, medium- and long-term guarantees of loans, direct loans, and export credit insurance. It has assisted small- and medium-sized U.S. exporters and 80 percent of Ex-Im's business has been directed to this sector in recent years. Ex-Im cooperates with U.S. private consortia such as Foreign Credit Insurance Association and Private Export Funding Corporation, with foreign export credit agencies, with U.S. government agencies such as the Small Business Administration and the Department of Agriculture, and with U.S. and foreign banks that finance international trade.

Ex-Im faces increasing competition from ECAs in other countries. In the past decade, export credits issued by foreign ECAs have increased by 22 percent.[38] Ex-Im supporters have argued that this is the major reason why the U.S. government should increase funding for the Ex-Im. However, the George W. Bush administration has proposed a nearly 25 percent cut in the appropriations to Ex-Im in FY2003. Ex-Im has had an excellent repayment record during its history. Losses have been only 1.4 percent of disbursements, although these losses have been somewhat higher during the past decade because of Ex-Im financing of trade with developing countries.[39]

The agency has been criticized for a number of its operations in recent years. Groups have criticized Ex-Im for financing environmentally unsound projects in foreign countries. It is seen by some as financing trade of large companies that could easily obtain the assistance from trade finance banks while ignoring small- and medium-sized U.S. firms. The evidence seems to show that more than 80 percent of transactions assisted by Ex-Im in recent years have been for small- and medium-sized businesses. However, the magnitude in money directed toward large company assistance may be much larger than the total of small- and medium-size company support in dollar terms. After the examination of foreign ECAs in Chapter 9, more comparative evaluation of Ex-Im relative to other ECAs will be made concerning these and other criticisms.

After the pros and cons of Ex-Im have been examined, it seems that the agency has served a useful purpose over the past five decades. Its operations have improved over time and the agency has become more competitive. On the other hand, the privatization of export trade insurance and guarantee programs in some industrialized countries, the advent of electronic means to finance trade, and the growth of international banking operations have all added to the handwriting on the wall: that some ECAs may be headed for obsolescence. For the present, Ex-Im is performing a creditable job in facilitating international trade by U.S. exporters. The decision to insure its own trade credits rather than rely on FCIA is a sign that the administrators of Ex-Im have become more aggresive in competing with a variety of foreign ECAs. The agency, however, will need the support of the U.S. government if it is to maintain this more competitive position. By the time this book is published, the final decision to make drastic cuts in Ex-Im's budget will have been made and implemented. Time will tell whether the U.S. government considers the agency to be a part of its foreign relations policy as well as a tool to promote and assist the U.S. economy.

NOTES

1. This section is based on material found on-line September 6, 2002, at www.exim.gov/history.html, p. 1.

2. U.S. Export-Import Bank, "Working Capital Guarantee Program," available on-line September 6, 2002, at www.exim.gov/wcgp.html, p. 1.

3. Angela M. Phifer, "Ex-Im Bank's Support for Small Business," *Business America* 118 (October 1997): 32–33.

4. Richard Barovick, "Most Exporters Use Brokers to Guide Them through Maze," *Journal of Commerce*, September 1, 1999, p. 9.

5. "Raytheon Says Brazil Extends Big Contract," *Wall Street Journal*, November 28, 1995, p. B6.

6. Laurie Morse, "Eximbank Backs Huge Caterpillar Deal with Russians," *Financial Times*, February 26, 1993, p. 4.

7. Available on-line September 6, 2002, at www.exim.gov/mover.html, p. 4.

8. Ibid., pp. 7–8.

9. "Shin Satellite Seeks $140m Ex-Im Loan," *Bangkok Post*, May 9, 2001, p. 1.

10. Bruce Gilley, "Reforming Zeal," *Far Eastern Economic Review* 162 (May 27, 1999): 50.

11. Sabrina Tavernise, "World Business Briefing: Europe; Russian Banking Partnerships," *New York Times*, December 6, 2000, p. W1.

12. Robert E. Duncan, "Knowledge of Financing Options Can Make U.S. Exporters More Competitive," *Business America* 118 (October 1997): 44.

13. Angela M. Phifer, "Ex-Im Bank's Support for Small Business," *Business America*, 118 (October 1997): 32.

14. Ibid., p. 33.

15. Ibid.

16. U.S. Export-Import Bank, *General Overview* (Washington: U.S. Export-Import Bank, n.d.), p. 6.

17. "Boost for South Korea," *Financial Times*, June 11, 1998, p. 4.

18. "U.S. Eximbank to Provide $1bn Trade Financing," *Financial Times*, March 17, 1998, p. 4.

19. Stephen Fidler and Khozem Merchant, "US, India Announce Deals of Dollars 4bn," *Financial Times*, March 25, 2000, p. 10.

20. "China Attracts Global Leaders," *Engineering News Record* 238 (June 9, 1997): 14.

21. Richard Barovick, "Small Firms in Bind to Get Export Financing in China," *Journal of Commerce* 421 (October 13, 1999): 9.

22. "Ghana National Petroleum Corporation," available on-line December 13, 2002, at www.winne.com/ghana/SOCS/GNPC.html, 1–2.

23. Roy C. Smith, *The Global Bankers* (New York: E. P. Dutton, 1989), p. 142.

24. Richard Barovick, "Forest Products Sector Gives Export Credit Its Due," *Journal of Commerce* 418 (November 12, 1998): 10A.

25. Export-Import Bank of the United States, *Annual Report FY2001* (Washington: Author, 2002), p. 3.

26. Ibid., p. 14.

27. Gilley, "Reforming Zeal," pp. 50–51.

28. James A. Harmon, "A Look at Africa and the AIDS Loan. . .," *The Washington Post*, September 17, 2000, p. B3.

29. J. Fred Weston and Barthold Sorge, "Export Insurance: Why the U.S. Lags," *Columbia Journal of World Business* 2 (September–October 1967): 67–76.

30. Friends of the Earth International, "Environmentalists Agree with President Bush: US Export-Import Bank Needs Appropriations Cut," press relase, February 22, 2001, available on-line September 7, 2002, at www.foe.org/act /gs4pr.html, pp. 1–2.

31. Nancy Dunne, "Earth Day Fowl Play for Green Americans," *Financial Times*, April 23, 1999, p. 7.

32. "US Eximbank Faces Environmental Criticism," *International Trade Finance* 206 (February 25, 1994): 7.

33. Peter Krouse, "Ex-Im Bank Revisiting Foreign Aid for Business," *Cleveland Plain Dealer*, July 25, 2001, p. C2.

34. Aaron Lukas and Ian Vásquez, "Dump the Export-Import Bank," available on-line September 7, 2002, at www.cato.org/dailys/03-19-02.html, pp. 1–2.

35. Aaron Lukas and Ian Vásquez, "Rethinking the Export-Import Bank," Trade Briefing Paper No. 15, March 12, 2003, available on-line September 7, 2002, at www.freetrade.org/pubs/briefs/tbp-015es.html, p. 1.

36. Edward Alden, "U.S. and Canada: Hefty Cuts Proposed in Export Finance Schemes," *Financial Times*, April 10, 2001, p. 5.

37. Richard Barovick, "Swiss Insurers Shine in Credit, Political Risk," *Journal of Commerce* 416 (August 27, 1998): 8A.

38. Joseph Guinto, "Should Gov't Be in the Business of Subsidizing U.S. Firms Abroad?" *Investor's Business Daily*, May 16, 2001, p. A18.

39. Chairman, Hearings of U.S. Senate Committee on Banking, Housing, and Urban Affairs, Comments by Paul Sarbanes, June 19, 2001, available on-line at www.senate.gov., accessed March 15, 2002.

5

Foreign Credit Insurance Association (FCIA)

Two private firms supplement the work of the U. S. Export-Import Bank (Ex-Im) and facilitate international trade finance for U.S. exporters. These are the Foreign Credit Insurance Association (FCIA) and the Private Export Funding Corporation (PEFCO). FCIA is the subject of this chapter. PEFCO and its operations will be the topic of Chapter 6.

FCIA was established in 1961 during the presidency of John F. Kennedy by 50 leading insurance firms. President Kennedy believed that U.S. exports were vital to the U.S. balance of international payments, that these exports had to be financed, that Ex-Im needed assistance in this area, and that private enterprise should be more involved in financing U.S. export trade. FCIA has pioneered export credit insurance in the United States.[1]

FCIA is backed by the economic strength of Great American Insurance Company. The latter is a specialty and multi-line property and casualty insurer and is part of the Great American Insurance Group, a consortium of some four dozen United States–based insurance companies which provide property and casualty insurance coverage. Great American is headquartered in Cincinnati, Ohio, and oversees property and casualty insurers throughout the United States. Great American is owned by American Financial Group, a New York Stock Exchange–listed corporation.[2] Great American Insurance Company also operates three other divisions, which provide ocean and inland marine insurance, surety bonds covering contractors and subcontractors, and fidelity bonds, which cover employees of financial institutions, mercantile companies, and government entities.

FCIA was formed to insure the foreign receivables of U.S. exporters against nonpayment resulting from political or commercial risks, or both. As such, it acts as an agent of Ex-Im. The latter is responsible for covering FCIA's expenses which exceed premiums it charges for insuring trade credits. FCIA administers and markets the export insurance program offered by Ex-Im including premium collection, claims handling, and claims recovery.

In 1983, 41 of the original FCIA founding members withdrew from the venture because they had suffered large commercial losses, particularly after the Mexican government defaulted on sovereign loans advanced to the country by leading international banks. Ex-Im began to insure exporters against both commercial and political risk at that time. After that date, FCIA acted as the marketing and service agent for Ex-Im.[3] FCIA currently has 60 private insurance companies which are owners of the consortium.

In 1991, the relationship between FCIA and Ex-Im changed. FCIA Management Company, Inc., (FCIAM) was formed as a subsidiary of Great American Insurance Company to provide underwriting and administrative services of Great American's credit insurance programs. Its policies are issued in the name of FCIA or Great American Insurance Company. FCIAM now services export credit insurance policies on behalf of Ex-Im and sells FCIA export credit insurance. The agreement between FCIA and Ex-Im was terminated in 1992 because Ex-Im assumed responsibility for the operation of its own insurance program.

FCIA is a member of the International Union of Credit and Investment Insurers, more commonly known as the Berne Union. This organization is a worldwide association of government and private insurance entities and was established to facilitate information exchange, promote sound underwriting principles, and assist in enforcement of foreign purchasers' payment obligations. The Berne Union is discussed in more detail in Chapter 9.

TRADE CREDIT INSURANCE

Export credit is the credit offered by the exporter, directly or indirectly through its bank, to the importer in the contract for sale of goods or the loans given to finance the sale. Risks, either commercial or political, may arise in the conduct of export business resulting in nonpayment by the importer. Thus, export credit insurance is a product which will eliminate or reduce such risks.

Credit insurance began in Europe in the middle of the nineteenth century when domestic credit risks were insured, especially in France, Germany, Switzerland, and the United Kingdom. One of the first instances of the use of export credit insurance occurred in Great Britain near the end of the nineteenth century when British merchants shipping goods to Australia demanded that these goods be insured. The first official export credit insurance scheme was introduced by the British Government in 1919 when British exports to East Europe were encouraged. That region was considered highly risky and the exports would not have been made without some type of government insurance program.

Trade credit insurance presents the exporter with advantages and benefits. On the other hand, some problems do stem from the use of such insurance. These advantages and disadvantages are discussed next.

Benefits of Trade Credit Insurance

Credit insurance is a method designed to reduce various risks in business accounts receivable caused by minimizing the risk of nonpayment stemming from financial, economic, or political uncertainties. According to FCIA, trade credit insurance has a number of benefits.[4] First, it can improve financial performance by enabling a firm to achieve its financial objectives and to develop more favorable financing alternatives. Second, trade credit insurance can be used to strategically increase export sales with less risk. Third, such insurance can protect the firm's accounts receivable at a relatively low cost. In short, exporters use credit insurance to mitigate risk, to meet the competition's selling terms, and to increase financing of international trade. The latter reason is the most compelling for small exporters to use credit insurance.

U.S. companies have generally used letters of credit to transfer the risk of nonpayment.[5] However, the appeal of trade credit insurance has increased. It is paid for by the exporter whereas the buyer usually paid for the letter of credit. Credit insurance premiums are tax deductible. The cost of credit insurance is less than one percent of sales. Trade insurance eliminates the paperwork and handling of letters of credit and the necessity to check foreign credit reports. Letters of credit often have discrepancies which are, thus, alleviated with trade credit insurance. Credit insurance can cover both commercial and political risks.

FCIA appears to be the main option for U.S. companies which export less than US$5 million annually. FCIA's minimum premium is US$500 and, depending on the cause of a loss, FCIA insurance covers 90 to 100 percent of the loss, after a deductible.

Problems with Credit Insurance

Drawbacks can occur with credit insurance. In some cases, it is unavailable.[6] Accounts cannot be insured in, for example, Iraq or Iran.

Very little credit insurance can be found for trade in much of Africa. Only recently was it introduced into Brazil. The high inflation there had precluded the credit insurance business. Credit checks of importers or banks which extend trade credit may be difficult, time-consuming, and costly, especially if they are located in developing nations. FCIA coverage is generally available to customers worldwide but a few countries may be uninsurable because of the current political or economic climate or because of legal sanctions imposed on trade with that country, for example, embargoes such as those on North Korea or Iraq.

Types of Credit Insurance Programs

No typical credit insurance program can be found. They come in various forms. Some are government departments and some are private companies or consortia of private firms. Some are government agencies and some are quasigovernment corporations. Some are operated by export-import banks as has been the case in the United States since 1992. Some of these programs write part of their insurance policies on their own account, as is the case with many short-term commercial and political risks. In these cases, the trade credit insurance entity may use private sector reinsurance. In other cases, the entity writes policies on government account.

FCIA PROGRAMS

FCIA offers a number of programs all designed to insure export credits for shipments which originate from the United States as well as other countries. The key coverage features of FCIA export credit insurance include comprehensive protection against both commercial and political risks for worldwide coverage of exports made on credit terms. Coverage for short-term and medium-term sales is offered. FCIA coverage against political risks protects against events such as the following:[7]

1. an importer's inability to legally obtain U.S. dollars or other approved currencies for transfer to the exporter;
2. loss of transportation or insurance charges incurred after shipment because of an interruption caused by an act of the importer's government;
3. occurrence after shipment of any of the following when not the fault of the importer, credit-issuing bank, or the insured:
   a. cancellation or nonrenewal of an export license or imposition of restrictions on the export of products not subject to restrictions before the shipment;

b. cancellation of authority to import the products of the importer's country;

c. imposition of laws that prevent the importation of the products into the importer's country or that prevent conversion of local currency into the exporter's currency needed to pay for the imports.

4. the occurrence of any of the following after shipment but before default on the payment:

a. war, hostilities, civil war, rebellion, revolution, insurrection, civil commotion, or similar disturbances;

b. governmentally authorized requisition, expropriation, confiscation of, or intervention in, the trade transaction business of the exporter, credit-issuing bank, or guarantors.

Export Credit Insurance

A number of FCIA programs are discussed in the following section. Types of programs and some of the key features of their coverage are included in the discussion.[8]

Pay-As-You-Go Multibuyer Policy. This policy covers export sales only, or it may cover combined export and domestic sales. The policy covers an agreed-upon spread of the exporter's sales of goods made on credit terms up to 180 days. If the sales are combined, the domestic sales are covered if they are made on credit terms up to 60 days. The key features of this policy are that premiums are calculated on the actual shipments made; small premium payments can be made on a regular basis, and the policy usually imposes no country caps on receivables outstanding.

Noncancelable Limits Multibuyer Policy. This policy also covers either exports only or a combination of export and domestic sales. It imposes a restriction that the insurer will not amend or withdraw coverage during the twelve-month policy period. Coverage on exports is good for up to 180 days and, for the domestic sales part of the combined policy, 60 days. Key features of this policy include: locked-in credit limits on importers and countries; minimal policy administration; and one up-front premium payment with a year-end reconciliation.

Key Accounts Multibuyer Policy. This policy covers the exporter's top ten or twenty importer exposures named by the exporter with the smallest exposures retained for the exporter's own account. Coverage is similar to the first two programs previously discussed. Credit limits on the covered importers are approved by the insurer. This policy can be quoted with or without a deductible.

Short-term Single Buyer Policy. This policy covers export sales to only one buyer on credit terms up to 180 days. The coverage is noncancelable. If the importer is a public entity, political risks alone may be insured. The policy normally does not include deductibles.

Medium-term Single Buyer Policy. This policy covers export sales to only one importer and the coverage is noncancelable. Again if the importer is a public entity, political risk alone may be covered. A cash down payment is required as well as a promissory note.

Brokers arrange most export credit insurance policies.[9] That is especially true of private insurers such as FCIA. And it is true for the policies issued by American International Group in New York and Trade Underwriters Agency in Jericho, New York. In fact, 100 percent of their business is brokered. Brokers arrange some 85 percent of such policies issued by Ex-Im. The remainder of Ex-Im's policies are marketed by its regional offices in New York City, Chicago, Houston, Miami, and Los Angeles.

Repayment terms on short-term policies have payment terms of up to 180 days. On a case-by-case basis, short-term policies can be extended to coverage for 360 days for selected commodities, mostly agricultural products, and some capital equipment. Repayment terms for medium-term policies depend on the contract price and the product sold. If the export value is up to US$50,000, the maximum repayment term is two years. For US$45,001–100,000, the maximum repayment is three years. For US$100,001-200,000, the maximum term is four years. For any export value over US$200,000, the maximum term is five years. U.S. content must be at least 50 percent for short-term sales to be insured. For medium-term sales, U.S. content must be 85 percent of the export value. For sales with 50 to 85 percent U.S. content, coverage is available for only the U.S. content.

FCIA Coverage Procedure. The procedure for obtaining FCIA insurance coverage on U.S. exports is rather easy but may, in some instances, take time to implement, especially if a claim is made.[10] FCIA sells all these products through licensed independent insurance brokers or agents, who provide FCIA quotations free of charge. The cost to cover an entire portfolio is generally about 1 percent of sales. The actual rate may be a function of the applicant's type of business, sales volume, terms of sale, loss experience, and buyer quality. FCIA can provide a quotation within one week after receipt of a policy application.

Decisions on an FCIA policy are made by the insured via multibuyer policies. This is accomplished by using the Discretionary Credit Limit, which requires the credit decision to be based on specific information. The insurer sets the credit limits under key accounts and single buyer policies.

If a claim is made under an FCIA policy, the claim can be filed after a waiting period of at least 90 days but no more than 240 days after default. After the proper information is filed to support the claim, claims typically can be approved within 60 days of receipt of a satisfactory proof of loss and supporting documentation.

Under an FCIA policy, the insured has certain responsibilities. The pay as you go multibuyer policies require that insured shipments must be reported monthly by the buyer and premiums must be paid. Significant overdue receivables must be reported. Buyers should be creditworthy based on their past payment experience or financial information.

FCIA Special Risks Insurance

FCIA also offers insurance against special risks. This program includes policies for select risk credit insurance and contract frustration risk insurance. These are primarily programs that insure against specific types of political risk caused by government action in the importer's country, including expropriation of property, war and civil strife, currency controls, and breach of government operations.

Select Risk Credit Insurance Program. The Select Risk Credit Insurance Program protects small- to medium-sized companies needing to protect a small capital base as well as large companies with significant exposure to political risk. These policies can cover single buyer credit and political risks on foreign buyers as well as single buyer credit risks on domestic buyers. The buyer may be either a public or a private entity. Such policies can cover up to 90 percent of the transaction value, and repayment terms are 360 days for short-term coverage and three years for medium-term sales.

Contract Frustration Insurance Program. The Contract Frustration Insurance Program insures performance or payment obligations of either public or private importers. Risks of contract frustration include pre- and post-shipment contract risks, nondelivery risks, on-demand bond risks, and deprivation risks. The latter risk arises when a company owns mobile assets in a foreign country or holds products on consignment and incurs losses because of a local government action. Under the pre- and postshipment contract policy, contract repudiation can be covered if the buyer is a public sector entity. Coverage on contract frustration policies generally is granted up to 90 percent of the shipment's value, and the maximum exposure period is three years, including the pre- and postshipment periods. On-demand bond coverage insures the bid, advance payment, or performance bonds with a maximum policy period of three years. Deprivation policies cover consignment stocks and mobile assets held overseas by the insured. The maximum policy period on consignment stocks is twelve months and, for mobile assets, twenty-four months.

How to Apply for FCIA Coverage

FCIA has developed an application process for its policies designed to facilitate quick coverage for U.S. exporters. It sells its policies through licensed independent insurance brokers or agents, which are listed on the FCIA Web site. FCIA quotes on coverage are provided to brokers free of charge. Premium costs are typically a fraction of 1 percent of sales. A quotation can be provided within a week after receipt of a policy application provided complete documentation is provided by the exporter. Coverage can then be bound on receipt of the applicant's acceptance and deposit premium and a policy can be issued within a day or two.

FCIA Special Financial Institution Coverage

FCIA provides insurance coverage for special financial institutions.[11] The policy features include coverage against select credit risks and cross-border political risks, worldwide short- and medium-term coverage, customized policy wordings, and coverage for both U.S. and non-U.S. entities. The policies offered by FCIA are the bank letter of credit policy and the bank buyer credit policy. The former policy insures against the the issuing bank's failure to honor an irrevocable letter of credit that has been confirmed by the insured. Refinancings of sight letters of credit can be covered under this policy. Single or multiple letters of credit that have been issued during the policy period are covered. The latter policy provides coverage for failure of a foreign purchaser to pay its obligations to the insured which arise from trade transactions. Nonpayment caused by only political risks can be covered by this policy. The policy may cover short- or medium-term transactions. The short-term policy coverage is for 180 days. The medium-term policy insures a maximum of three year terms and requires at least semiannual amortization, a cash down payment, and a promissory note.

FCIA Country Update

FCIA performs one activity unrelated to its insurance and funding work. FCIA publishes a newsletter, *FCIA Country Update,* several times annually. The newsletter contains economic and political intelligence gathered and analyzed by FCIA's international economist. Individual countries are reviewed concerning their political risk situation as well as trade-related developments. A recent issue of *FCIA Country Update* was entitled, "Volatile International Environment, Uncertain Economic Recovery," and contained an overview about the United States, Venezuela, Argentina, Brazil, and South Korea.[12] This newsletter is disseminated to FCIA policyholders, brokers, and assignee banks.

BENEFITS OF FCIA'S OPERATIONS

Several reasons can be given why many firms that produce an exportable product do not, in fact, export. These include the burdensome documentation, the time taken to collect from customers in a distant country, and the risk of nonpayment. Export credit insurance can alleviate these problems. Many banks will not lend against foreign orders without insurance. Export credit insurance enables small companies to make export sales they could not finance on their own since the bank is usually assigned as beneficiary of an export credit insurance policy.

Credit insurance facilitates the achievement of several financial objectives and can improve the financial performance of an export company. It can result in income from fraudulent and slow-paying customers. It can increase industry competitiveness. It can limit customer and country risk which can in turn create higher company growth rates, improve cash flows and operating ratios and create confidence in the company's shareholders and potential investors when it is disclosed in the company's financial reports that the firm uses credit insurance.

FCIA's foreign credit insurance is comprised of five key elements: (1) it covers U.S. exports worldwide; (2) it protects against both commercial and political risks; (3) it covers shipments which originate from the United States or from other countries; (4) it covers short- and medium-term sales; (5) it provides a number of policies for different coverages.

FCIA ISSUES

FCIA was not always rated by critics as a total benefit to the U.S. export industry. In fact, it was once considered to be a possible hindrance to exports. An attitudinal study of U.S. exporters based on their 1978 export sales identified three programs in the United States that, according to the respondents, had a significant impact on their export activities.[13] This study found, however, that small firms did not perceive FCIA to present significant benefits to them. Several reasons were identified for this perception including high premium rates for export insurance, relatively high deductibles, restrictions on what activities FCIA could insure, administrative delays required by individual underwriting, and slow credit checks of foreign buyers. Changes were suggested in a subsequent application of this study to exporters' experience in the State of Georgia.[14] Several of these issues have been alleviated by subsequent changes in FCIA's operating methodology since this study was done.

Another issue may have prompted Ex-Im to provide its own trade credit insurance. After most of the original founders of FCIA left the consortium in 1983, FCIA's ability to provide adequate coverage for U.S. exporters seemed in doubt. Since Ex-Im began its own insurance operations in 1992, FCIA, with its reorganization and the financial backing of Great American Insurance Company, has slowly returned to its original position as a highly recognized provider of trade credit insurance.

SUMMARY AND CONCLUSIONS

FCIA was conceived as an idea of the John F. Kennedy presidency and was put into effect in the early 1960s. That idea was to supplement the work of the U.S. Export-Import Bank with private enterprise. In reality, this was an experiment in mixing public and private enterprise to accomplish one major objective. The expertise of the U.S. insurance industry was used to insure trade credits for the purpose of increasing U.S. exports and the experiment has been a successful one.

A consortium of insurance companies, now numbering sixty, was established to offer a variety of trade insurance programs, utilizing the experience of the insurance companies and their actuarial science to insure trade credits. FCIA supplemented the governmental variety of the Ex-Im with its programs. By 1992, Ex-Im broke off this partnership when it began to offer its own trade credit insurance. This move only made the FCIA program more efficient and allowed the organization to perform without the emphasis government policy sometimes imposed on its business.

Few countries have a public-private provision for trade finance assistance. The United States has enjoyed such an environment for the past forty years. If the Private Export Funding Corporation, the subject of the next chapter, is added to the mix, the United States must be regarded as having one of the most comprehensive trade finance systems in the world. Given the number of commercial banks offering trade credits and loans to international traders, the cooperative efforts of the public-private mix of trade credit guarantees and insurance make the U.S. system of international trade finance relatively competitive in a world of expanding trade and of facilities to finance that trade that are sponsored by national governments.

NOTES

1. Available on-line September 6, 2002, at www.fcia.com/aboutfcia.htm, p. 1.

2. Ibid.

3. Suk H. Kim and Seung H. Kim, *Global Corporate Finance: Text and Cases* (Oxford, England: Blackwell Publishers, 1999), pp. 333–334.

4. FCIA, "Why Credit Insurance?" available on-line November 21, 2002, at www.fcia.com/whycrins.htm, p. 1.

5. Gordon Platt, "U.S. Risk Managers Discover Export Credit Insurance," *Journal of Commerce*, April 26, 2000, p. 11.

6. Ibid.

7. David K. Eiteman, Arthur L. Stonehill, and Michael H. Moffett, *Multinational Business Finance* (Boston: Addison-Wesley, 2001), pp. 608–609.

8. Available on-line October 29, 2002, at www.fcia.com/exportinsurance .htm, pp. 1–2.

9. Richard Barovick, "Most Exporters Use Brokers to Guide Them Through Maze," *Journal of Commerce* 420 (September 1, 1999): 9.

10. Available on-line November 21, 2003, at www.fcia.com/apps-info.htm, pp. 1–4.

11. Foreign Credit Insurance Association, "FCIA Special Financial Institution Coverages," available on-line December 26, 2002, at www.fcia.com/spfininstcov .htm, pp. 1–2.

12. Foreign Credit Insurance Assocation, *FCIA Country Update*, April 2002, pp. 1–5, available on-line November 21, 2002, at www.fcia.com/CountryUpd-ate4-2002.htm, pp. 1–5.

13. Sandra M. Huszagh and Mark R. Greene, "FCIA: Help or Hindrance to Exports?" *Journal of Risk and Insurance* 49 (June 1982): 256–268.

14. Sandra M. Huszagh and Mark R. Greene, "How Exporters View Credit Risk and FCIA Insurance—The Georgia Experience," *Journal of Risk and Insurance* 52 (March 1985): 117–132.

6

Private Export Funding Corporation (PEFCO)

The system for financing international trade in the United States includes the traditional methods of trade finance offered by the banking system and means of guaranteeing or insuring export finance credits by the U.S. Export-Import Bank (Ex-Im) and the Foreign Credit Insurance Association (FCIA). One other organization supplements the U.S. system and its methods are entirely different from any of the other institutional methods previously discussed. This is the Private Export Funding Corporation (PEFCO), whose history and operations are the topics of this chapter.

PEFCO was incorporated in 1970. It is a private sector corporation that has issued its own stock. Its principal business is to make loans to foreign importers to finance purchases of goods and services which are manufactured in or originate in the United States. Thus, PEFCO works on the other side of the table, financing the importer of U.S. goods and services. Its principal mission is to facilitate U.S. exports through competitive financing in conjunction with Ex-Im, or, as stated in its 2001 Annual Report, "to assist in the financing of U.S. exports by mobilizing private capital as a supplement to the financing already available through Eximbank, commercial banks, and lending institutions."

PEFCO is essentially a consortium or joint international business venture. Its shareholders include major commercial banks that finance U.S. exports as well as industrial companies that export U.S. goods and services along with other financial services firms. PEFCO currently has thirty-six shareholders, including banks, industrial companies, and financial services companies. No shareholder can hold more than 18 percent of the total shares outstanding. See Table 6.1 for a breakdown of PEFCO's shareholders. PEFCO has a wholly owned subsidiary called PEFCO Financial Corporation. This subsidiary funds the debt that PEFCO acquires from foreign countries that import U.S. goods and services. It implements this objective by issuing collateralized notes that are neither obligations of PEFCO nor guaranteed by Ex-Im.

Several commercial banks, industrial companies, and investment banks joined together in 1970 to form PEFCO. The Bankers Association of Finance and Trade (BAFT), a trade association of banks engaged in foreign trade financing, sponsored the creation of PEFCO. The company was established with assistance of the U.S. Treasury Department and the U.S. Export-Import Bank (Ex-Im) as a supplement to the work of commercial banks, other lending institutions, and the Ex-Im in their financing of U.S. exports. Ex-Im guarantees the loans made by PEFCO to foreign importers. These guarantees save PEFCO the cost of evaluating the credit risk of the importers, country risk appraisals, and the review of factors which affect the collectibility of its loans.

In the early years of PEFCO operations, a majority of its lending projects involved the aircraft and power plant industries. Most of these loans were aimed at importers in developing countries. In 1979, PEFCO began a cooperative program with Ex-Im whereby it would purchase existing export loans from banks and financial institutions and Ex-Im would guarantee the loans. During the 1980s, the Third World debt crisis slowed the market for projects funded by PEFCO loans. In order to compensate for this loss of business, PEFCO created its small business program, which focused on short-term working capital loans to small exporters.

PEFCO'S FUNDING

Most of the funds raised by PEFCO are sourced from selling secured notes to public markets. These notes are underwritten by investment banks and are given the highest credit ratings by both Moody's and Standard & Poor's. (Moody's Investor Services and Standard and Poor's Corporation rate the quality and credit riskiness of financial instruments for the financial marketplace.) The notes are secured by PEFCO's portfolio of loans to foreign importers, which are, in turn, guaranteed by Ex-Im. Thus, these obligations are backed by the full faith and credit of the U.S. government. As of September 30, 2001, PEFCO had issued US$8.6 billion of secured notes, all rated Aaa by Moody's and AAA by Standard & Poor's.[1] One example of a PEFCO note issue can be demonstrated by a US$150 million offering of 5.75%

TABLE 6.1 PEFCO Shareowners

Commercial Banks	Shares
ABN AMRO, Chicago	1,249
Bank of America, Charlotte, NC	1,422
Bank of New York	710
Bank One, Chicago	708
Brown Bros. Harriman, NY	38
Chase Manhattan Bank, NY	1,422
Citibank, N.A., NY	1,066
Deutsche Bank, NY	1,066
1st Alabama Bank, Mobile	20
1st International Bank, Hartford, CT	266
Fleet Bank, Boston	502
Harris Bank, Chicago	150
Int'l Bank of Miami	100
Key Bank, Cleveland	165
Mellon Bank, Pittsburgh	158
Morgan Guaranty, NY	1,066
National Westminster, NY	300
PNC Bank, Pittsburgh	370
Riggs Bank, Washington, DC	83
Silicon Valley Bancshares	42
Société Générale, NY	100
Standard Chartered Bank, LA	300
Sterling Bancorp, NY	39
UBS AG, NY	137
Union Bank of California	93
United California Bank	79
U.S. Bank, Minneapolis	566
Wachovia Corporation	175
Financial Services Companies	
Asset Guaranty Insurance, NY	212
Exporters Insurance Corp.	100
Industrial Companies	
Asca Brown Boveri	80
Boeing Company	984
Cessna Aircraft Co.	40
General Electric Co.	200
Halliburton Co., Houston	113
United Technologies Corp.	200
Total	14,221

Source: PEFCO, *2001 Annual Report* (New York: PEFCO, 2001).

secured notes made in January 2001, due to mature January 15, 2008, and priced at par.[2] See Table 6.2 for a breakdown of PEFCO's borrowing by length to maturity.

PEFCO also raises additional funds for loan commitments from the commercial paper market. This commercial paper is rated P-1 by Moody's and A-1+ by Standard & Poor's. In addition, PEFCO has an agreement to borrow up to US$550 million on a revolving basis from eleven lenders that are also shareholders of PEFCO. No funds had been raised by this method as of September 30, 2001.[3]

Another example of the funding of PEFCO's operations can be demonstrated by a note offering by PEFCO's wholly owned subsidiary, PEFCO Finance Corporation, in 2001.[4] The issue was a US$100 million collateralized note offering managed by BNY Capital Markets Inc., a subsidiary of the Bank of New York. This was the second issue BNY Capital Markets managed for PEFCO and came only days after the World Trade Center terrorist attack. The notes mature in ten years and were priced to yield 5.66 percent. These and other issues by PEFCO are rated Aaa by Moody's Investor's Service and AAA by Standard & Poor's.

LENDING PROGRAMS

PEFCO administers a number of lending programs. All are designed to advance funds to foreign importers for the objective of purchasing U.S. goods and services. Among these programs are the following: (1) primary long-term loans, (2) secondary long-term loans, (3) small business loans, and (4) work with the Ex-Im. These programs will be discussed in the following sections. See Figures 6.1, 6.2, and 6.3 for features and restrictions of the programs dealing with primary and secondary long-term loans. In 2001, PEFCO made new loan commitments totaling US$1.8 billion, compared with US$1.5 billion in 2000.

TABLE 6.2   PEFCO Funding Sources

Long-term Notes	2001	2000
Average Balance*	3,282.60	3,044.60
Interest Rates	6.62%	6.64%
Short-term Notes		
Average Balance*	1,673.70	1,440.80
Interest Rates	5.39%	6.11%

Source: PEFCO, 2001 Annual Report.
*Millions of US$.

Interest Rate– Setting Options	Features	Restrictions
Prior to Disbursement	1. gives borrower maximum security	1. PEFCO must be direct lender
	2. fixed rates often below CIRR	2. interest rate must be fixed no later than final disbursement
	3. originator may charge structuring & L/C fees	3. no additional spread may be added for originator
	4. originator may earn underwriting income	4. PEFCO must be disclosed to Ex-Im Bank as possible lender prior to Ex-Im's final approval of guarantee
During or at End of Disbursement Period	1. gives borrower flexibility of using floating rates to lower average cost of funds	1. same as above, except while interest rate is floating, originator may charge borrower additional spread over PEFCO's rate
	2. maintains borrower's security of being able to fix rate prior to end of disbursements	
	3. allows originator to be lender of floating-rate loan	
	4. PEFCO will participate in floating-rate loan at thin spread over LIBOR and originator may charge borrower additional spread over PEFCO's floating interest rate	
	5. originator may charge structuring and L/C fees	
	6. originator may earn underwriting income	

Source: Brent Schrock, "PEFCO," unpublished research report, Kent State University, Fall 2001, p. 6.

Figure 6.1 PEFCO's Primary Long-Term Loan Program

Its loan portfolio totaled US$5 billion at the end of its FY2001, compared with US$4.6 billion one year earlier.[5] PEFCO's net profits in FY2001 were US$7.5 million, unchanged from one year earlier. See Table 6.3 for a list of the loan commitments by industry made by PEFCO in 2001.

Primary Long-Term Loan Program

Under the primary long-term loan program, PEFCO commits loans to foreign importers of U.S. goods and services. These loans are made

Interest Rate–Setting Options	Features	Restrictions
At or After End of Disbursements	1. gives borrower increased flexibility because interest rate may be fixed after end of disbursement period	1. fixed and floating rates slightly higher than under Primary Program
	2. while interest rate is floating, originator may be direct lender or may have PEFCO be direct lender	2. reduces borrower's security because interest rate cannot be fixed until end of disbursements
	3. originator may charge borrower additional spread over PEFCO's interest rate loans on fixed and floating rate	3. when interest rate is fixed, PEFCO must take over as direct lender
	4. originator may charge structuring and/or L/C fees	4. not necessary to disclose PEFCO to Ex-Im Bank on borrower until interest rate fixing
	5. in some case, originator may earn underwriting income	

Source: Brent Schrock, "PEFCO," unpublished research report, Kent State University, Fall 2001, p. 7.

Figure 6.2 PEFCO's Secondary Long-Term Loan Program, Fixed Interest Rate

at fixed interest rates. They are of two types: fixed-rate pricing and deferred fixed-rate pricing.[6]

Loans with Fixed-rate Pricing. With loans that are priced with a fixed rate, PEFCO fixes the interest rate, which it holds for up to forty-five days. If market rates decline from this fixed rate before the importer

Interest Rate–Setting Options	Features	Restrictions
No fixed rate	1. gives borrower maximum flexibility because no requirement to fix interest rate	1. gives borrower no security because interest rate cannot be fixed
	2. originator may be direct lender or may have PEFCO be direct lender	2. PEFCO's interest rate higher than under Primary Program
	3. originator may charge borrower additional spread over PEFCO's interest rate	3. not necessary to disclose PEFCO
	4. originator may charge L/C fees	

Figure 6.3 PEFCO's Secondary Long-Term Loan Program, Floating Interest Rate

TABLE 6.3   Loans by Industry (FY 2001)

No. of Loan Commitments	Products	Amounts (in millions)
3	Aircraft	$ 761
2	Telecommunications	20
1	Power Generation	425
1	Mixed	287
287	Small Business	275
294	Total	$1,768

Source: PEFCO, 2001 Annual Report, p. 3.

accepts the loan, PEFCO will change the fixed rate to the lower market rate.

Deferred Fixed-rate Loans. Some importers wish to use temporary financing from a commercial bank or from PEFCO before the latter fixes the rate on a long-term loan. This can be facilitated via a deferred fixed-rate loan from PEFCO, whereby the latter offers to establish a fixed-interest borrowing rate for some future time selected by the borrower. Alternately, PEFCO will agree to offer a fixed differential over the yield on an average-life U.S. Treasury security and cap this fixed spread for some specific period until the borrower gives instructions to PEFCO to fix the rate on the loan.

PEFCO sets these fixed rates based on its estimate of the cost of funds at the time the rate is calculated. Disbursement and repayment characteristics of the loan are taken into consideration when the cost of funds is estimated. PEFCO charges a commitment fee on the committed, undisbursed, and uncanceled amount of the loan commitment to the foreign importer if the borrower cancels some or all of an unused loan or prepays the loan. However, it must pay PEFCO a fee equal to the present value of the reinvestment loss that might be incurred by PEFCO.

Secondary Long-Term Loan Program

PEFCO assists other lenders of long-term funds to foreign importers of U.S. goods and services by buying their loans in some cases. These loans must be guaranteed against nonpayment by a comprehensive Ex-Im guarantee, that is, one that guarantees against both commercial and political risk. Furthermore, they must have an Ex-Im–guaranteed value of more than US$10 million, and their maturity to repayment is five years or more. This program may be combined with PEFCO's primary long-term loan program.

Medium-Term Facilities

Two medium-term facilities are available from PEFCO for lenders financing multiyear export loans. These are the guaranteed note facility, for notes guaranteed by Ex-Im, and the insured note facility, for notes insured by an Ex-Im policy. PEFCO also offers special programs for special needs of lenders, including a discount facility and an associated lender program.

PEFCO also purchases medium-term loans in the secondary market. These loans are bought from the lender which may be a bank, finance company, asset-based lender, or state agency. These loans are made without recourse. If less than 100 percent of the notes are covered by Ex-Im, PEFCO purchases only the covered part of the loan.

PEFCO charges either a floating interest rate or a fixed rate. The floating rate is three- or six-month London Interbank Offer Rate (LIBOR), that is, the rate charged by banks to each other in the Eurocurrency interbank money market, plus a PEFCO spread of .250 to .325 percent. The fixed rate is the yield on three- or five-year Treasury obligations plus a PEFCO spread of 1.4 to 1.5 percent.

The lender derives a number of benefits from the PEFCO medium-term secondary market facility. Its profitability can be improved. Fixed rates charged are without an up-front fee. The lender's loan portfolio can be reduced and small or low-income loans can be removed from the balance sheet.

Small Business Program

PEFCO's small business program was established to assist banks and other lenders by buying their short- or medium-term export loans that have been guaranteed or insured by Ex-Im. This program includes short-term loans and working capital loans.

Short-term Loans. Under the small business program, PEFCO offers lenders a secondary market buyer of export-related working capital and letter of credit loans that are guaranteed by Ex-Im. PEFCO also buys from lenders loans that were made to finance short-term export receivables when these loans are also guaranteed by Ex-Im.

Working Capital Loans. Under its working capital program, PEFCO buys loans from lenders when the loans are to finance working capital of U.S. exporters, usually small businesses, and guaranteed by Ex-Im's working capital guarantee. PEFCO can purchase the 90 percent guaranteed part of the loan, while the lender maintains the risk of the remaining 10 percent. The lender retains control over the administration of the loan including loan servicing, documentation, and the Ex-Im guarantee. This facility solves the problem whereby many banks refuse to hold multiyear export loans. Thus, these banks sell their loans to PEFCO.[7]

Two specialized programs under the working-capital facility have been established by PEFCO: the underserved markets program and the accessible lender program. The former program serves small exporters with minority or female ownership, rural or urban development locations; it also serves environmental businesses. Ex-Im guarantees 100 percent of these loans. In the latter program, the exporter cannot obtain financing but is commited to a working-capital guarantee. Ex-Im guarantees 100 percent of the loan and refers the exporter to PEFCO, which introduces the exporter to a participating lender.

Other Work with Ex-Im

PEFCO cooperates in export trade finance with Ex-Im in other ways.[8] These include short-term insured loans, medium-term loans, an insured note facility, a guaranteed note facility, and a discount facility.

Short-term Insured Loans. PEFCO operates a program in which it purchases short-term insured loans from lenders involving export financing. These loans are made by a lender to finance U.S. exports and are insured by Ex-Im. The loans may be made to the overseas buyer or foreign bank, they may be obligations purchased from the exporter, or they may consist of an advance of funds to the exporter which is secured by buyer obligations. These purchases are made without recourse to the exporter and PEFCO purchases 90 to 95 percent of the insured portion while the lender assumes the risk for the remainder of the loan.

Medium-term Loans. PEFCO operates a small business program that offers lenders with a dependable secondary market buyer of multi-year export loans insured or guaranteed against non-payment by an Ex-Im Medium-term Comprehensive Insurance Policy or Medium-term Comprehensive Guarantee. Again all loans purchased under this program are without recourse to the lender. These medium-term purchases have a minimum per loan of US$100,000 and a maximum per loan of US$10 million.

Insured Note Facility. PEFCO offers an insured note facility, which offers to purchase medium-term insured loans and leases. A fixed or floating interest rate is set at the time PEFCO purchases the loan. The lender retains the servicing of the loan as well as the Ex-Im insurance policy.

Guaranteed Note Facility. The PEFCO-guaranteed note facility, operates in the same manner as the insured note facility and either a fixed or floating interest rate is set at the time of the purchase. These loans are guaranteed rather than insured.

Discount Facility. PEFCO operates this facility under the guaranteed note facility, but only a fixed interest rate is determined before the items are shipped. PEFCO collects the payments and maintains the Ex-Im guarantee.

CASE STUDIES

In June 1996, PEFCO priced a US$125 million offering of 7.03% secured notes due October 31, 2003, sold at par with interest payable semiannually. Chase Securities Inc. was lead manager among a group of nine comanagers. The notes received the highest rating possible by both Moody's and Standard & Poor's. PEFCO will use the net proceeds from the notes issue to fund its outstanding loan commitments. Payment of the principal was backed by the full faith and credit of the United States, and the interest payments were guaranteed by Ex-Im.[9]

In December 1999, PEFCO participated in a loan facility of US$1.94 billion for the delivery of thirty-five aircraft exported from the United States by Boeing Company and McDonnell Douglas for Saudi Arabian Airlines. The aircraft consisted of eleven Boeing 777-220s, two Boeing 737-400s, and twenty-two MD-90 airliners.[10] This was a twelve-year loan priced very tightly at five basis points over LIBOR.[11] The loan was arranged by Chase Manhattan Bank, National Westminster Bank, and Société Generale, which provided US$1.04 billion of the financing. The remaining US$.9 billion was furnished by PEFCO, and the loan, which was guaranteed by Ex-Im, was the largest loan it supported. The aircraft were purchased by Air Finance, a lessor of commercial airliners, to be leased to Saudi Arabian Airlines, and were delivered by the end of 1999. Saudi Airlines had already financed eighteen of the aircraft with a commercial loan. An extra US$662.5 million was obtained to finance the delivery of the final eight airliners between 2000 and 2001.[12]

In June 2002, PEFCO entered into a US$850 million, 364-day revolving credit facility with a syndicate of banks led by JP Morgan Chase Bank. The syndicate consisted of JP Morgan Chase Bank, Citibank, Bank of America, Lloyds TSB Bank, ABN AMRO Bank, The Bank of New York, BNP Paribas, Wachovia Bank, PNC Bank, and Fleet National Bank. The revolving credit agreement was reached to support PEFCO's commercial paper.

FINANCIAL RESULTS

According to the PEFCO Annual Report for 2001, the organization made 294 new loans totaling US$1.8 billion, and its total portfolio amounted to US$5 billion, most of which is guaranteed by Ex-Im. Interest income from its loans rose in 2001 to US$319.7 million, primarily a result of the large increase in primary long-term loans. Income resulting from prepayment fees and commitment fees also increased in 2001. PEFCO's earnings in 2001 were US$7.5 million, and a dividend of US$100 per share was paid to shareholders. See Table 6.4 for a breakdown of interest income on PEFCO loans by program.

TABLE 6.4   PEFCO's Interest Income by Program

	2000	2001
Primary Long-Term Loan		
Average Balance*	3,264.10	2,795.5
Interest Rate	6.64%	7.06%
Secondary Long-Term Loan		
Average Balance*	970.1	923.9
Interest Rate	6.19%	6.37%
Investment Securities Portfolio		
Average Balance*	391.3	565
Interest Rate	5.71%	5.83%
Medium-Term Programs		
Average Balance*	394.1	187.7
Interest Rate	6.02%	6.71%
Working Capital Programs		
Average Balance*	27.5	18.4
Interest Rate	6.98%	9.12%
Short-Term Insurance Program		
Average Balance*	12	1.7
Interest Rate	6.33%	7.39%

Source: PEFCO, *2001 Annual Report.*
(*)millions of US$

SUMMARY AND CONCLUSIONS

PEFCO has become a key component in the U.S. international trade financing system in its short life of three decades. PEFCO's operations have assisted U.S. exporters in a very competitive world market by alleviating the risk of nonpayment for the trade finance lender. Its cooperative efforts with Ex-Im's trade credit insurance and guarantee programs have benefited developing countries in their need for U.S. goods and services and small business exporters in the United States in their efforts to gain a piece of the world trade pie.

PEFCO has become an established trade lender and purchaser of export loans. Its operations have simplified Ex-Im's procedures and helped to reduce rates on smaller transactions. PEFCO, in concert with the work of FCIA, has combined with Ex-Im to make the U.S. trade financing system one of the most comprehensive in the world and has helped to reduce some of the disadvantages of Ex-Im working alone in competition with foreign export credit agencies.

PEFCO's shareholders do not perceive the organization to be a major investment. Very few shares of the company trade. The shareholders remain close to PEFCO's daily operations by providing loans for PEFCO to purchase or to assist in funding their securities. In short, the shareholders use PEFCO to facilitate their own business and, from that viewpoint, the organization has been a good investment.

From the borrower's viewpoint, PEFCO offers a broad spectrum of financing trade. It facilitates short-, medium-, and long-term financing; assists developing countries and small businesses in the United States; and can support its lending with Ex-Im insurance or guarantees.

PEFCO has remained a low-key organization that has successfully met its major objective. U.S. exporters have been assisted in ways which the Ex-Im by itself could not have fulfilled. Exporters and shareholders alike have been rewarded. Lenders' worries about nonpaying customers have been alleviated by PEFCO loans guaranteed by Ex-Im. In conclusion, the PEFCO methodology in facilitating U.S. exports and their financing has been a succcessful supplement to the programs of the U.S. Export-Import Bank and the Foreign Credit Insurance Association. Thus, this combination, which is unique among the industrialized nations of the world, has made the U.S. trade-financing system one of the most comprehensive facilities anywhere in the world.

NOTES

1. Private Export Funding Corporation, *2001 Annual Report* (New York: PEFCO, 2001), p. 4.
2. "Secured Note Offering, Series L," *Business Wire*, January 23, 2001.

3. Ibid., p. 5.

4. "Press Release by The Bank of New York," available on-line December 13, 2002, at www.bankofny.com, p. 1.

5. Private Export Funding Corporation, *Annual Report 2001*, p. 2.

6. "Press Release by the Bank of New York," p. 1.

7. Gordon Platt, "Financing Trade—PEFCO Expands Export Financing Deals to Small Businesses with Success," *Journal of Commerce* 409 (October 2, 1996): 9.

8. Ibid., p. 7.

9. LexisNexis, "Financial News," *Business Editor*, November 6, 2002.

10. "Saudi Arabia Inks $1.9 Billion Plane Finance Deal," *Singapore Business Times*, November 24, 1999, p. 16.

11. LIBOR is the London Interbank Offered Rate, the interest rate at which banks in the Eurocurrency market lend to each other.

12. "Saudi Mandates Chase to Arrange Largest Eximbank Financing," *Airfinance Journal* 223 (December 1999): 14.

7

U.S. and Foreign Private and Public Export-Financing Facilities

In addition to the U.S. banking system, the major export-financing institutions in the United States are the U.S. Export-Import Bank (Ex-Im), the Foreign Credit Insurance Association (FCIA), and the Private Export Funding Corporation (PEFCO). These organizations were the focus of attention in Chapters 4, 5, and 6. Several other financing facilities assist U.S. exporters. Among them are those agencies of the U.S. government: the Department of Agriculture, the Small Business Administration, and other, lesser institutions. Various national, state, and city trade associations and other financial and nonfinancial organizations also furnish assistance in some way for U.S. exporters. These public and private sources of export trade assistance will be discussed in this chapter.

In addition to these United States–based agencies and organizations, other institutions around the world facilitate some aspect of international trade. Among these tools are world trade centers, international factoring firms, foreign banks and financial institutions, insurance firms, and e-commerce companies. A representative sample of these will also be discussed in this chapter.

The chapter, however, will begin with a discussion of multilateral trade assistance which may be valuable to exporters, especially those that sell into developing countries. This assistance is performed by the Trade Point Global Network, a service of the United Nations Conference on Trade and Development (UNCTAD). The chapter will conclude with a discussion of foreign trade zones, a service available to international trade firms, which is not an agency or an organization.

In addition to a descriptive analysis of the export-financing facilities, this chapter will also contain a discussion of the working interrelationships between these institutions and those discussed in the previous four chapters. Given this analysis, the U.S. system of export finance will be seen to be one of the most complex of any other national system covered in this treatise.

Finally, in addition to U.S. facilities other than export credit agencies and firms, U.S. and foreign banking firms have specialized operations that facilitate international trade. The functions of these institutions will also be discussed in this chapter.

MULTILATERAL TRADE ASSISTANCE

Before discussing the U.S. public and private agencies, organizations, and firms available to assist U.S. exporters, one multilateral agency should be mentioned. This is the Trade Point Global Network (TPGN) established by the UNCTAD, a UN organization whose primary mission is to increase the economic development of the low-income countries. The TPGN was formed in 1992 to lower the costs of trading internationally. Information is transmitted in electronic form through a network of Trade Points around the world. Participants in international trade submit data about their operations. These participants include customs officials, foreign freight forwarders, insurance firms, banks, transportation companies, and related businesses. Business opportunities and statistical data are available to all members over this network. Trade Points are located in fifty places including one in Columbus, Ohio. The TPGN cooperates with a similar organization known as the World Trade Centers Association, which will be discussed later in this chapter.

U.S. GOVERNMENT ACTIVITIES

Several U.S. government agencies are involved in various aspects of international trade and finance. Their principal objective is to expand U.S. international trade, particularly exports. They include the U.S. Department of Agriculture, U.S. Small Business Administration, the Bureau of Industry and Security of the U.S. Commerce Department, the U.S. Commercial Service, the Trade Information Center, the U.S. Customs Service, the National Trade Data Bank, U.S. Agency for International Development, and the Trade Promotion Coordinating Committee of the U.S. Department of State. These agencies will be discussed in the following sections.

U.S. Department of Agriculture

The U.S. Department of Agriculture (USDA) operates export credit guarantee programs through the Commodity Credit Corporation (CCC) for agricultural exports to emerging markets. These programs are authorized by the Agricultural Trade Act of 1978 as amended. A 1990 amendment to this law directed at least US$1 billion in direct credits or export credit guarantees for the 1996–2002 period.[1] These programs benefit both U.S. farm products exporters and the recipient developing countries which import the U.S. farm products.

The USDA offers four different programs: (1) the GSM-102 Export Credit Guarantee Program, (2) the GSM-103 Intermediate Export Credit Guarantee Program, (3) the Supplier Credit Guarantee Program, and (4) the Facility Guarantee Program. These programs will be discussed in the following sections.[2] The export credit guarantee programs are aimed at commercially financed sales of agricultural products. They are not designed to be foreign aid or subsidy programs. The CCC must qualify exporters for participation in these programs before guarantee applications are accepted. The CCC also evaluates each country and foreign bank for their ability to service debt guaranteed by the CCC. The interest rate charged by participating banks is usually determined by the level of the U.S. prime rate or the London Interbank Offered Rate (LIBOR).[3]

CCC-guaranteed programs require that the applicant specify the importing country, commodity, quantity, estimated value, shipping period, credit period desired, and the name of the foreign bank which will issue the letter of credit, if it is available. Importers can inquire at U.S. embassies for the appropriate information concerning the availability of CCC guarantees.[4]

Export Credit Guarantee Program. The Export Credit Guarantee Program guarantees credit granted by U.S. banks to approved foreign banks for the purpose of financing imports of U.S. agricultural goods. The program offers terms up to three years provided a U.S. dollar–denominated letter of credit has been issued. The guarantees cover 98 percent of principal and some interest, and they cover most U.S. agricultural products.

Intermediate Export Credit Guarantee Program. The Intermediate Export Credit Guarantee Program guarantees credit granted by U.S. banks to approved foreign banks for the purpose of financing imports of U.S. agricultural goods. The terms of these guarantees are offered for from three to ten years provided a U.S. dollar–denominated letter of credit has been issued. Again, 98 percent of principal and some interest can be covered. Most U.S. agricultural products can be covered.

Supplier Credit Guarantee Program. The Supplier Credit Guarantee Program guarantees short-term credit offered by U.S. exporters directly to foreign importers of most U.S. agricultural products. Terms extend up to 180 days on an importer's promissory note. At least 65 percent of the principal is covered.

Facility Guarantee Program. The Facility Guarantee Program guarantees credit offered by U.S. banks to approved foreign banks. Terms can be arranged for up to ten years with a U.S. dollar–denominated letter of credit. This program covers 95 percent of principal and some interest and is designed to apply to U.S. goods and services to be used by the importing country for agricultural infrastructure projects.

Some of the CCC programs have been criticized for their cost to the taxpayer. When CCC guarantees agricultural trade credits, the taxpayer often foots the bill. Congress does not need to approve these guarantees. They have little immediate impact on the federal budget. And U.S. exporters and farm interests are pleased that they are available. In the early 1990s, the U.S. government had to pay US$1.9 billion of a total of US$5 billion in guarantees made to Iraq on agricultural commodity loans. At the same time, the former USSR republics presented an imminent liability on US$5 billion of guaranteed loans made to these nations. The CCC programs have been special targets for criticism. A former administration aide to the Ronald Reagan presidency stated that the CCC was little more than a slush fund to support personal diplomacy objectives of the administration toward Iraq and Russia.[5]

U.S. Small Business Administration

The U.S. Small Business Administration (SBA) offers three programs for small U.S. exporters that offer guarantees and loans. These are the Export Working Capital Program, the International Trade Loan Program, and the SBA Export*Express* Program.

SBA assistance to small business firms, no matter what the financial assistance, requires the recipient firms to be a certain size. In general, SBA size standards are: for retail and service, US$3.5 to 20 million; for construction, US$7 to 17 million; for agriculture, US$.5 to 19 million; wholesale, no more than 100 employees; manufacturing, 500 to 1,500 employees.

Export Working Capital Program. The Export Working Capital Program usually assists small firms that cannot obtain export financing or guarantees from any other source. Under SBA's Export Working Capital Program, the agency can guarantee 90 percent of a loan of up to US$1 million. Loans in excess of this amount can be made to small exporters by Ex-Im. Features of export working-capital loans include low fees, flexible terms, fast turnaround, a streamlined application process, and preliminary commitment. Proceeds can be used to purchase finished goods for export or acquire inventory to be exported, to finance pre-export costs of labor and materials used in the manufacture of goods for export, to finance costs of U.S. labor and overhead for service-company exports, to finance standby letters of credit used for bid or performance bonds, and to finance foreign accounts receivable.

International Trade Loan Program. The SBA's International Trade Loan Program offers medium- and long-term working-capital loans to small business firms for up to twenty-five years. SBA can guarantee up US$1.25 million to the borrower. Loans are made to the export-financing lending institution, with SBA guaranteeing part of the loan. These loans are for small businesses engaged in, or about to enter into, international trade. They are also made to firms facing foreign competition from imports. Collateral for loans made under this program must be located in the United States, its territories or possessions.

*SBA Export*Express. The SBA Export*Express* Program offers guaranteed loans to participating lenders who make loans to small U.S. exporters. This program streamlines and expedites the loan review and approval procedures and, thus, makes funds available to the small exporter much more quickly than other export-financing programs. The loans can be used for export market development activity, general lines of credit for exporting, working capital, and fixed asset acquisition. In addition to obtaining guaranteed loans, exporters can use the SBA Export*Express* program to participate in a foreign trade show, to translate product brochures or catalogs for use in foreign markets, to obtain general lines of credit for exporting, for service contracts from foreign buyers, for transaction-specific financing needs associated with the completion of actual export orders, and for the purchase of real estate and equipment to be used in the production of goods or services to be exported.

SBA extends this program to participating lenders with a repayment guarantee of 85 percent on SBA Export*Express* loans up to US$150,000 and a 75-percent repayment guarantee on loans above US$150,000, up to a maximum loan amount of US$250,000.

Business Education and Training. The SBA also provides U.S. Export Assistance Centers for exporters as part of its Business Education and Training Program. These are centers where the exporter can find local export assistance of various kinds in one location. These centers are located in nineteen U.S. cities and exporters can receive personalized help at these centers from SBA, U.S. Department of Commerce, Ex-Im, and other public and private organizations.

Bureau of Industry and Security

The Bureau of Industry and Security (BIS) is a branch of the U.S. Department of Commerce.[6] BIS offers services to exporters and potential exporters covering export administration regulations. BIS holds training sessions throughout the United States on such topics as the essentials of export controls, technology controls, and export compliance for forwarders. BIS offers advice to exporters about export management, compliance with antiboycott movements, sensitive products that may require clearance from some branch of the U.S. government, and the identities of unverified end-users.

Since much of international trade is regulated in some way by governments, this service is a valuable tool for exporters that may produce and sell a product that is sensitive to one or more such regulations. Many bureaucratic snafus of the trade process can be alleviated or eliminated if the exporter is knowledgeable about, and uses, BIS.

U.S. Commercial Service

The U.S. Commercial Service is a part of the U.S. Department of Commerce.[7] The major service rendered by this branch is a Web site from which an exporter can obtain a global listing of trade events, international market research, and assistance in all phases of the export procedure. The site covers awards given to U.S. exporters that are designed to motivate others to enter the world of international trade. From the Web site, an exporter can directly contact a U.S. commercial service trade specialist for advice on any aspect of international trade.

Trade Information Center

The Trade Information Center (TIC) is located in the USA Trade Center of the U.S. Department of Commerce in Washington.[8] It offers comprehensive export-counseling programs for companies needing export assistance. Among the services that TIC trade specialists offer exporters are: advice on how to find and use government programs, guidance through the export process, market research sources and trade leads, information on overseas and domestic trade events, sources of public and private export finance, and direction of companies to state and local trade organizations, some of which are discussed later in this chapter. TIC trade specialists can help exporters with import tariffs and taxes as well as customs procedures, foreign commercial laws and regulations, and distribution channels for their goods.

U.S. Customs Service

The U.S. Customs Service is a branch of the U.S. government that offers information to exporters about duty rates, customs rulings and regulations in the United States and foreign countries, and trade publications and forms.[9] It offers a Web site that discusses current trade issues, exporting, commercial enforcement, information for the infrequent traveler or importer, information about antidumping or countervailing duties, duty rates, trade regulations and rulings, international agreements, and a host of data about all phases of exporting and importing.

National Trade Data Bank

The National Trade Data Bank (NTDB) was authorized by the Omnibus Trade and Competitiveness Act of 1988. This data bank compiles information on international trade, export promotion, trade contacts, country profiles, and a variety of other international economic data. Exporters can obtain this information on a computer disk, which is sold, individually or by twelve-month subscriptions, by the U.S. Department of Commerce.

U.S. Agency for International Development

The U.S. Agency for International Development (USAID) is the official agency of the U.S. government for the administration of the U.S. foreign economic aid program. The agency operates the Global Trade and Technology Network from its Office of Business Development. This network is comprised of domestic and international partners available to assist U.S. small- and medium-sized companies which seek access to overseas markets. The network also facilitates the transfer of technology to less-developed countries by matching firms in these countries with U.S. firms that can provide the appropriate technology.

U.S. Department of State

The U.S. Department of State issues an annual National Export Strategy Report written by its Trade Promotion Coordinating Committee. This committee coordinates efforts of the Departments of State and Treasury, USAID, and other U.S. government agencies. The objective of this committee's work is to promote U.S. trade and expand U.S. exports.

U.S.-Asia Environmental Partnership

The U.S.-Asia Environmental Partnership (US-AEP) is a program of the U.S. Agency for International Development and was established 10 years ago. Its objectives are to build partnerships among governments, businesses and non-governmental organizations in Asia and the United States in economic and technological matters. Its website contains links to U.S. export leads for environmental projects in various Asian countries.

U.S. Trade and Development Agency

The U.S. Trade and Development Agency (TDA) was established in 1981 and funds feasibility studies in developing countries. Its primary objective is to create U.S. jobs by assisting U.S. companies to pursue overseas projects. In addition to feasibility studies, TDA funds orientation visits by project managers, specialized training grants, business workshops, and trade conferences.

Office of the U.S. Trade Representative

The U.S. trade representative develops and coordinates U.S. international trade, commodity, and direct investment policy. As a cabinet member, the trade representative advises the President of the United States on trade and related investment matters. The trade representative is the major U.S. trade negotiator and proponent of U.S. interests in the adoption and enforcement of international intellectual property agreements. The offices are in Washington and Geneva.

One example of the work of the U.S. trade representative can be demonstrated by the November 2001 negotiations between the United States and agricultural exporting nations and developing countries to move toward free trade in agricultural products.[10] The U.S. trade representative proposed, for the United States, that all export subsidies be abolished within five years. At the same time, a drastic reduction in agricultural tariffs was proposed, cutting the average farm tariff allowed from 62 percent to 15 percent. Finally, the U.S. position called for a reduction in allowable trade-distorting subsidies by more than US$100 billion. The U.S. trade representative, Robert Zoellick, presented the initiative to other countries at the World Trade Organization in Geneva, in July 2002. While such proposals reduce trade barriers for U.S. exporters, they also result in increased trade worldwide because the reduction or abolition of these barriers can affect other countries' trade in a favorable way by making their trade less costly.

On the other hand, the work of the U.S. trade representative can have unilateral impact since the primary objective of the office is to benefit U.S. exporters. For example, the trade representative defended U.S. trade policy that imposed new and higher U.S. tariffs on imported steel.[11] China, Japan, South Korea, and the European Union had protested the tariffs of up to 30 percent that took effect on March 5, 2002. Trade Representative Zoellick held that overcapacity in the steel market and unfair practices created a need for negotiations. In the meantime, the U.S. steel industry needed some additional protection against the alleged unfair practices of dumping steel imports into the U.S. market at prices below manufacturing costs.

U.S. Council for International Business

The U.S. Council for International Business advances the global interests of American business firms at home and abroad. It represents American business in principal intergovernmental bodies and to foreign business communities and their governments. Thus, U.S. trade development is one of the council's objectives.

National Institute of Standards and Technology

A rather obscure U.S. government agency, the National Institute of Standards and Technology (NIST), should be included in this study because of its importance in working toward a world of measurements and standards that promote order, efficiency, and fairness in the global marketplace in nearly every facility throughout the world. NIST is a non-regulatory agency in the U.S. Department of Commerce Technology Administration. It is responsible for establishing, maintaining, and improving the nation's measurement and standards infrastructure. Its role in international trade is to reduce or eliminate the arbitrary "local" standards implemented by foreign governments that impose conflicting technical requirements that force companies to modify their products to meet these subjective standards, thus presenting a barrier to international trade. NIST cooperates with the World Trade Organization (WTO) and the General Agreement on Tariffs and Trade (GATT) to accomplish its objectives. GATT is a multilateral trade treaty, as well as an agency, among governments, which embodies rights and obligations. It facilitates the reduction of tariffs on a worldwide basis. WTO is a multilateral organization that develops rules to guarantee that international trade will carried out in a fair manner.

The United States is not innocent of imposing arbitrary local standards. A good example of such a trade barrier imposed by the United States can be found in the historical treatment of beef produced in Argentina. Argentinians produce some of the best beef products in the world, and they consume more beef per capita than any other country in the world. However, the United States has long imposed an administrative barrier against Argentinian beef imports. The reason given for this restriction stems from a health threat to both Americans and U.S. livestock, that is, the threat of anthrax. Argentinian beef cattle have been free of this disease for many decades, perhaps more than a century, yet the U.S. cattle producers have effectively lobbied the U.S. government to place such restrictions on Argentinian beef imports. Thus, U.S. trade policy comes into conflict with the objectives of agencies such as NIST.

District Export Councils

The U.S. Department of Commerce has established a District Export Council (DEC) in each of the agency's fifty-one districts. Each DEC is an organization of leaders from local business communities whose members are appointed by the U.S. secretary of commerce. Their membership is composed of volunteer business and trade experts who organize workshops for exporters and arrange for consultation between experienced exporters and those which may be prospective exporters. An annual national conference is held to honor the volunteer efforts to assist U.S. business firms to become successful exporters.

Michigan District Export Council. The Michigan District Export Council (DEC) is one of several such organizations centered in cities where U.S. Department of Commerce regional offices are located.[12] The forerunner of the District Export Councils program was the program of U.S. Export Expansion Councils of the 1960s and 1970s. The Export Expansion Councils were composed of bankers, exporters, and academicians who had expertise in international business and exporting and who were appointed by the U.S. secretary of commerce. The Michigan council is representative of the new DEC programs. Occasional forums, seminars, and conferences are held by the Michigan DEC on topics concerning international trade. A recent forum, held in December 2002, examined credit and political risk analysis in emerging economies, Ex-Im loans, and project finance. The objective of these councils is to educate firms in their respective districts about export trade and international business in general.

STATE AND LOCAL EXPORT FINANCE PROGRAMS

Several states and cities have public and private export financing programs. Some thirteen states have passed legislation authorizing the provision of export financing. Most of these states have export finance offices now operating. These programs provide combinations of pre- and postshipment working-capital loans and guarantees, accounts receivable financing, and export insurance.

These programs usually require a letter of credit or credit insurance coverage. Some of these programs also require a certain minimum amount of state or local content in the product shipped. Some require that a certain state or local port be used. The state and local programs discussed in the following sections are representative of all such programs.

Ohio Export Finance Initiative

The Ohio Export Finance Initiative (OEFI) gives assistance to Ohio-domiciled companies in solving their export finance needs.[13] OEFI works with other agencies and banks to fulfill its role including Ex-Im, SBA, Ohio banks, and other U.S. Government agencies such as Overseas Private Investment Corporation (OPIC), U.S. Agency for International Development (USAID), and the U.S. Trade and Development Agency (TDA). Exporters can also use OEFI for alternative trade financing such as factoring and forfaiting.

Missouri Development Finance Board

The Missouri Development Finance Board is representative of a number of state agencies which provide services to exporters. It offers a number of programs to Missouri exporting companies.[14] These include export working capital guarantees, foreign buyer financing, and export credit insurance. This agency partners with Ex-Im and SBA to gain access to working capital and export credit insurance.

Florida Export Finance Corporation

The Florida Export Finance Corporation (FEFC) is a nonprofit corporation formed in 1993 to assist Florida-based exporters with export transactions.[15] Although FEFC is not a state agency, it is supported by the State of Florida. FEFC guarantees bank loans made to exporters for up to 90 percent of a loan. Small- or medium-sized companies are given priority for these services and transactions up to US$500,000 may be guaranteed. Small business firms in Florida which might otherwise be unable to obtain export funding can use the services of FEFC. However, the organization has a limited capitalization and the borrower must meet all of the required qualifications.

California Export Finance Office

The California Export Finance Office (CEFO) is administered by the California State World Trade Commission. CEFO provides working capital loan guarantees to financial institutions for loans made to small- and medium-sized California exporters. These guarantees can cover 90 percent of a loan amounting to a maximum of US$833,000. When CEFO cooperates with SBA, a loan of up to US$1,500,000 can be guaranteed. These guarantees can be used to finance the purchase of materials, services, and labor to prepare for an export sale. They can support working capital loans of up to twelve months, revolving line of credit loans, or direct loans and/or standby letters of credit.

Tennessee Small Business Development Center

The Tennessee Small Business Development Center, in Clarksville, offers advice and consulting services on a variety of areas for small- and medium-sized firms. Topics covered include an introduction to international trade. A five-seminar series on international trade is offered by specialists. The series includes an introduction to exporting and importing, export operations, trade finance, and legal aspects of exporting. Freight forwarding and documentation are also covered in this course.[16]

TRADE ASSOCIATIONS

Several trade associations have been established in the United States to facilitate and expand U.S. international trade. The most significant function performed by these associations is to educate corporate executives of large and small firms in methods designed to increase exports by these companies. Some of these associations represent manufacturing sectors, some are associations of banking firms, and many are city trade associations. A representative group of these trade associations will be discussed in the following sections.

Bankers Association for Finance and Trade

The Bankers Association for Finance and Trade (BAFT) is an association of banks involved in financing international trade.[17] BAFT has established six committees which deal with various aspects of international business. Its Trade Banking Committee identifies issues of importance to international trade bankers and makes suggestions for their solution. It works closely with organizations such as the World Bank, Ex-Im, OPIC, and the Trade Development Association, as well as non-U.S. export credit agencies (ECAs). BAFT's Project Finance Committee works with national ECAs and studies issues that impact banks' ability to provide competitive project financing. Another committee formed by

BAFT which is closely involved in international trade issues is the Small Business Export Committee. This committee works with Ex-Im and SBA to assist small export companies to compete better in the world of international trade.

City International Trade Associations

Several cities host international trade associations. Among the more active local associations are the Baltimore World Trade Association, Cleveland World Trade Association, and San Francisco World Trade Association. The Cleveland Association is quite representative of these associations and will be discussed in the following section.

Cleveland World Trade Association. The Cleveland World Trade Association (CWTA) is a division of the Greater Cleveland Growth Association, a quasi–chamber of commerce. CWTA performs both educational and lobby functions designed to inform citizens and company officials in Northeast Ohio about international trade and how to expand exports. Its members consist of company and bank officials and educational institution faculty and staff.

CWTA organizes and hosts a number of functions designed to fulfill its objectives. It holds monthly luncheon meetings with speakers involved in international trade and finance. It is the seat of at least four committees involved in international trade activities including committees on foreign trade policy and international trade development. CWTA holds occasional half-day executive seminars that cover international trade topics in detail. It sponsors courses on trade and documentation and an annual World Trade Conference, whose speakers are well experienced in some aspect of international trade and finance. Some of its committees study trade issues and form opinion letters which are sent to key officials of the U.S. government or Congress.

WORLD TRADE CENTERS

World Trade Centers have been established around the world to promote world trade with a variety of programs. Some 330 of these are located in one hundred countries. In the United States, 42 have been established in most major cities. The activities of 4 of these trade centers have been selected as representative of these centers. See Appendix 3 for a list of world trade centers.

World Trade Centers take a wide variety of organizational shapes and operate in a wide variety of methods. Some, such as the World Trade Center Cleveland, network with other foreign chambers of commerce and industry associations around the world. Most offer educational services for international traders and give global business training courses. Some host world trade conferences bringing together international exporters and importers and other international businessmen and bankers. The work of the average world trade center stimulates the economy of the region it serves and offers a network for international trade services, organizations, and individual international business executives for the generation of expanded international trade. Some, like the World Trade Center of New Orleans, serve as a means for international business-oriented people to socialize at receptions, luncheons, and dinners held to recognize leading international business and banking experts.

Others serve a role different from a trade-oriented center. The World Trade Center Boston includes the Seaport Hotel, with 426 first-class hotel rooms, a gourmet restaurant, and conference rooms. A variety of exhibitions, conferences, and special events are held there. World Trade Center Geneva offers conference rooms, e-commerce links, trade seminars, and furnished offices for trade associations.

World Trade Centers Association

The World Trade Centers Association (WTCA) was founded by the New York–New Jersey Port Authority and is a tool for new exporters.[18] The WTCA has licensed more than sixty world trade centers worldwide. Exporters and importers have access to an on-line trading system called NETWORK. Exporters can use a computer and modem to post offers to sell in an electronic database, much like someone posting something for sale on E-bay.com. Importers can send messages to exporters' e-mail addresses if they accept an advertised price or initiate electronic negotiations. Access to this system can be obtained with a local telephone in eight hundred cities in more than sixty countries.

U.S. AND FOREIGN PRIVATE FIRMS' SPECIALIZED ACTIVITIES

In this section, a representative group of private firms, banks and financial institutions will be discussed. They specialize in some area of international trade finance.

Factors Chain International

Factors Chain International (FCI) is an umbrella organization formed in 1968 to coordinate the activities of independent factoring companies worldwide.[19] FCI is the world's largest factoring network and is located in Amsterdam. Factoring is the purchase of a seller's accounts receivable by a firm or bank acting as a factor. The purchase is usually without recourse to the seller and the factor assumes the responsibility for the debtor's financial ability to pay. When the seller and buyer are from different countries, the activity is referred to as international factoring.

This organization was established at a time when few international factors operated, especially outside of North America and Europe. FCI was formed to introduce factoring into countries where the process was not then available and to develop a framework for members to cooperatively work together.

The factors in each country operate independently and take into consideration the local customs and culture in financial operations. However, each member of the network operates within a standard communications system and according to a global code of conduct.

FCI currently has more than 150 members located in fifty-three countries. Members must demonstrate a commitment to high service standards and have met FCI's criteria of financial strength. Otherwise the factoring operations are carried out in the same manner whereby the accounts receivable of an international trading company are purchased by the member factors.

International factoring has grown significantly during the recent past. Total world factoring increased from 305.6 billion euros in 1996 to 720.2 billion euros in 2001, an increase of 135 percent in only five years. A total 965 companies factored their accounts receivables in 2001. By that year, the total cumulative volume factored by FCI members during the past twenty-five years amounted to 298 billion euros.[20]

Steven Gilbert Companies Inc.

Steven Gilbert Companies Inc. is a Brownsville, Texas, firm that offers an export finance program for manufacturers and exporters of U.S. manufactured goods and services to foreign buyers by financing direct sales to end users. The minimum transaction size is US$150,000 and, depending on the size of the transaction, the interest rate ranges from 6.7 to 9.2 percent and is usually 1.0 to 3.5 percent over the London Interbank Offered Rate (LIBOR) in the Eurocurrency market. Steven Gilbert finances only 85 percent of the amount loaned after a 15 percent down payment. The typical export documentation is required, and the firm cooperates with Ex-Im or private sector risk protection systems in obtaining trade finance guarantees.

Wells Fargo Bank

Wells Fargo Bank in San Francisco offers a variety of services for U.S. exporters.[21] The bank's products and services include export letters of credit, including on-line service and trade documentation. These services are available from the Trade Bank at Wells Fargo. The Trade Bank can arrange financing for amounts ranging from US$1 to $25 million. Financing options available to exporters include trade finance online with electronic documentation, coverage by the Ex-Im Working Capital Guarantee Program, short- and medium-term financing, forfaiting, and insurance for export receivables.

Wells Fargo makes available two trademarked services to expedite international trade transactions. These are ExportExpress™ and Document Express™. With the former program, the process can be expedited and an exporter's account can be credited within twenty-four hours when the transaction is supported by a letter of credit. Under the latter program, the entire letter of credit documentation for an export transaction can be accomplished by Wells Fargo staff who are experienced in international trade documentation procedures.

The Bank of New York

The Bank of New York has a history of operations as a bank for more than two hundred years. The bank offers a full range of services for exporters, importers, and financial institutions in the field of international trade.[22] Importer services include the issuance of letters of credit involving the use of sophisticated software and Internet-based initiation. Importers can also take advantage of the bank's Trade Internet Query[sm], a secure, on-line access to details on a letter of credit, amendments, and payments routed through the bank's trade-processing centers.

The Bank of New York assists exporters with letters of credit, internet direct collections, the on-line access just mentioned, and ECA programs in other countries. These same services are available for other financial institutions and, in addition, the bank offers these institutions bank-to-bank reimbursements, trade outsourcing solutions, and trade asset distribution. Its eleven trade-processing centers are located in the United States and eight other countries.

HSBC Holdings plc

HSBC Holdings plc is one of the largest international banking firms in the world and is headquartered in London.[23] The company has seven thousand offices in eighty-one countries and territories. It furnishes a comprehensive range of financial services and operates an e-commerce business. HSBC provides trade finance and all foreign exchange services and operates as a specialist in offshore banking. Its Hong Kong office was named best trade finance bank in the world for 2002 by the monthly publication *Global Finance*.

General Bank

General Bank is a California-chartered, full-service commercial bank headquartered in Los Angeles. This relatively young bank, established in 1980, specializes in international trade financing among other areas and serves primarily medium-sized business firms. General has strong ties with the Asia-Pacific region and has correspondent relationships banks located in more than one hundred cities worldwide.

General's international trade finance business caters to medium-sized firms. It is capable of financing as much as US$30 million in a given trade transaction. Its financing cooperates with the Ex-Im and SBA guarantee programs and with the California Export Finance Office Guarantee Program. Its range of services includes negotiation, issuance, and settlement of letters of credit, assignment of proceeds, international collections, wire transfers abroad, and foreign exchange. It was voted most efficient bank holding company in California in 2002.[24]

World's Best Trade Finance Banks of 2002

The trade publication, *Global Finance*, recently selected the best trade finance banks in the world for 2002.[25] Banks were chosen based on their prowess in international trade finance including on-line trade functions. The criteria used to select these banks included volume, scope of global coverage, customer service, competitive pricing, and innovative technologies.

The best trade finance bank on a global basis was Citigroup in New York. Citigroup makes extensive use of ECA programs worldwide. The transactions which it has arranged have been guaranteed by Ex-Im for several years. It is the largest foreign bank arranger of export credits.

Other banks chosen as best trade finance institutions in 2002 on a regional or national basis included ABN AMRO, the Netherlands bank for Europe. This bank was selected for, among other reasons, its paperless cross-border transactions. The best trade finance bank in Asia was HSBC Holdings in Hong Kong. This bank was established in 1865 to finance trade between the United States and China. Individual banks in thirty-three countries were selected as best national trade finance banks in 2002 and included Mizuho Holdings in Japan, Grupo Financiero Banamex in Mexico, United Bank for Africa in Nigeria, Alfa Bank in Russia, Korea Exchange Bank in South Korea, Banco Bilbao Vizcaya Argentaria in Spain, and Credit Suisse Group in Switzerland The best on-line trade finance providers selected by *Global Finance* for 2002 were Actrade Financial Technologies for transaction settlement/credit business, and TradeCard for finance and trade logistics.

Hibernia National Bank

Hibernia National Bank in New Orleans has decades of experience in international banking and is a leader in export service. Hibernia offers a variety of services for U.S. exporters including trade finance, foreign exchange, letters of credit, standby letters of credit, foreign drafts, international funds transfer, documentary collections, and clean collection and cash letters. Its trade finance operations include Ex-Im guarantees and insurance of trade credits and cooperative work with the Working Capital Guarantee programs of the U.S. Small Business Administration and the GSM Programs of the U.S. Department of Agriculture. Hibernia is a member of the Society for Worldwide Interbank Financial Telecommunications (SWIFT), an automated processing system capable of sending standardized messages, which are encoded through computer systems that support international funds flows. This system offers a low-cost, very quick, secure method for sending messages underlying funds flows of multinational corporations.[26]

Export Insurance Services, Inc.

Export Insurance Services, Inc. (EIS) is an insurance brokerage firm specializing in commercial credit, export credit, and political risks insurance for domestic and international trade and finance.[27] It is headquartered in Augusta, Georgia, with representatives in four other states. It is, in reality, a network of affiliates that are experts in the provision of insurance services for international trade.

It can connect exporters with a wide variety of international trade specialists. These include credit reporting agencies, tax and legal firms, marketing, finance, and some governmental programs. EIS is administrator for the Ex-Im Umbrella Export Credit Insurance Policy for smaller exporters, discussed in Chapter 4.

EIS can provide government credit insurance as well as private credit insurance. It is in contact with U.S. credit insurance underwriters such as AIG Global Trade & Political Risk, EULER American Credit Indemnity, CNA, U.S. Ex-Im, Exporters Insurance Company, FCIA, Lloyd's of London, NCM Americas, and Trade Underwriters Agency, Inc.

EIS makes available to exporters a trade credit insurance policy and trade finance management service known as Trade Banker®.[28] This is trade finance software designed to manage receivables insured under Ex-Im and private trade credit insurance policies. This software was developed by Lex-Tek International, a software company based in Atlanta, Georgia, and one of the largest specialty credit insurance brokers in the United States. It is marketed by Lex-Tek and is available for a onetime set-up fee and monthly service charges. The software reduces policy administration costs for exporters, manages export receivables, and offers buyer credit.

Business.com

Business.com is an on-line search engine providing export assistance and information.[29] It has links to the major government departments and agencies discussed earlier. It offers links to a variety of import-export resources such as trade articles, books, and seminars. Links are available to state and local trade development agencies; to ExportHotline.com, a membership-based service that provides market research, industry analysis, trade show listings, and business protocol information; and to foreign trade information centers.

Miscellaneous Export-Facilitating Organizations

The work of several organizations that service exports or work to increase exports should also be addressed. These are export management companies, export-trading companies, and foreign sales corporations. Export management companies are chartered firms specializing in being the export department for firms which, for some reason, cannot perform this function by themselves. The export-trading company is a wholly owned subsidiary of an American company permitted by U.S. law to join with other export trading companies without penalty of violating antitrust laws. Foreign sales corporations are special subsidiaries permitted U.S. firms, which receive special tax treatment for their foreign sales. These special organizations are discussed in the following sections.

Export Management Companies. Export management companies (EMCs), formerly known as combination export managers, act as the export department for noncompeting manufacturers that lack the personnel or funds to support their own international marketing department.[30] They are, in essence, intermediaries. EMCs can transact the international business operations of their principals and handle routine details of shipping their exports. Usually, they take possession of the goods shipped but do not take ownership. They conduct this business function for a commission, usually a percentage of the shipment's value. EMCs can also pay the manufacturer for the goods and resell the product to a foreign purchaser. Thus, they can act either in the name of the firms they represent or in their own name. These entities are usually located in port cities.

Export Trading Companies. Export trading companies (ETCs) were authorized by the Export Trading Company Act of 1982. This new indirect export trading channel is a tool for exporters to avoid anti-trust regulations in that businesses can join together to form ETCs and, thus, avoid violations of laws against companies combining operations without government approval. The Export Trading Company Act eliminated two disadvantages which had faced U.S. exporters. First, bank holding companies were permitted to invest in export trading companies. Federal law had prohibited such acquisitions before 1982. Second, competing companies could combine export operations without fear of violating antitrust regulations of the federal government. Any potential exporter can apply to the U.S. Department of Commerce for approval to form an ETC with one or more other companies. Trade associations can also form ETCs. Examples of the latter include the National Tooling and Machining Association and the American Film Marketing Association.[31]

Foreign Sales Corporations. Foreign Sales Corporations (FSCs) replaced the Domestic International Sales Company program in 1985. The latter, DISCs as they were called, received an indefinite tax deferral for taxes due on one-half of their foreign sales. DISCs had been authorized in 1972. Foreign businesses criticized DISCs for their supposedly unfair use of direct tax revenues to subsidize U.S. exports. In addition, DISCs were supposed to encourage small companies to initiate export programs. Instead, large U.S. firms took advantage of the tax law permitting the tax deferral. DISCs were also criticized because they were not operating companies but merely shell operations. Some companies still operate a watered-down version of the DISC and can defer a portion of their undistributed profits.

U.S. companies were authorized by the U.S. government to establish wholly owned subsidiaries referred to as FSCs. Under the Tax Reform Act of 1984, a company can get a 30 to 32 percent tax reduction for the export business done by an FSC.[32] In addition, special transfer pricing rules permit an exporter to sell goods to an FSC at prices below an arm's length price. And a dividends-received tax deduction is allowed by the Internal Revenue Service. The FSC must be located in a U.S. possession, except for Puerto Rico, or in a foreign country. It must have economic substance. In other words, it cannot be solely a paper corporation.[33] The export operations which the FSC performs must be done outside the United States. Under this arrangement, as many as twenty-five exporters can share one FSC. The FSC tax reduction is still under fire from GATT member countries, especially in Europe, which hold that the tax break is not proper according to GATT rules.

One example of an FSC is Infocus Systems, Inc., a U.S. manufacturer of liquid crystal display projection panels and video projection systems. The company decided in 1990 to export its products through an FSC based in the Virgin Islands. The FSC cost only U.S. $5,000 to establish and has saved hundreds of thousands of dollars in taxes since then.[34]

Although FSCs seem to be complicated entities permitted by Federal law, they do offer some tax savings. Small firms can benefit from this form of organization and some states have established FSCs for small firms.[35] This is a departure from the predecessor DISCs, which were used by large firms to exploit the tax advantage.

FOREIGN TRADE ZONES

In addition to the public and private agencies and services discussed so far in this chapter, which service exporters and importers in one way or another, the benefits of foreign trade zones (FTZs) should be included. The foreign trade zone is the American version of the free trade zone.[36] A free trade zone is an enclosed area, usually a warehouse, considered to be external to the customs territory of the country in which it is located. Products of foreign origin can be moved into the free trade zone pending transshipment, re-exportation, or importation into the country. The goods can remain in the free trade zone without being levied with import duties. These also may be referred to as duty-free zones.

The foreign trade zone is the U.S. version of the free trade zone, there are more than four hundred FTZs located in the United States. They may be located at seaports but are also found inland. Goods may come into the FTZ disassembled and, thus, incur a lower duty than fully assembled goods. Importers may store parts in FTZs and incur no duty until the parts are withdrawn.

The savings in costs to the importer from a FTZ operation may be obvious. Benefits to the exporter may also be apparent in that the FTZ can accelerate the export process and result in export tax rebates and smoothing of the customs process. The exporter can apply for such a rebate or customs facilitation as soon as the goods enter the FTZ. No duties may be paid if final assembly or manufacturing is performed in the FTZ. Firms may use an FTZ for final assembly or manufacture in a country with low labor costs and, thus, benefit from the cheap labor.

SUMMARY AND CONCLUSIONS

The U.S. Export-Import Bank, Foreign Credit Insurance Association, and Private Export Funding Corporation are generally considered the foundation of the U.S. export financing system in conjunction with commercial banks in working to increase U.S. exports. However, several other agencies, firms, banks, and specialized programs supplement the activities of the major export credit agencies and firms. These include services offered by the U.S. Department of Commerce and the U.S. Small Business Administration. Other U.S. government agencies educate firms in export procedures or identify overseas markets for U.S. goods and services.

Specialized private firms, banks, and associations offer services to exporters. These include world trade centers and city world trade associations. Factoring banks and networks bring individual factors together to purchase accounts receivable of exporters. Foreign trade zones facilitate cost reduction in trade by eliminating some customs duties.

Exporters should examine the services of these and other specialized agencies and firms to assist them in some aspect of international trade and financing of that trade. These resources can ease the complicated entry into world trade and reduce the costs of export operations. Two of the best local places to obtain export finance information are the regional U.S. Department of Commerce offices and the nearest city world trade association. Information on almost any aspect of export procedures, documentation, and financing can be found in these places.

When the auspices of the numerous federal and state governmenal agencies, coupled with the wide variety of public and private miscellaneous firms and organizations, are considered, the U.S. system has a vast array of resources for the facilitation of financing the international trade of U.S. firms. However, when one considers the small proportion of U.S. firms which export are compared with the number of firms actually producing exportable goods and services, one can surmise that even the most comprehensive of international trade financing systems needs to do more. As discussed in Chapter 2, trade is an extremely important part of a nation's economy. Facilities which finance this trade must do a more diligent job in expanding U.S. exports. Given the very large current account deficits in the U.S. balance of payments, a time might come when the capital account will not offset these deficits. Our capital market may not always elicit the inflows which ameliorate the current account problems. The result will be a depreciating dollar, which might be replaced as a reserve currency by some other currency, such as the euro. This might be a favorable event for some U.S. exporters, but it might also be disastrous for the U.S. economy as a whole.

NOTES

1. U.S. Department of Agriculture, "Commodity Credit Corporation: 7CFR Part 1493," August 1, 1997, p. 5.

2. U.S. Department of Agriculture, *Will You Get Paid for the Sale You Just Made?* (Washington: Author, 1999), p. 2.

3. U.S. Department of Agriculture, "U.S. Export Credit Guarantee Programs: What Every Importer Should Know about the GSM-102 and GSM-103 Programs," November 1996, p. 5.

4. Ibid., p. 6.

5. Gerald F. Seib, "Export Credits, a Useful Tool Abroad, Can Leave Taxpayer Holding the Bag," *Wall Street Journal*, June 5, 1992, p. A12.

6. Available on-line November 29, 2002, at www.bxa.doc.gov/, pp. 1–2.

7. Available on-line November 29, 2002, at www.usatrade.gov/website /website.nsf, pp. 1–2.

8. Available on-line November 29, 2002, at web.ita.doc.gov/, pp. 1–2.

9. Available on-line November 29, 2002, at www.customs.gov/impoexpo /imex_txt.htm, pp. 1–6.

10. Robert Zoellick, "Bringing Down the Barriers," *Financial Times*, July 25, 2002; available on-line December 23, 2002, at www.usconsulate.org.hk/pas /pr/2002/072901.htm, pp. 1–2.

11. "US Trade Representative Defends Steel Tariffs," *People's Daily*, April 10, 2002; available on-line December 23, 2002, at www.china.org.cn/english /30426.htm, p. 1.

12. Available on-line November 29, 2002, at www.exportmichigan.com/ calendar.htm, pp. 1–4.

13. Available on-line November 29, 2002, at www.odod.state.oh.us/itd /oefi.htm, pp. 1–2.

14. Available on-line November 29, 2002, at www.mdfb.org/export.htm, pp. 1–2.

15. Available on-line November 29, 2002, at www.manateeedc.com/flor- ida.asp, pp. –2.

16. Available on-line November 29, 2002, at www.apsu.edu/ext_ed /small_business/, pp. 1–4.

17. Available on-line November 29, 2002, at www.baft.org/pages/committees .html, pp. 1–3.

18. Donald A. Ball and Wendell H. McCulloch, Jr., *International Business: The Challenge of Global Competition* (Chicago: Irwin, 1996), p. 525.

19. Available on-line September 6, 2002, at www.factors-chain.com/b2/ b2_main.html, p. 1.

20. Available on-line December 6, 2002, at www.factors-chain.com/b5 /stats2001/fl_main.html, pp. 1–6.

21. Available on-line September 6, 2002, at www.wellsfargo.com/inatl /trade_sves/exporters.jhtml, pp. 1–5.

22. Available on-line September 10, 2002, at www.bankofny.com/pages /ccbs_tradeservices.htm, pp. 1–6.

23. Available on-line December 6, 2002, at www.hsbc.com, p. 1.

24. Available on-line December 6, 2002, at www.generalbank.com, p. 1.

25. Gordon Platt and Adam Rombel, "World's Best Trade Finance Banks 2002," *Global Finance*, August 2002; available on-line September 6, 2002, at www.globalf.vwh.net/content/?article_id=186, September 6, 2002, pp. 1–8.

26. James C. Baker and Raj Aggarwal, "SWIFT as an International Funds Transfer Mechanism: User Satisfaction and Challenges," in Yong H. Kim and Venkat Srinivasan (eds.), *Advances in Working Capital Management: A Research Annual*, Vol. 2 (Greenwich, CT: JAI Press, 1991).

27. Available on-line December 13, 2002, at www.exportinsurance.com/company .htm, pp. 1–2.

28. Available on-line December 13, 2002, at www.exportinsurance.com /insloanex.htm, pp. 1–2.

29. Available on-line December 13, 2002, at www.business.com/direc- tory/government_and_trade/international_trade/export_asp?query, pp. 1–5.

30. Ball and McCulloch, *International Business*, p. 432.

31. Ibid., pp. 434–435.

32. James C. Baker, *International Finance: Management, Markets, and Institutions* (Upper Saddle River, NJ: Prentice-Hall, 1998), p. 470.

33. Lee H. Radebaugh and Sidney J. Gray, *International Accounting and Multinational Enterprises* (New York: John Wiley and Sons, 1997), p. 626.

34. Baker, *International Finance*, p. 470.

35. Radebaugh and Gray, *International Accounting and Multinational Enterprises*, p. 627.

36. Ball and McCulloch, *International Busienss*, pp. 533–534.

8

Cooperation among U.S. Trade Finance Institutions

The financial institutions, government agencies, and private associations and firms covered in Chapters 3–7 have all facilitated some aspect of trade financing for U.S. exporters. Their major objective during their many years of operations has been the expansion of U.S. exports. In many cases, one institution or agency has cooperated with another institution or agency to fulfill this objective. These collaborative efforts will be the focal point of this chapter. An evaluation of the benefits of this teamwork will be included in the discussion.

THE INTRABANK SYSTEM AND COOPERATIVE EFFORTS

In Chapter 3, the role of commercial banks in the international trade finance system was examined. Commercial banks finance the vast bulk of international trade by making loans to either the exporter or the importer. When these loans are made with a letter of credit and a draft, the lending bank, in a manner cooperates with the short-term financial markets when it accepts the draft, thus creating a banker's acceptance, and then sells it at a discount into a banker's acceptance market where a dealer sells it to an investor specializing in these short-term negotiable instruments called banker's acceptances.

However, in recent years, use of the banker's acceptance has declined drastically. Other means of funding trade credits or reducing their riskiness have replaced the banker's acceptance because the alternatives may be less costly or easier to arrange. Banks, through their holding companies, can issue commercial paper in the short-term financial markets and use this market source of funds to finance export trade.

Banks may collaborate with other banks in the à forfait market. In this nontraditional method for financing certain types of international trade, a medium- or long-term loan is divided into a series of short-term notes (usually six-month notes), which are guaranteed by either the original bank or some other bank. These guaranteed short-term notes, each with an interest rate set commensurate with its length to final maturity, can be retained by the original bank or discounted to another bank in the system or they may be sold to investors specializing in forfaited notes.

Forfaited trade transactions, once an important part of the arsenal of European banks, have become a profitable business for more and more U.S. banks. Cases of forfaiting were examined in Chapter 3. It appears that a number of U.S. manufacturers make products conducive to this nontraditional form of trade finance, and U.S. banks should continue to find such business a growing prospect.

EX-IM AND ITS COOPERATIVE EFFORTS

Ex-Im initiates cooperative efforts with several sectors of the international trade financing system in the United States. These include guaranteed and insured loans made by commercial banks, relationships with the Foreign Credit Insurance Association (FCIA) and the Private Export Funding Corporation (PEFCO), and operations with other U.S. governmental agencies.

Banks and the U.S. Export-Import Bank

Banks do not like to retain all the risk of their loans, even if that risk is low. They like to hedge or spread risk by securitizing a loan, as with the banker's acceptance, or they prefer another party to guarantee the loan. In some cases, the loan may be insured against nonpayment. In the United States, the U.S. Export-Import Bank (Ex-Im) can provide a guarantee for a bank loan or it can insure the loan against the risk of nonpayment. The guarantee and insurance programs of Ex-Im were discussed in Chapter 4. The guarantee requires that some of the risk be borne by the exporter, some by the importer, and some by the lending bank. Commercial or political risks can be insured by Ex-Im and a comprehensive policy can also be issued under some circumstances covering both commercial and political risk. For example, General Bank of Los Angeles participates with Ex-Im and SBA guarantee programs as well as with the California Export Finance Office Guarantee Program. Citibank of New York is another bank whose loans have been guaranteed by Ex-Im for several years. These are just a few of the U.S. banks which have collaborated with Ex-Im to facilitate the financing of U.S. exports.

Ex-Im and the Small Business Administration

The U.S. Small Business Administration (SBA) and Ex-Im have a cooperative program of coguarantees provided to small business exporters and export trading companies. This program applies to loans in principal amounts ranging from US$200,000 to 1,500,000. These guarantees cover up to 85 percent of the amount of a loan. The principal objective of this program is to encourage small companies to export their products. This program has been relatively successful because nearly 80 percent of Ex-Im's trade finance operations have involved small firms in recent years.

Ex-Im and Miscellaneous Cooperative Efforts

Ex-Im incorporates several cooperative relationships in the fulfillment of its primary objective: to increase U.S. exports of goods and services. In the implementation of its Small Business Environmental insurance policy, Ex-Im uses the services of specialty brokers such as Export Insurance Services in Atlanta to deliver its umbrella policy service. Until 1992, Ex-Im collaborated with the FCIA, a private consortium of insurance companies discussed in detail in Chapter 5, to provide insurance of loans granted by banks to facilitate exports. Since 1992, Ex-Im has provided its own trade credit insurance facilities. Other U.S. insurance companies have been encouraged to insure trade credits especially in cases where the importer is located in an industrialized country and when the trade credits are issued by a large money center bank. Such policies written by U.S. companies can be profitable and low in risk.

Ex-Im and PEFCO

Ex-Im has a strong working relationship with the Private Export Funding Corporation (PEFCO). PEFCO is a consortium of banks, industrial companies, and financial services firms which makes loans to foreign importers to buy U.S. goods and services. The organization was discussed in detail in Chapter 6. Ex-Im guarantees the short-term and medium-term loans which PEFCO makes to foreign purchasers. It also purchases short-term loans from U.S. exporters which are guaranteed by Ex-Im. Ex-Im also insures the PEFCO note facility which offers to purchase medium-term loans and leases. PEFCO also borrows in world capital markets to fund its operations and these loans can be guaranteed by Ex-Im. Ex-Im guarantees save PEFCO the cost of a credit risk evaluation of the importers as well as country risk appraisals and the review of any elements which might affect the collectibility of PEFCO loans.

The cooperative relationship between Ex-Im and PEFCO benefits developing countries, which need U.S. merchandise goods and services, as well as small business exporters in the United States, in their efforts to sell their products into the world marketplace. Their role is to reduce the riskiness of foreign trade transactions so that more small firms will initiate export business, especially to developing nations.

PEFCO, thus, combines cooperative efforts with a number of institutions public and private and with short- and long-term capital markets. It makes loans to importers, purchases Ex-Im-guaranteed loans from U.S. exporters, borrows operating funds from the money and capital markets, and obtains Ex-Im guarantees for its loans and for its own borrowings. PEFCO has found a different way to provide a comprehensive system of trade finance designed to increase U.S. exports.

U.S. GOVERNMENT AGENCIES AND THEIR COOPERATIVE ACTIVITIES

The major U.S. government agencies concerned with international trade finance covered in this book are the U.S. Department of Agriculture (USDA) and the U.S. Small Business Administration (SBA). The USDA operates export credit guarantee programs through its Commodity Credit Corporation (CCC) for agricultural exports, especially to developing countries and works with the banking system in guaranteeing trade credits made to exporters or importers by commercial banks. The CCC can also provide direct credits in some cases.

The SBA has a comprehensive trade finance program to encourage exporting by small firms in the United States. The agency can make short-term working capital loans as well as medium- and long-term capital loans. It can provide guarantees of trade credits made by qualified banks. The U.S. Export Assistance Centers operated by SBA offer exporters a variety of international trade information and can connect small firms to Ex-Im and other export trade finance facilities.

SBA has guaranteed loans made by a number of U.S. banks. Hibernia National Bank of New Orleans is a typical example of a U.S. commercial bank which has participated in the Working Capital Guarantee programs of SBA. SBA's primary mandate is to support small U.S. business firms. By teaming with Ex-Im's relatively new thrust toward small business, this cooperative effort between two U.S. agencies has made a significant impact in the encouragement of small U.S. firms to recognize the benefits of export trade.

Many small firms which produce an exportable good are discouraged from following up trade leads or queries because of the complexity of the average export trade transaction. The operations of Ex-Im and SBA can facilitate such transactions. The result may be profits for the exporter and improvement in the U.S. balance of payments.

STATE AND LOCAL EXPORT FINANCE PROGRAMS

Several state and local export finance programs have been established throughout the United States. Many of these have cooperative relationships with U.S. Government agencies such as Ex-Im, SBA, and the Overseas Private Investment Corporation (OPIC). The Ohio Export Finance Initiative is one such state agency which, in addition to cooperative activities with other government agencies is able to offer exporters alternative trade financing such as factoring and forfaiting by facilitating arrangements with commercial banks offering such programs.

TRADE ASSOCIATIONS AND COOPERATIVE PROGRAMS

Several trade associations that provide special trade finance facilities were discussed in Chapter 7. Many of these organizations cooperate with commercial banks, export credit agencies (ECAs) such as Ex-Im, and other government agencies, as well as foreign organizations. Bankers Association for Finance and Trade (BAFT) is one example of a trade association of banks involved in financing international trade and which cooperates with Ex-Im, OPIC, and non-U.S. ECAs. Its Small Business Export Committee has a working relationship with SBA.

City world trade associations also promote the activities of major elements of the international trade finance system in the United States. For example, the Cleveland World Trade Association (CWTA) works very closely in the development of its educational programs with the Cleveland Regional Office of the U.S. Department of Commerce. Educational conferences, seminars, luncheon speakers, and courses are offered by the CWTA. The objective of these programs is to expand exports by firms located in Northeast Ohio. Other city world trade associations throughout the United States have similar programs and similar goals.

World Trade Centers are located around the world and promote world trade with numerous programs. More than three hundred of these centers have been established in one hundred countries, with forty-two located in the United States. They are listed in Appendix 3. The centers cooperate with local business firms and banks in hosting seminars, courses, and other programs designed to educate business-ment about the benefits of international trade and how to facilitate such transactions.

U.S. TRADE LEGISLATION

The U.S. Congress has also cooperated in efforts to expand U.S. exports with selected legislation. Laws have been enacted that permit U.S. firms to establish export trading companies and foreign sales corporations (FSCs). Export trading companies are wholly owned subsidiaries permitted to combine their efforts without the risk of violating U.S. antitrust laws. In addition, U.S. companies have been authorized by law to establish FSCs. Tax relief can be obtained for the firm's exports which are shipped through these entities.

International organizations have formulated quasi-legislation designed to promote world trade including trade by U.S. firms. The General Agreement on Tariffs and Trade (GATT) organizes periodical tariff cutting negotiations and supervises international trading rules to maintain fairness in world trade. The World Trade Organization (WTO) also works toward trade-enhancement programs aimed at multilateral programs which can benefit nations.

SUMMARY AND CONCLUSIONS

Banks are responsible for the vast bulk of trade finance. Banks cooperate with exporters, with federal and state government agencies, and with other banks in providing export trade credits. They also fund some of this trade finance by securitizing trade drafts and by borrowing in such markets as the commercial paper market.

Ex-Im works with a variety of commercial banks, export finance institutions, federal, state, and local agencies, and private organizations in cooperative efforts designed to enhance U.S. exports. It guarantees or insures loans made by commercial banks to U.S. exporters and loans made by PEFCO to foreign purchasers of U.S. merchandise goods and services. It guarantees loans made by the U.S. Department of Agriculture and the U.S. Small Business Administration. Before the early 1990s, Ex-Im and FCIA had a ccoperative working relationship. FCIA insured trade credits as a supplement to Ex-Im's guarantees or lending operations. Since then, Ex-Im has initiated its own trade credit insurance program.

Federal and state government agencies whose objectives are aimed at expanding U.S. exports carry out cooperative activities with each other and with banks, nonbank financial institutions, and foreign ECAs in the fulfillment of these goals. They guarantee loans and trade credits provided by these entities, promote small firm export business, and sponsor training programs aimed at educating potential exporters in the procedures necessary for selling their goods to foreign purchasers.

Trade associations and world trade centers work with Federal and state governmental agencies and educational institutions in the presentation of programs aimed at U.S. export expansion. They sponsor conferences and seminars whose speakers stress topics which educate and inform businessmen about international trade finance procedures.

These cooperative efforts weld together a large variety of institutions which have the same goal: the expansion of U.S. exports. They have been successful in these endeavors and the result has been one of the most comprehensive international trade finance systems available in any country. The relationships among the agencies, institutions, and firms involved in the U.S. trade financing system have demonstated that successful combinations of the public and private sector can be accomplished if all involved are on the same wave length.

Net exports is a small, but not insignificant, part of any country's gross national product. It has been said that only about five percent of the U.S. companies which make an exportable good actually export. If means can be found to convince the other 95 percent of the benefits of international trade, U.S. national income and the balance of payments should benefit. The cooperative efforts of the agencies, institutions, and associations discussed in this chapter should be successful in this objective.

9

Major Foreign Export Credit Agencies

Export credit agencies (ECAs) have become prevalent around the world. As international trade has increased, the number of government and quasigovernmental agencies that facilitate the expansion of trade finance has increased greatly. At the present time, ECAs of some type can be found in as many as seventy-three nations, both industrialized and developing. At least forty-eight ECAs operate in thirty-five countries, all of which are members of the Organization for Economic Cooperation and Development (OECD). About half of all export trade credit support rendered by ECAs worldwide is extended by ECAs in the seven largest industrial nations, the so-called Group of Seven (G-7) nations, comprising Canada, France, Germany, Italy, Japan, the United Kingdom, and the United States. Details of these organizations can be found in various editions of the *World's Principal Export Credit Insurance Systems*, published by the International Export Credits Institute in New York. This chapter is devoted to a discussion of those ECAs found in a representative group of these nations: Australia, Canada, France, Germany, India, Japan, Korea, and United Kingdom.

Most of these are government agencies. Some are quasigovernmental institutions or private firms. The main export finance institution in Germany is Hermes, a private insurance company, which acts as an agent for the government. Some of the activities of the ECA that handles trade finance in Great Britain have been privatized in recent years. See Appendix 2 for a listing of the ECAs located in OECD countries. Other

Country	Agency	Acronym
France	Coface Scrl	SCRL
Germany	Gerling Credit Insurance Group	GCIG
Hong Kong	Hong Kong Export Credit Insurance Corporation	HKEC
India	Export-Import Bank of India	Eximbank-India
Indonesia	Asuransi Ekspo Indonesia	ASEI
	PT. Bank Ekspor Indonesia (Persero)	BEI
Israel	Israel Foreign Risks Insurance Corp. Ltd.	ITRIC
	Israel Discount Bank	Discount bank
Italy	Societa Italiana Assicurazione Credit SpA	EULER-SIAC
Malaysia	Malaysia Export Credit Insurance Berhad	MECIB
New Zealand	EXGO	EXGO
Oman	Export Credit Guarantee Agency, Oman Development Bank	ECGA
Singapore	ECICS Credit Insurance Ltd.	ECICS
Slovenia	Slovene Export Corporation, Inc.	SEC
South Africa	Credit Guarantee Insurance Corp. of Africa	CGIC
Sri Lanka	Export Credit Insurance Corporation	SLECIC
United Kingdom	EULER Trade Indemnity plc	EULER

Source: Available on-line April 12, 2002, at www.oecd.org/ech/act/xcred/ecas.htm, p. 2.

Figure 9.1   Miscellaneous Non-OECD Export Credit Agencies

miscellaneous agencies that perform some functions in international trade finance are shown in Figure 9.1.

INTRODUCTION TO WORLDWIDE EXPORT CREDIT AGENCIES

ECAs operate around the world with a variety of methodologies and in a variety of nations. Lending by ECAs, including the U.S. Export-Import Bank, increased by 400 percent between 1988 and 1996, from US$26 billion in 1988 to US$105 billion in 1996. During this period, ECAs' shares of developing country debt increased to 25 percent of total debt and of developing country official debt increased to 56 percent.[1] In this section, a general discussion will cover ECAs located in Europe, Asia, and other areas of the world.

European ECAs

The ECAs with the longest history and most significant operations are located in Great Britain, France, and Germany. These institutions are Export Credits Guarantee Division (ECGD) in Great Britain, Compagnie française d'assurance pour le commerce extérieur (Coface) in France, and Hermes Kreditversicherungs AG (Hermes) in Germany. These are hybrids as far as government ownership and operation are concerned. ECGD is a branch of the British government but has had some of its operations privatized. Coface is completely government controlled. Hermes is a private insurance company which operates as an agency of the German government in the export trade financing function.

Asian ECAs

The most significant ECAs in Asia are located in Japan, Korea, and India. The Japan Bank for International Cooperation, formerly the Japan Import-Export Bank, handles export financing operations for the Japanese Government. The Export-Import Bank of Korea is the major ECA operation in South Korea. The Export-Import Bank of India has financed, facilitated, and promoted foreign trade in India for the past two decades. All three of these agencies are government owned and operated; they will be discussed in detail in subsequent sections of this chapter. In addition, the ECAs of Thailand and Malaysia, lesser developed nations of Asia, will also be discussed. These are the Export-Import Bank of Thailand and the Export-Import Bank of Malaysia Berhad and they operate in two of Asia's leading developing nations.

ECAs in Other Areas

ECAs in two other areas are worth noting. These are North America and the South Pacific. In addition to the U.S. trade finance system, one other ECA is located in North America and has significant operations. This is the Canadian Government's Export Development Corporation (EDC), a branch of the Canadian Government. The major ECA located in the South Pacific is the Export Finance and Insurance Corporation (EFIC) located in Australia. EFIC is also an agency of the Australian government.

Multilateral ECAs

Several export credit and financing functions are performed by multilateral agencies, or ECAs which are regional in composition and provide services for a number of countries in the area. These include the African Export-Import Bank; Corporación Andina de Fomento (CAF), which services the Andean Pact countries; the European Bank for Reconstruction and Development, which services the East European and former Union of Soviet Socialist Republics; the Inter-American

Development Bank, which services Latin American nations; the Islamic Corporation for the Insurance of Investment and Export Credit (part of the Islamic Development Bank), which services Islamic nations, and the Multilateral Investment Guarantee Agency (MIGA), an affiliate of the World Bank. These agencies perform some export financing and trade credit guarantee functions.

OFFICIAL EUROPEAN EXPORT CREDIT AGENCIES

Major national export credit agencies located in Europe will be discussed in the following sections. These include Compagnie française d'assurance pour le commerce extérieur (Coface) of France, Export Credit Guarantee Department (ECGD) of Great Britain, and Hermes Kreditversicherungs AG (Hermes) of Germany.

Coface

The Coface Group, a French ECA, is a world leader in the provision of export credit insurance. It has more than fifty years of experience in trade finance and insurance. Coface provides more than seventy-eight thousand customers worldwide with international credit insurance, guaranty insurance, prospecting and credit information, receivables management and collection, and access to two global networks based on shared risk management and an integrated product and service assistance. Coface operates with more than 3,700 employees in fifty-six countries. Its receivables management business includes factoring and securitization of receivables.

During 2002, Coface purchased the CNA Credit business line in North America. This division of CNA Property & Casualty Operations provides commercial credit protection to companies domestically or internationally on credit terms. This acquisition will enable Coface to compete more intensively with financing of U.S. exports by U.S. institutions. In 1998, Coface and CNA formed Worldwide Credit Managers LLC to market credit insurance in the United States and Canada. The Coface-CNA partnership is thought to be the world's largest supplier of private export credit insurance.[2]

The Coface Group, comprised of Coface and Coface Scrl, provides exporters with two online networks designed to assist with foreign credit checks.[3] These are @rating Credit Scores and @rating Credit Opinions. These on-line systems were launched in 2000 and provide tools for assessing credit risk and the quality of companies with which exporters deal. Financial institutions involved in trade finance can also take advantage of these on-line systems.

The Coface Group has done relatively well financially during a period of export decline. Its consolidated turnover for the first half of 2002 increased by 4.8 percent over the same period for 2001. During this period, Coface booked 357.2 million euros of insurance premiums, an increase of 18 million euros over the same period in 2001.[4] During this period, the euro traded in a range of US$0.90 to 1.00.

Export Credits Guarantee Department

The Export Credits Guarantee Department (ECGD) is the official export credit agency of the United Kingdom. It operates as an autonomous department of the government. ECGD was established in 1919, making it the oldest ECA in the world. In 1991, the British government considered that the risks encountered by ECGD were too high so a portion of ECGD was sold to the private sector. Transactions involving credit terms of less than two years were taken over by the privatized portion. ECGD now concentrates on credit insurance and financing for longer-term commitments. These new powers, including specialization in markets in developing countries and non-OECD member developed countries, are derived from the Export and Investment Guarantees Act of 1991. ECGD officials now report directly to the British Secretary of State for Trade and Industry. The primary objective of ECGD is to assist exporters, project sponsors, banks, and buyers so that they can compete effectively in overseas markets where private sector assistance may be unavailable. International trade is very important to Great Britain. In 1996, for example, trade accounted for nearly 60 percent of the United Kingdom's gross domestic product (GDP).[5]

Funding ECGD Operations. Many ECAs finance their operations by borrowing in the international capital markets. ECGD, on the other hand, borrows through a separate organization, the Guaranteed Export Credit Corporation (Gefco) by issuing bonds to the latter organization. Gefco is a discretionary trust established in 1986. Royal Exchange Assurance is the trustee for Gefco. Gefco was originally formed by Lloyds Bank to refinance overdue debt issued by large European banks. Gefco's primary business now is to fund ECGD's operations. ECGD acts as the guarantor of these borrowings. Some evidence exists that ECGD's borrowing costs would be lower if it operated on its own in the capital markets.[6]

The process by which ECGD issues bonds to Gefco is time-consuming and slow. Gefco is permitted to borrow only US$1 billion annually. If a bank makes a sound proposal to ECGD, the latter must gain the approval of the Bank of England, the British Department of Trade and Industry (of which ECGD is a part), and the British Treasury, all of which must attest that the loan to the bank will be guaranteed by the British government. In addition, Gefco can only borrow in sterling so any arbitrage possibilities are impossible since other currencies cannot be used. In any case, the procedure for funding ECGD is cumbersome and fraught with bureaucracy. In the competitive world of ECAs and global trade finance, ECGD is at a disadvantage vis-a-vis other newer ECA operations, especially those in the emerging markets.

ECGD Services. ECGD offers three major services: financial services enabling British exporters of capital goods and services in markets that might be inaccessible in the absence of private sector financing; credit insurance is offered by ECGD, which protects exporters of capital goods and services against nonpayment, and ECGD offers political risk insurance for British companies that invest overseas, against loss on such investments caused by political unrest and instability. These major services will be discussed in subsequent sections of this chapter.

In FY2001, ECGD issued trade credit guarantees and policies totaling £5.66 billion, which generated net contributions to the government treasury of £205 million. Given the average foreign exchange rate for the year, these figures amount to US$8.25 billion and US$300 million, respectively.[7]

Financial services offered to exporters by ECGD include guarantees of private sector bank loans which finance trade by UK exporters. These guarantee activities include buyer credits, supplier credit financing, lines of credit, and project financing. Buyer credits enable exporters to obtain lower interest and better terms than possible from a private bank. Long-term credit for up to 85 percent of the amount financed can be guaranteed. The value of the contracts guaranteed must total at least £5 million for at least two years. These guarantees are extended, however, with recourse to the exporter. The exporter, thus, must obtain insurance on the credits or face default risk.

ECGD makes Supplier Credit Financing available for trade contracts for at least £25,000 with credit terms in excess of two years. Under this program, the exporter can receive immediate payment by selling bills of exchange or promissory notes to a commercial bank. If a bill of exchange is used, payment can be received as soon as the goods are shipped. If a promissory note is used, the exporter receives payment as soon as the buyer accepts the goods. Risk of nonpayment is transferred to the bank, and the transaction is without recourse to the exporter should the buyer default.

Line of Credit financing is offered by British banks and supported by a guarantee from ECGD. The guaranteed loan funds are used to pay British exporters once the goods are exported. An exporter can use this program to gain entry to an overseas market by financing unrelated contracts, with either different buyers in different countries or a particular buyer in a particular country.

The ECGD Project Financing Program is used for projects of £20 million when repayment is expected from a project's revenues. This financing is made with limited recourse. The borrower must make sure the project is finished but does not need to make up all of the shortfall in the project's earnings.

ECGD also offers credit insurance to British exporters. Again, this insurance is available for transactions beyond the capability of the private sector and to underwrite reasonable payment risks. The two major insurance programs available from ECGD are the Export Insurance Policy (EIP), the Bond Insurance Policy, and the Tender to Contract or Forward Exchange Supplements. Most ECGD insurance is transacted with the EIP, which covers cash and credit contracts involving large capital goods shipments. Both commercial and political risks are covered for up to 95 percent of the loss incurred and when the contract is for £50,000 or more.

The Bond Insurance Policy is available only when the Buyer Credit or EIP is used and it provides the exporter additional coverage if the buyer requires a contract or performance bond. It protects the exporter if the bond is called or if some political risk causes a loss.

The Tender to Contract/Forward Exchange Supplement protects exporters with the ability to provide quotes in foreign currencies. This program is a unique offering from ECGD. The insurance helps the exporter commit to a firm price since it covers adverse currency fluctuations during the period between the currency quotation and the time when the contract is actually signed by the parties.

ECGD has developed a close relationship with the manufacturers of Airbus, a joint British-French venture to manufacture large commercial jet airliners. As a result, it has developed a fixed-rate finance package allowing it to offer a fixed interest rate for up to three years prior to delivery. Such an option can provide a significant benefit to the buyers of Airbus aircraft in an environment of rising interest rates.

ECGD offers another program in addition to the Contract to Tender Program which is unique. This is the International Debt and Development Program. With this program, ECGD has written off US$1 billion during 1998–2000 under an activity referred to as the Heavily Indebted Poor Country Initiative. Countries that have benefited from this program include Bolivia, Cameroon, Guyana, Guinea Republic, Madagascar, Mali, Nicaragua, Uganda, and Zambia. When the World Bank and the International Monetary Fund agree that this initiative has reached a so-called "decision point," according to criteria set by these organizations, ECGD will write off debt owed it by a particularly needy developing country.

Beginning in 1991, ECGD privatized its short-term trade financing business. Since then, the major portion of this business has been performed by four organizations in Great Britain: EULER Trade Indemnity, the NCM Group, Coface UK, and the British Insurance and Investment Brokers Association. These private insurers establish credit limits for qualified importers and generally cover losses from 75 to 90 percent of the contracted limit. These firms, short in number, are valuable to British exporters since their experience in foreign countries helps exporters establish trade relationships. These firms have modern on-line systems, which offer exporters real-time information about any problems that might result in nonpayment by foreign buyers.

A down side can be pointed out in the case of ECGD operations. Like the U.S. Ex-Im, it is considered the financier of last resort. Both ECAs have found it increasingly more difficult to compete with other governments that offer export financing, especially the emerging markets of the Third World. In addition, both agencies have been at a disadvantage when competing with government-subsidized financing. They both rely heavily on private sector participation in their export financing programs. ECGD has privatized its short-term business, and Ex-Im relies heavily on FCIA and PEFCO to supplement Ex-Im activities or to cooperate with U.S. official programs. Their programs have been found to be relatively much smaller in relation to the national exports they finance in their respective countries than ECAs in Japan and France.

However, ECGD has had the reputation of having one large advantage over ECAs from other industrialized nations. At least until recently, ECGD has been praised for its ability to quickly determine the riskiness of a foreign purchaser. The reason often given for this ability is the relatively longer history of the agency when compared with other ECAs. ECGD has been able to build a better credit-rating system, which includes more in-depth country analysis as well as a broader range of credit ratings of potential foreign purchasers. This favorable characteristic seems to have been retained by ECGD despite the desire to privatize some of its operations.

Hermes

Hermes-Kreditversicherungs-AG (Hermes) is the leading credit insurer and provider of credit management services for exporters in Germany; it is headquartered in Hamburg. Hermes has been a subsidiary of EULER & HERMES S.A., located in Paris, since 2002. The latter is a holding company established by Allianz and AGF, two European insurance companies, for the purpose of combining their credit insurance operations. EULER & HERMES is a worldwide leader in credit insurance, a leader in Europe in the factoring business, and a market leader in guarantee insurance. One of its affiliates, EULER Indemnity, has taken over some of the short-term financing operations of ECGD in Great Britain. The firm has a 37 percent share of the international credit insurance market, generated by its six thousand employees located on five continents.[8]

Hermes is the largest credit insurer in Germany, with about 50 percent of the market. It is a private firm but has handled the German State Export Guarantee Scheme from 1926 until World War II and since 1948 for the Federal Republic of Germany. Hermes's major business is credit insurance. It insures accounts receivable generated from both domestic and export transactions. Every day Hermes rates the companies that are customers of German exporters. Its model for rating companies includes economic and sector analyses, balance sheet evaluation, status information analysis, payment terms checks, and enterprise-specific developments evaluation. Hermes has access to economic data on 40 million companies worldwide. The organization may, in fact, compete favorably with ECGD in its ability to rate the credit risk of foreign purchasers.

Hermes offers credit insurance covering bad debt losses in Germany and abroad. Coverage can involve payment terms of up to five years. Hermes also provides bonds and guarantees that are comparable to bank guarantees. Its guarantee operation relieves the emphasis on bank credit and increases liquidity for the exporter. Hermes' consumer credit insurance covers banks and other financial services companies against risks involved in overdrafts, term loans, credit cards, and electronic cash transactions.

OFFICIAL ASIAN EXPORT CREDIT AGENCIES

Major export credit agencies located in Asia will be discussed in the following sections. The ECAs included are Export-Import Bank of India, Export-Import Bank of Korea, the Korea Export Insurance Corporation, and Japan Bank for International Cooperation. Discussion of the ECAs of Thailand and Malaysia, developing countries of Asia, are included as well. These are the Export-Import Bank of Thailand and the Export-Import Bank of Malaysia Berhad. These agencies located in more underdeveloped countries in Asia are added as a contrast to those ECAs from the more developed nations and are fairly representative of ECAs located in less-developed nations.

Export-Import Bank of India

At least twelve developing countries have an official ECA. India is one of these countries.[9] Its ECA is the Export-Import Bank of India

(India Ex-Im). India's agency is relatively young having been established in 1981 by the Export-Import Bank of India Act. It began operations in 1982 and is wholly owned by the government of India. The purpose of this agency is to finance, facilitate, and promote foreign trade in India.

The India Ex-Im provides many of the services offered by the U.S. Ex-Im or by most other ECAs. It supports all aspects of the business cycle including foreign investment by Indian companies, pre- and postshipment, export production and marketing, export product development, and technology imports. For example, India Ex-Im offers short-term foreign currency financing to exporters with its preshipment credit program. The agency supports investment abroad by Indian companies, unlike the U.S. Ex-Im, by its equity lending program for overseas joint ventures and wholly owned subsidiaries of Indian companies.

One key difference between the Indian and U.S. ECAs involves the emphasis each puts on proposals for support. Ex-Im of the United States examines its applicants using a net present value (NPV) approach which considers the company's track record and estimated profitability of the project to be financed. This approach can be taken because the U.S. agency has a longer track record with a major presence in most major world markets. However, India looks at each project less from a NPV viewpoint but with more of a broad analysis of the prospect that it will improve India's international business operations as a whole. In other words, India uses a less scientific approach but one that results in a more qualitative credit analysis. India does not have a major presence in many of the major world markets and its trade infrastructure is still in the development stage. In 2001, India Ex-Im supported export contracts worth US$377 million. When compared with the US$15.5 billion of support provided in 2000 by U.S. Ex-Im, this amount is miniscule.

India Ex-Im works more closely with the government than do most ECAs. Its goals are geared toward a developing economy. Diversification of markets is one of those goals while focus on other developing areas is another. For example, it has focussed on Latin America and Africa in its export financing. It recently provided a US$10 million line of credit to Corporación Andina de Fomento (CAF) and Banco Industrial de Venezuela to promote India's exports to the Latin American market. CAF is a multilateral ECA, which will be discussed later in this chapter.

India Ex-Im offers a wide range of finance services. These include: lending to export-oriented companies, production equipment finance, import finance, export marketing finance, lending for software training institutes, financing research and development activities, port development, lending for export vendor development, foreign currency pre-shipment credits, and working capital loans for exporters. All of these financial services have the objective of increasing India's exports. India Ex-Im finances exports by extending credit to foreign governments, importers, or financial institutions which permit foreign buyers to purchase Indian exports on deferred payment terms.

The agency also offers a variety of nonfinancial export services and, therefore, has a broader approach to trade support than does, for example, the U.S. Ex-Im. These include advisory services to Indian companies to improve their prospects for securing business in projects funded by multilateral agencies. In addition, India Ex-Im acts as a consultant to other foreign trade–oriented nations, and organizes seminars and workshops on international trade and investment, export marketing, and business opportunities. India Ex-Im also publishes research studies on issues relevant to international trade and investment and furnishes information on all aspects of exporting, international trade and investment, and trade regulations.

One final note of comparison between the U.S. and Indian ECAs involves the difference in capital availability in the two countries. The per capita gross domestic product in India is about 5 percent of that in the United States, and the U.S. Ex-Im has ten times more assets than India Ex-Im. U.S. companies can raise capital more easily than their Indian counterparts and can raise these funds more efficiently from private sources than from government agencies. Indian firms, on the other hand, must look to their government more in raising capital for business operations, including export activities. Thus, India Ex-Im is motivated to offer a broader range of services than its counterparts in industrialized nations.

Export-Import Bank of Korea

The Export-Import Bank of Korea (Exim Korea) is a special governmental financial institution established in 1976 under the Export-Import Bank of Korea Act. Its primary objectives are to facilitate the development of the national economy and to enhance economic cooperation with foreign countries. The agency offers three types of guarantees and three types of export credit, among other services.[10]

Exim Korea Guarantees. Exim Korea provides guarantees to Korean commercial banks, local branches of foreign banks and foreign banks that participate in transactions that are financed by Exim Korea. These are financial guarantees, advance payment guarantees, and performance guarantees. Financial guarantees are for private sector loans which meet Exim Korea's eligibility requirements and, in the event of a default by the purchaser, Exim Korea will repay all of the principal and interest on the loan. Advance payment guarantees provide foreign importers with 100 percent guarantees to refund their advance cash payment for medium- and long-term transactions when the domestic exporter is unable to perform its part of the contract. Performance guarantees provide foreign importers with a 100 percent guarantee that a domestic exporter will perform according to the contract.

Exim Korea's Export Credit Programs. Exim Korea offers three export credit programs: export loans, direct loans, and relending facilities. Export loans are supplier credits which provide eligible borrowers with funds to finance exports. The exporters must be Korean nationals and certain capital goods can be covered. Foreign currencies as well as Korean won can be used. Coverage is for 100 percent of the contract price on medium- and long-term transactions after at least 15 to 20 percent has been paid in cash. Interest rates charged are the minimum rates under OECD guidelines. Direct loans have the same requirements as the export loans just discussed except that the contract price of a transaction must be more than US$1 million. The relending facility is a line of credit granted to foreign banks to assist foreign buyers to obtain loans from their local banks for the purchase of Korean exports. The foreign banks must be creditworthy, and the line of credit covers 100 percent of the contract price minus the required cash down payment. The maximum repayment period is 10 years.

Other Exim Korea Services. Exim Korea also offers a number of other services designed to facilitate the fulfillment of its primary objective. These include technical service credit for Korean firms, overseas investment credit for Korean nationals who invest abroad when the projects financed promote economic cooperation with foreign countries, overseas project credit for Korean firms engaged in business outside Korea and overseas subsidiaries of Korean firms, major resource development credit for Korean nationals which investigate and acquire mining and other natural resource rights abroad, and import credit for Korean importers for the purchase of essential materials and major resources needed for the national economy

Exim Korea Fund Operations. Exim Korea also operates two funds. These are the Economic Development Cooperation Fund (EDCF) and the South and North Korea Cooperation Fund (SNKC). The EDCF makes funds available for developing countries to foster a beneficial economic relationship with Korea. Loans from this fund are made for development projects, equipment, and project preparation. The SNKC is used by the Korean government to promote mutual exchange and cooperation with North Korea.

Exim Korea played a significant role in alleviating the financial crisis which began in Korea in 1997. The major reasons for this crisis were: (1) an economic system failure in that Korea had pursued economic liberalization without a concomitant monitoring system; (2) a highly leveraged expansion by corporations, which resulted in weak financial structure; (3) Korean banks and nonbank financial institutions relied too heavily on short-term foreign borrowings; (4) worsening of Korea's terms of trade, coupled with overvaluation of the Korean won. An "unofficial" further reason for the crisis is the same found in Indonesia, Malaysia, and Thailand, which suffered in the same Asian economic crisis. All four countries had a high level of business corruption as a result of cronyism with political bureaucrats.

Exim Korea alleviated some or all of these problems. The agency became very aggressive in filling the gap left by commercial banks through supplying, not only export credits, but also short-term loans. Exim Korea first expanded export credits in 1998 and 1999. In 1998, the agency increased export credits to US$5 billion to support exports of industrial plants, ships, machinery, and other capital goods. This represented 4 percent of Korea's total exports. Second, Exim Korea had concentrated on medium- and long-term loans in the past, but introduced short-term financing in 1998. The lack of commercial bank credits for imports of raw materials necessary to produce export goods caused Exim Korea to introduce special import credits by obtaining funds from the World Bank, Japan's ECA, and the Bank of Korea. During the first year, Exim Korea disbursed US$4.2 billion for such imports. Exim Korea next introduced refinancing of export bills. This move increased foreign exchange liquidity in commercial banks permitting them to expand their provision of export credits. Finally, Exim Korea increased assistance to small businesses by supporting seventy-seven venture companies in 1998 in the amount of US$133 million. These operations by Exim Korea facilitated the country's emergence from the economic crisis in much less time than the Korean government working alone would have taken.

The financial operations of Exim Korea have done quite well in recent years. In 2001, the agency provided total export credits amounting to US$9.829 billion. Of this, 55 percent was extended as loans and 45 percent was provided in the form of guarantees of trade credit. The agency plans to increase this activity by 7.4 percent in 2002.[11]

Korea Export Insurance Corporation

The Korea Export Insurance Corporation (KEIC) was established in 1992 as a supplement to Exim Korea's work. KEIC is committed to the promotion of sound international transactions. Its primary product is export credit insurance. During 2001, the volume of its export insurance amounted to 37,316 billion won in support of 17.6 percent of Korea's total exports. Its services have been concentrated on small Korean exporters.

Japan Bank for International Cooperation

The Japanese government sponsors two agencies that facilitate trade by Japanese firms and perform related functions. These are the Japan Bank for International Cooperation, formerly the Import-Export Bank of Japan, and the Development Bank of Japan. Programs of the Japan Bank for International Cooperation (JBIC) will be discussed in this section.

The primary purpose of JBIC is to undertake lending and other financial operations which will promote Japanese exports, imports, and other international economic operations. JBIC operations consist of two financially independent activities, International Financial Operations (IFOs) and Overseas Economic Cooperation Operations (OECOs). The objective of IFOs is to promote Japanese exports, imports, and foreign economic activities. The Japanese government facilitates imports, whereas most ECAs do not. This is because Japan requires imports, especially of raw materials, in order to survive economically. Indeed, the U.S. embargoes on scrap iron and petroleum shipments to Japan prior to World War II are said to have provoked the Japanese attack on the United States. These import loans are designed to increase Japanese imports of manufactured goods, providing the country with high-quality, inexpensive goods and equipment while raising the level of sophistication of Japanese industry.

IFOs consist of loans for Japanese exports of goods and services; loans for imports of natural resources, manufactured products, and technology; loans to Japanese firms that undertake foreign direct investment in local production and natural resource development; and loans to Japanese firms for activities to improve the environment. They also include: short-term bridge loans in hard currencies for less-developed countries facing balance of payments difficulties in financing their external transactions, equity participation in Japanese joint ventures that undertake foreign operations, and the financing of studies that require the implementation of any of these activities. JBIC obtains funds for these loans by borrowing from the fiscal investment and loan program of the Japanese government, bond issues, and internally generated funds.

The primary purpose of OECOs is to assist developing countries in their efforts to develop economic and social infrastructure in their economies. This purpose is implemented in the form of loans to assist self-help efforts made by these countries in sustaining their economic development. These loans are low-interest, long-term commitments to build economic and social infrastructure in these countries. Another form of OECO assistance takes the form of investment finance by making loans or equity investments to private sector firms in developing countries. This operation also funds studies that are required to implement these activities in developing countries. OECOs are funded with capital appropriations from the general budget, borrowing from the fiscal investment and loan program, and from internal funds from repayment of principal and interest on loans or dividends from equity investments.

The operational goals of these JBIC programs consist of: maintenance and expansion of international business activities of Japanese firms, the improvement of the environment for foreign business activities for Japanese firms, support of international business activities of small- and medium-sized Japanese firms, promotion of a harmonious international division of labor, guarantee of a stable supply of energy resources, and appropriate transfer of technology, especially inward to the Japanese industry.

JBIC operates according to a set of principles. By law, it is restricted from competition with Japanese private-sector financial institutions and must, in fact, encourage their activities. It is tied to the implementation of Japan's external economic policies. Its operations are based on the principle of loan repayment certainty but it hedges its operations with capital appropriations and grants from the Japanese government. JBIC operates on a control mechanism whereby its functions use performance measurement for strategic management. As a public institution, JBIC attempts to maintain a high degree of public accountability and transparency.

One JBIC project that is representative of the agency's lending function involved the financing of a gas pipeline between Bolivia and Brazil.[12] Bolivia's economic growth has been slow as a result of relatively slow modernization of its transportation infrastructure. However, it is a country with large energy resources. Brazil has a growing economy in need of those energy resources. Petrobras, a Brazilian company, became the lead company in both construction and funding of the pipeline project. JBIC provided an export loan of yen 35 billion to supplement the financing of this project and this facilitated export orders for 540,000 tons of steel pipes from Japanese steel companies. The orders represented 20 percent of the annual export volume of major Japanese steel producers.

A representative example of a JBIC import loan can be demonstrated by the development of a copper mine in Chile to supply copper ore to Japan. The Escondida Copper Mine in Chile supplies

15 to 20 percent of the Japanese annual copper ore demand. A JBIC import loan facility was used to supplement financing of a copper mine project operated by Escondida, a mining company which has 1.7 billion tons of reserves of high-quality copper deposits. The company produces 760,000 tons of ore annually, and Japan imports half of this annual production.

Export-Import Bank of Thailand

The Export-Import Bank of Thailand (Thai Ex-Im) was established in 1993 by the Export-Import Bank of Thailand Act of 1993 and is wholly owned by the Royal Thai government under the supervision of the Ministry of Finance.[13] Thai Ex-Im is permitted to operate a number of functions. It can offer short- as well as long-term credits for either domestic or foreign transactions in Thai baht or any foreign currency denominations. The agency can borrow from local or foreign financial institutions, both domestically or internationally and can offer short- or long-term financial instruments for sale domestically or internationally to financial institutions or the general public. In short, the Thai Ex-Im can perform any banking function except to take deposits. The Export-Import Bank of Thailand Act was amended in 1999 to permit the Thai Ex-Im to also offer services to Thai investors abroad and to local investors in businesses relating to exporting.

Cases of Thai Ex-Im Financing. The following cases are representative examples of the type of financial activities performed by the Thai Ex-Im. In 2002, the agency issued two tranches of senior unsecured bonds with fixed interest rates to refinance the agency's debt and to fund its export financing operations. One issue was for three billion baht with a three-year maturity. The other issue was also for three billion baht but with a five-year maturity and the option of an additional amount of up to one billion baht. In 2001, the Thai Ex-Im made a loan to Cambodia Air Traffic Service Company to finance an air traffic control system project in Cambodia. The loan was for US$15 million, with a maturity of seven years, and is to be used for payment of all equipment installed at three airports and for the interest payment during construction and preconstruction expenses. The agency initiated a new facility in 2001, the Express Export Credit designed to provide small and new exporters with faster access to credit lines before shipment of their exports. These types of exporters will be able to receive financing under this program within three working days after all documentation has been completed. The Thai Ex-Im will then finance up to 80 percent of the letter of credit value, with a credit limit not to exceed 2 million baht per exporter.[14] Finally, the Thai Ex-Im approved thirteen international projects in 2000 valued at 1,292 million baht, including projects located in Morocco, Myanmar, Cambodia, Taiwan, Laos, Malaysia, and the United States.

Export-Import Bank of Malaysia Berhad

The Export-Import Bank of Malaysia Berhad (MEI) was established in 1995 and is a wholly owned subsidiary of the Bank of Industry and Technology of Malaysia Berhad, a leading Malaysian development bank. The agency provides medium- to long-term trade credits to promote Malaysian exports with emphasis on exports to nontraditional markets.[15]

MEI offers a number of export trade financing facilities. These include the buyer credit facility, the overseas investment credit facility, the supplier credit facility, the export of services financing facility, and a guarantee facility. Under the buyer credit facility, MEI can make direct or indirect loans to foreign importers of Malaysian capital goods and other approved exports. The overseas investment credit facility permits MEI to make loans to Malaysian companies or their joint venture partners for foreign projects that involve Malaysian exports. MEI makes working capital loans to Malaysian exporters under the supplier credit facility. The agency makes loans to Malaysian exporters of professional services in the form of technical consultancies under the export of services financing facility. Finally, MEI can guarantee loans made by Malaysian banks and other local financial institutions which are involved in a financing arrangement with MEI. The agency also developed an export credit refinancing operation in 1977. Under this program, MEI makes loans to Malaysian commercial banks for lending to qualified Malaysian exporters. This program was initiated by the Central Bank of Malaysia but transferred to MEI in 1998. Export credit refinancing of both pre- and postshipment transactions is possible under this program.[16]

MAJOR ECAs IN OTHER AREAS

Two major ECAs located in other areas are sufficiently significant to be included in the discussion of foreign trade finance institutions. These are Export Development Corporation of Canada and the Export Finance and Insurance Corporation of Australia. These agencies will be discussed in the following sections.

Export Development Corporation

Export Development Corporation (EDC) is a Canadian financial institution authorized by the Export Development Act and established in 1969. The agency provides trade finance services for Canadian exporters. It replaced the Export Credits Insurance Corporation which started operations in 1943. EDC is accountable to the Canadian Parliament through the Minister of International Trade. In 2001, Canadian business made C$45.4 billion in export and domestic sales and investments using EDC trade finance services. Many of these sales would not have been made without EDC assistance. EDC concentrates on small business firms and 90 percent of its customers are small businesses. Its services include credit insurance, bonding and guarantees, political risk insurance, direct loans to buyers and lines of credit in foreign countries to encourage imports of Canadian products. EDC underwrites across a wide variety of risks and is self-sustaining since, by managing its own treasury operations, it raises funds in domestic and international financial markets and generates sufficient income to support itself.

EDC, when compared with most other ECAs, operates under a different mandate. It serves both commercial and social policy objectives.[17] It performs this latter objective by serving as a bridge between the support provided by private sector lenders and what the exporter needs to be successful in export markets. One EDC tool by which this social policy mandate is performed can be demonstrated by export credit insurance. The insurance frees up the exporter's working capital advanced by its bank because the bank is secure in the fact that the exporter will be paid either by the buyer or by EDC.

EDC's Loan Portfolio. As of December 1999, commercial loans accounted for 64 percent of EDC's performing loans. Its commercial loan portfolio is diversified across four industry sectors: air transportation (27 percent), information technology (24 percent), resource industries (24 percent), and surface transportation (23 percent). Its sovereign loan portfolio is concentrated mainly in China (20 percent), Canada (19 percent), and Peru, Venezuela, and Algeria (7 percent each).

EDC is more heavily involved in Europe than is its counterpart to the south. Ex-Im finances projects in more risky areas such as Asia, Latin America, and Africa. EDC concentrates more on North America and Western Europe. Again this operational method may stem from EDC's philosophy of operating as a commercial entity whereas Ex-Im is more influenced by governmental policy.

EDC's Programs. EDC sponsors two broad areas of trade finance. These are insurance and export finance. Three types of insurance policies are provided to exporters. These are accounts receivable insurance, documentary credits insurance, and political risk insurance. The exporter's foreign accounts receivable are covered to 90 percent of their value with the accounts receivable insurance policy. Documentary credits insurance provides support to Canadian exporters whose customers pay with letters of credit. EDC also offers political risk insurance, which covers 90 percent of the exporter's losses as a result of currency transfer and inconvertibility of funds, expropriation, or political violence.

EDC also offers financing of Canadian exports to foreign buyers. Three variations of finance are provided. They are direct loans, lines of credit, and equity investments in transactions which will result in the export of Canadian goods and services. Direct loans are made by EDC to foreign banks which will then lend to the purchaser of the Canadian goods. The line of credit works in the same way whereby money is loaned to a foreign bank based on the line of credit and then the foreign bank lends funds to the foreign purchaser of Canadian goods and services.

During the past few years, EDC has become active in the development of e-business solutions for Canadian exporters. One such program developed to expand business over the internet is Export Check, a Web site that permits exporters to investigate 64 million companies in one hundred markets.

Evaluation of EDC. Canada relies on exports to a greater extent than does the United States. According to the OECD, Canadian exports in 2000 were 43.7 percent of the country's gross domestic product (GDP). Exports from the United States were only 10.7 percent of the U.S. GDP. Canadian export trade is highly concentrated with five firms accounting for 20 percent of Canadian exports.[18] Although EDC is a government agency, it operates as though it were a commercial entity with its aim to be financially self-sustaining. Finally, Ex-Im is considered by most business firms to be the last resort for a U.S. exporter needing a loan or a guarantee. EDC, on the other hand, may be one of the first sources a company will look to for assistance with trade finance. At least, it may be considered among a group of private sources for trade financing. A possible reason for this is that only a handful of Canadian banks operate in the country whereas hundreds of U.S. banks are available for financing international trade.

Export Finance and Insurance Corporation

The official export credit agency in Australia is the Export Finance and Insurance Corporation (EFIC), which was established as a statutory corporation of the Commonwealth of Australia under the Export Finance and Insurance Corporation Act of 1991. Its primary objective is to increase Australian exports. Its operations consist of two activities: the Credit Insurance Group and Export Finance.

Credit Insurance Group. Australian exporters and banks are protected by the Credit Insurance Group against nonpayment by foreign buyers and banks. Its main products include export credit insurance and export payment protection. An export credit insurance policy provides insurance cover for Australian exporters with more than US$10 million in total sales. It covers both commercial and political risk. Among the features of this policy are: (1) up to 100 percent coverage against nonpayment as a result of political risk; (2) up to 90 percent coverage against nonpayment as a result of commercial risk; (3) customized policies; (4) access to industry specialists knowledgeable about the exporter's business; (5) on-line declaration capabilities; (6) coverage available for pre-shipment; and (7) cover available for indirect exports, those to suppliers selling goods for export where the payment obligation remains with an Australian company.[19] Under the export payment protection service, EFIC targets small- and medium-sized companies with annual turnover of less than US$10 million in sales. The features of the export payment protection policy include coverage of up to 100 percent against political risk and up to 90 percent against commercial risk when the risks result in nonpayment, minimal paperwork and administration, and flexible payment options.

Export Finance Group. EFIC's Export Finance Group provides buyers of Australian exports with over two-year finance facilities to purchase Australian capital goods or services. Political risk insurance is available under this program. The major products offered by the Export Finance Group include direct loans, export finance guarantees, documentary credit guarantees, political risk insurance, medium-term payments insurance, and bonds and guarantees.[20]

Direct loans are made to Australian exporters after the Export Finance Group has entered into an agreement with a foreign buyer. The foreign buyer pays back the principal and interest on the loan to the Export Finance Group. The goods shipped must have high Australian content and the contract amount must be in excess of A$1 million.

The Export Finance Guarantee Program encourages banks or other commercial lenders to make direct loans to foreign buyers of Australian capital goods or services. Under this program, the Export Finance Group does not make the loan but offers a guarantee to the lender which provides the loan.

Under the Documentary Credit Guarantee Program, a bank confirms an irrevocable documentary credit and provides trade facilities without recourse to an Australian exporter. EFIC guarantees that the issuer of this credit pays both principal and interest to the confirming bank and, thus, shares the nonpayment risk with the confirming bank.

EFIC provides political risk insurance against losses caused by expropriation, war damage or political violence, currency inconvertibility, and exchange transfer blockage. This coverage is as extensive as that issued by most other ECAs.

EFIC's Export Finance Group offers medium-term payments insurance. Exports are eligible for this program if they have high Australian content, the contract amount exceeds A$500,000, and payments are to be made over two years.

Foreign buyers sometimes require Australian exporters to provide a bond as security for shipment of the ordered goods. EFIC, under its Export Finance Group, may issue a bond directly or it can provide guarantees to a bank to issue a bond.

In its promotional material, EFIC offers a number of benefits from its financing or insurance. Its staff has extensive industry, regional, and international experience. Its services can be tailored to meet the needs of the Australian exporter. It offers flexible terms and innovative financial solutions. The agency is globally organized.

EFIC can offer most of the services expected from an ECA. However, its operations are much smaller than those of, for example, the Ex-Im, according to a comparison of the two agencies' annual reports. Its authorized support of Australian exports amounted to U.S. $6.8 billion in 2001, whereas Ex-Im authorized US$9.2 billion in loans, guarantees, and export credit insurance. Ex-Im's total assets in 2001 were nearly four times those of EFIC. EFIC has been profitable in every year except one since 1991.

As a government agency, EFIC is regulated and supervised much as is the case of Ex-Im in the United States. The Export Finance and Insurance Corporation Act of 1991 set a maximum limit on EFIC loans and for liability for contracts entered into as well as for guarantees issued by EFIC. Ex-Im has slightly more authority to operate its programs but, since it is funded by Congress, it is subject to budgetary cuts ordered by the U.S. president during recessionary periods.

MULTILATERAL ECAs

Some ECAs are groupings of international or multilateral members. These ECAs work in a manner similar to the national ECAs except their focus is on a regional geographical area comprised of several countries. Among these are the African Export-Import Bank, the Corporación Andina de Fomento, the Islamic Corporation for Insurance of Investments and Export Credit, the European Bank for Reconstruction and Development, and the Multilateral Investment Guarantee Agency. The first three of these are representative of multilateral ECAs and will be examined in the following sections.

African Export-Import Bank

The African Export-Import Bank (Afreximbank) is a multilateral ECA headquartered in Cairo. Afreximbank offers a number of programs to assist African exporters with their foreign sales.[21] The bank's Line of Credit Program assists small- and medium-sized exporters whose size and export sales volume does not qualify them for direct loans. Afreximbank provides funded and unfunded credit lines to qualified banks to be used for lending to exporters. The agency's Direct Financing Program provides pre- and postexport financing directly to companies with at least US$2 million in assets and annual sales of at least US$10 million. This financing is short-term and for trade-related purposes. The Project Financing Program supports the import of equipment needed for export manufacturing. The Syndications Program uses trade leverage and project finance derived from Afreximbank's collaboration with other international banks and, thus, is able to attract more international funding to Africa. Afreximbank provides a forfaiting program operated in the same manner as forfaiting programs described in other sections of this book. Its Special Risk Program guarantees credit exposures of international and African banks against certain risks including political risk. Afreximbank provides a Factoring/Invoice Discounting Program whereby the agency purchases and sells debt receivables. It provides a Note Purchase/Discounting Program under which the agency issues promissory notes guaranteed by a bank of acceptable credit standing. Afreximbank operates a Finance Future-Flow Pre-Financing Program, under which future-flow debt offerings that are not generated by export sales are financed by Afreximbank. Afreximbank also operates an Infrastructural Services Financing Program and an Investment Banking Program. Under the former program, Afreximbank finances exporters of infrastructure services necessary for the manufacture of export goods. Under the latter program, Afreximbank finances the development of entrepreneurship and capital markets in Africa by providing advisory services, underwriting services backed by export-secured debt, and assistance with the securitization of local and foreign currency receivables.

Corporación Andina de Fomento

Corporación Andina de Fomento (CAF) is a multilateral financial institution whose mission is to promote sustainable development of its shareholder countries and regional integration. Its membership is comprised of twelve countries in Latin America and the Caribbean. The agency was established in 1970, with headquarters in Caracas.

Its major operations include mobilizing financial resources from industrialized countries into the region, financing the development of productive infrastructure in the region, development of the financial and capital markets in the Andean region, promotion of trade and investment, support of small-, medium-, and large-sized corporations in the region, and support of modernization of regional economies. Most of its activities are directed toward project investment in the region and financing of infrastructure improvements in member countries.

CAF is only peripherally involved in trade finance when exports of its member countries need trade credits or when imports of goods and services important to development in the region are the subject of financing needs or guarantees. It cooperates with other multilateral development agencies such as the Inter-American Development Bank, national and local government agencies in other countries, foreign ECAs, and other private international financial institutions.

CAF is comprised of member countries in Latin America and the Caribbean. Its authorized capital is US$3.0 billion, with US$990 million paid in as of the end of 2000. Its Series A and B shares are subscribed by the five major countries of the Andean Region. Series B shares may also be held by individuals residing in the region. Its Series C shares may be subscribed by governments or public or private entities outside the Andean Region as well as by international organizations.

Islamic Corporation for Insurance of Investments and Export Credit

The Islamic Corporation for Insurance of Investments and Export Credit (ICIEC) is an affiliate of the Islamic Development Bank and is located in Saudi Arabia.[22] ICIEC was established in 1994. The agency offers Islamic compatible insurance for investments and export credit, that is, it operates according to Shariah, the law stemming from the Koran.

To be eligible for ICIEC export insurance, the exporter must be: (1) the Islamic Development Bank, (2) a corporation or bank whose shares are owned in the majority by a member state or a national from a member state, or (3) a juridical person whose office may be located in a nonmember state where at least 50 percent of the shares are owned by nationals from a member state. To obtain export credit insurance, the covered goods must be wholly or partially produced, manufactured, assembled, or processed in one or more member states.

ICIEC insures exports against both commercial and political risks. Commercial risks include insolvency of the buyer, repudiation of a contract by the buyer, or nonpayment of part or all of the purchase price.

Political risks covered include transfer restrictions, expropriation, breach of contract, or war and civil disturbance.

ICIEC offers three export credit insurance policies. They are a comprehensive short-term policy, a supplemental medium-term policy, and a bank master policy which applies to all contracts financed by a bank in accordance with the principles of Islamic Shariah law.

THE BERNE UNION

In any analysis of ECAs on a global basis, the Berne Union should be included.[23] This organization, whose official name is the Union d'Assureurs des Credits Internationaux, was established in 1934 with four countries as members. It now includes fifty-one members from forty-two countries and locations. This organization works for international acceptance of sound principles and practices of export credit and foreign investment insurance.

The Berne Union was established at the time when export credit insurers began to value cooperation in the development of underwriting techniques. Information sharing was seen by them as being in their best mutual interests. After World War II, the Berne Union resumed its work at a time when political and commercial risk insurance became even more important, especially during reconstruction of wartorn countries. State controlled agencies and private insurance companies began to join the union in their role as direct insurers and not as agents of their governments.

The Berne Union resembles a cooperative clearinghouse of ECA activities. Its leadership speaks on behalf of ECA management worldwide. Its work includes assistance with the growth of the reinsurance market for short-term political risks. Its statutes were amended in 1998 to recognize the significant changes in the market for export credit insurance. The reinsurance market for short-term political risks was one of the significant growth areas. Since 1998, it has established three technical working committees: the short-term export credit insurance committee, the medium- and long-term export credit insurance committee, and the investment insurance committee.

The objectives of the Berne Union are as follows:

1. the global acceptance of sound principles of export credit insurance and the establishment and maintenance of discipline in terms of credit for international trade;
2. the maintenance of sound principles of foreign investment insurance and the encouragement of a favorable investment climate;
3. the provision of the exchange of information, assistance, expertise and advice in relation both to the commercial and political risks

involved in export credit insurance and to the political risks involved in foreign investment insurance.

Members of the Berne Union, in order to accomplish these objectives, have agreed to :

1. exchange information and furnish the Union with the information necessary to accomplish its work;
2. maintain and adhere to the maximum credit terms and starting points of credit formulated in a series of agreements and understandings;
3. consult together on a continuing basis, carry out studies, and participate in agreed projects;
4. cooperate closely and, where appropriate, take coordinated action; and
5. cooperate with other international institutions concerned with these matters.

Its member ECAs have been highly instrumental in the growth of world trade during the past two decades. From 1982 to 2001, its members have assisted worldwide exports amounting to US$7.334 trillion and supported foreign direct investments totaling US$174 billion. Its headquarters is located in London.

EVALUATION OF NON-U.S. EXPORT CREDIT AGENCIES

ECAs have financed, insured, or guaranteed a tremendous amount of world trade during the past few decades. World economic development has improved concomitantly as these agencies have helped companies in their respective countries to significant increases in the export of goods and services. In this section, the benefits of global operations of ECAs will be examined. In addition, the major complaints raised against the operations of these agencies will also be discussed.

Benefits of Global Operations of Export Credit Agencies

National ECAs support more than US$100 billion of investments globally each year. These projects have significant impact, especially from an environmental viewpoint, some good and some bad. Some of these projects involve the financing of wastewater treatment plants, which improve the water quality in developing countries. Few ECAs apply environmental standards to their financing decisions, nor do many of them collect information on the environmental impact of the projects they assist in addition to disclosing to the public what information they do obtain.[24]

Complaints against Export Credit Agencies

ECAs have not been found by some groups to be totally beneficial to the world economy. Their operations have elicited a number of complaints from some organizations and individuals. The most significant charge leveled against ECAs is the major complaint discussed in the coverage of the U.S. Export-Import Bank (Ex-Im) in Chapter 4, that is, financial assistance to projects that are environmentally unsound or which actually damage the environment. Some of the projects funded or whose funding is guaranteed or insured by ECAs include inefficient coal plants, dirty factories, and unsafe mining operations, according to their critics.

For example, one such project assisted by foreign ECAs was the Aginskoe gold mine in the Russian far east. This project, it was alleged, might endanger the brown bear, mountain goat, and other wildlife. Another project located in Russia involved logging joint ventures, assisted by, among other agencies, the U.S. Overseas Private Investment Corporation (OPIC). This project was alleged to involve the elimination of irreplaceable forests. These projects were needed by the Russian government because of its shortage of hard foreign currencies. Another project assisted by European ECAs involved funding for the US$1.52 billion Ilisu Dam, a hydroelectric project on the Tigris River in Turkey.[25] The European ECAs asked Ex-Im to join them in the project. The U.S. agency agreed only if conditions were attached to the agreement. The dam would require the resettlement of 15,000 Kurds, including the flooding of an ancient archaeological site that they revered. In addition, Turkey could use the dam to block the flow of water to Iraq for several months each year.

Globalization. The process of globalization is frequently criticized for perceived human rights violations. Globalization, or global economic integration, has been praised for improving the allocation of resources, promotion of technology transfer, and the enhancement of living standards. It has also been blamed for growing trade imbalances, increased financial market volatility, and the formulation of ineffective domestic macroeconomic policies.[26] Projects are financed in developing countries by foreign direct investment made by MNCs, which may displace whole villages. Roads must be built to the site location of some of these projects. Homes of citizens are often acquired by the government with little or no due process of law. Often these projects are insured by a government entity such as OPIC or trade credit guarantees or insurance is obtained from some ECA to finance the exports of goods and equipment to the project site.

Global warming is one of the environmental issues of concern to some groups that criticize ECAs for their trade finance operations. Some countries have worked to reduce greenhouse emissions at home only to subsidize projects in foreign countries that, in fact, increase such emissions. Hermes of Germany does not disclose information about greenhouse emissions from the projects it assists.[27] On the other hand, British, Australian, and Japanese ECAs have incorporated environmental information in their decision making in recent years.

The U.S. administration of George W. Bush has not had a very good record on the global warming issue. And yet, his policies may outpace those of European governments on this issue. It may be that European finance ministers wish to maintain control over their particular ECAs and, thus, compete on the basis of low environmental standards. The European agencies have not given the issue much attention and the bureaucratic inertia found in many European governments may also contribute to this problem.

CONCLUSIONS

More than three dozen ECAs have been established in the member countries of the Organization for Economic Cooperation and Development (OECD). Many more operate in non-OECD countries, especially in some of the developing nations. The facilitation of international trade finance which these agencies accomplish has been a major reason for the increases in world trade during the post–World War II period. The export trade credit guarantees and insurance have reduced the risk encountered by the banking system in financing international trade. Thus, more banks have been encouraged to make loans to exporters. The increase in trade finance available has encouraged more companies producing goods and services to enter the world of international trade.

These foreign ECAs have a variety of ownership types. Most are owned and operated by the national government of the country in which they are located. Some are publicly owned but their shares are traded on a stock exchange, as is the case with Coface in France. Some are private companies but act as an agent for the government, as is the case with Hermes in Germany. Some have had some of their operations privatized, as is the case in Great Britain with ECGD, whose short-term operations have been sold to a private company.

Regardless of the ownership type, their objectives remain the same: to expand exports from their respective countries. In all cases, they seem to have accomplished this major objective.

Some of the foreign ECAs are very versatile in the programs which they offer. This is especially true of ECAs in some developing countries. For example, the Export-Import Bank of Thailand can do most of the familiar trade financing operations while performing all of the functions of a commercial bank, except for the taking of deposits. The Export-Import Bank of Malaysia Berhad can make loans to exporters as well as guarantee trade credits offered by banks. In addition, it offers an export refinancing program in which the agency makes loans to qualified commercial banks which then on-lend these funds to Malaysian exporters.

In any case, the growth in the numbers of ECAs can be attributed to the sharp acceleration in world trade during the past several decades, the desire of the banking system to hedge trade credit risks with the assistance of agencies that can guarantee or insure these credits, and the desire of governments, both industrialized and developing, to promote government assistance in financing exports.

NOTES

1. Nancy Dunne, "Export Credit Agencies See Business Soar," *Financial Times*, February 4, 1999, p. 6.

2. Gordon Platt, "US Risk Managers Discover Export Credit Insurance," *Journal of Commerce* 424 (April 26, 2000): 11.

3. Press release available on-line December 10, 2002, at www.coface.com /rub05_actus/pres/021008gb.htm, pp. 1–4.

4. Press release available on-line December 10, 2002, at www.coface.com /rub05_actus/pres/020916gb.htm, pp. 1–2.

5. World Bank, *Economic Growth Research,* (Washington: World Bank, 1997); this is a pamphlet on world development indicators.

6. Geoff Dyer, "Agencies Sidestep the Sovereign Squeeze," *Euromoney*, May 1993, pp. 93–94.

7. ECGD, *Annual Report and Resource Accounts 2000/01* (London: Her Majesty's Stationery Office, 2001), p. 2.

8. Available on-line September 23, 2002, at www.hermes-kredit.com, pp. 1–2.

9. Information about the India Ex-Im was available on-line February 4, 2002, at www.eximbankindia.com.

10. www.coudert.com/practice/ecawebkorea.htm, pp. 1–4.

11. "2001 Results and Prospects for 2002," available on-line February 4, 2002, at www.koreaexim.go.kr/english/eximnews/20020115.htm, pp.1–3.

12. Available on-line November 26, 2002, at www.jbic.go.jp/english/profile/about/finance/A22/p08.php, November 26, 2002, pp. 2–3.

13. Available on-line January 16, 2002, at www.exim.go.th, p. 1.

14. Ibid.

15. Available on-line January 15, 2003, at www.exim-bank.com/about.html, p. 1.

16. Ibid.

17. Available on-line April 12, 2002, at www.edc.ca/corpinfo/whoweare/index_e.htm, pp. 1–2.

18. Gary C. Hufbauer and Rita M. Rodriguez, eds., *The Ex-Im Bank in the 21st Century: A New Approach?* (Washington: Institute for International Economics, 2001), p. 228.

19. Available on-line September 6, 2002, at www.efic.gov.au/creditinsurance.asp, pp. 1–2.

20. Available on-line September 6, 2002, at www.efic.gov.au/exportfinance.asp, pp. 1–2.

21. Available on-line December 10, 2002, at www.afreximbank.com/docs/productinfo.aspx, pp. 1–3.

22. Available on-line November 26, 2002, at www.iciec.org/, pp. 1–11.

23. "About the Berne Union," available on-line December 10, 2002, at www.berneunion.org.uk/about.html, pp. 1–3.

24. David Sandalow, "Exports and the Environment," *Financial Times*, July 19, 2001, p. 17.

25. Nancy Dunne, "Export Credit Agencies See Business Soar," *Financial Times*, February 4, 1999, p. 6.

26. George A. Kahn, "Global Economic Integration: Opportunities and Challenges—A Summary of the Bank's 2000 Symposium," *Federal Reserve Bank of Kansas City Economic Review* 85 (Fourth Quarter 2000): 5–12.

27. David Sandalow, "Exports and the Environment," *Financial Times*, July 19, 2001, p. 17.

10

Evaluation of the U.S.
System and Conclusions

Five major elements make up the U.S. system of finance, insurance, and guarantee of U.S. exports of goods and services: (1) the banking system, (2) the U.S. Export-Import Bank (Ex-Im), (3) the Foreign Credit Insurance Association (FCIA), (4) the Public Export Funding Corporation (PEFCO), and (5) miscellaneous U.S. governmental agencies and organizations, state and local governmental agencies, trade associations, and specialized firms. Although U.S. exports are a relatively small portion of the nation's gross domestic product, in absolute terms, they are very large. They are a significant part of the nation's economy and require a large amount of financing in order to facilitate their sale to foreign countries.

The U.S. system of international trade financing is one of the most comprehensive found in the world. Most countries have banks that engage in financing trade and one or, at the most, two governmental agencies whose primary objective is to insure or guarantee trade credits granted by the banking system. Some of these countries also host one or more private insurance companies, which offer trade credit insurance or supplement the activities of the nation's government institution responsible for trade finance. These export credit agencies (ECAs) are government owned and operated in nearly every case. In a few cases, the ECA is a private firm, as in Germany; some functions of the ECA have been privatized, as with short-term insurance of exports in Great Britain, or the government-run ECA attempts to operate as though it were private enterprise, as with the Export Development Corporation in Canada.

In the United States, the banking system is composed of financial institutions owned by shareholders. Ex-Im is an operation of the federal government. FCIA and PEFCO are consortia of private insurance firms, banks, industrial companies, and financial services firms. As discussed throughout this book and particularly in Chapter 8, these elements of the U.S. system cooperate with one another and, in some cases, supplement each other's services.

BENEFITS OF THE U.S. SYSTEM

The Ex-Im has functioned for five decades as the primary federal ECA involved in financing international trade or guaranteeing or insuring trade credits issued by banks. The organization has evolved over the years into an agency which offers a comprehensive variety of services for U.S. exporters. It has been involved in facilitating more than US$400 billion of U.S. exports during the past fifty years.

FCIA evolved from a vision of the U.S. presidency of John F. Kennedy, who believed that private enterprise should play a larger role in financing U.S. exports. A group of U.S. insurance companies established FCIA in the early 1960s for the purpose of insuring trade credits granted by the banking system. This experiment in private enterprise supplementing a government operation worked so well that the Ex-Im decided in the early 1990s to act alone in insuring trade credits. Until then, it had specialized in short- and medium-term lending and guarantees of trade credits.

COMPLAINTS AGAINST THE U.S. SYSTEM

Major complaints lodged against the U.S. system of international trade financing centered on the relative lack of competitiveness of Ex-Im vis-a-vis foreign ECAs, especially in the early years of its operations. Another major problem often cited by critics focussed on the U.S. system of foreign credit insurance. These and other problems of the U.S. system will be discussed in this section.

Ex-Im seemed to be another slow moving bureaucracy of the federal government. U.S. exporters often obtained trade financing from foreign ECAs instead of their own government agency. Ex-Im often seemed slow to approve exporters' applications for trade credit insurance or guarantees, usually because the agency was slow to evaluate the credit of the foreign purchaser or because insufficient information about the importer had been obtained. The Export Credits Guarantee Division

(ECGD) of the British government could approve guarantees or insurance much faster than Ex-Im. One of the reasons for this problem was that ECGD had a much longer history of evaluating the credit of foreign purchasers than did Ex-Im. Where political risk was involved, especially in developing countries, ECGD seemed to have a better database of information on overseas buyers. Some U.S. exporters have used the services of an ECA in a developing country such as the Korean Export-Import Bank, to obtain guarantees of trade credits for exports to a third country because they were able to obtain approval much faster than if they had dealt with the U.S. Ex-Im.

Many of these criticisms were leveled at Ex-Im in its first two decades of operations. Foreign credit insurance was one of the first problem areas.[1] Private foreign credit insurance was introduced in the United States in 1921, but the concept failed to make inroads in trade finance before the Great Depression of the 1930s. In 1961, President John F. Kennedy gave Ex-Im the mandate to establish a credit insurance program which would make U.S. trade finance competitive with other nations. The result was FCIA, a consortium of private insurance companies.

This new system of foreign credit insurance was compared in its early years with the British and German systems. These were the principal competitors in trade finance operations to the United States. The comparisons were unfavorable. In most cases, the foreign systems were judged to be better than the new U.S. credit insurance. The objective of credit insurance was to alleviate the effects of three types of risk faced by the exporter: commercial risk, foreign exchange risk, and political risk. The U.S. system offered protection against commercial and political risks only. Foreign exchange risk would have to be hedged by other means. Insurance policies could be written for either short- or medium-term credits.

One criticism leveled at the U.S. system dealt with what exports could be covered, especially with short-term policies. The U.S. exporter had to decide whether its goods transacted on a short-term basis are to be covered with a comprehensive risk policy, which covers both commercial and political risk, or with a political risk policy only. The exporter could not elect to cover some goods with a comprehensive risk policy and some with a political risk policy. With medium-term coverage, the exporter could opt to cover some goods with a comprehensive risk policy and some with a political risk policy.[2]

In the United Kingdom, the ECGD permitted the exporter to use a comprehensive policy but still use the political risk-only policy for shipments to subsidiaries. Hermes in Germany provided insurance for any sale on a single-transaction basis. German exporters had several other options that Ex-Im did not offer. It appears that U.S. exporters had fewer choices of policies from Ex-Im than did exporters under the systems in Great Britain and Germany, at least in the first few decades of Ex-Im's operations.

Another complaint with the U.S. credit insurance system was concerned with the option to exclude certain types of sales from coverage.[3] The insurer ideally desires to cover all of an exporter's short-term exports in order to hedge its risk. If the exporter wants to exclude some shipments from coverage, the insurer's risk increases. ECGD requires that all short-term transactions must be insured and none may be excluded. The U.S. system permits exclusion of transactions on a cash or fully secured basis. The German system permits the most flexibility in that the exporter may obtain blanket coverage or single-transaction coverage only.

In terms of premiums charged, ECGD's premium was the lowest because no transactions could be excluded. The U.S. premiums were in the middle, with some exclusions. The German premiums were highest among the three systems because of the freedom to exclude shipments from coverage. When setting premiums, the U.S. and British systems classify countries into four classes according to their risk level. The German system charges the same premium for all countries, regardless of risk. It does, however, refuse to cover shipments to countries deemed risky.

In terms of currencies used in the insurance transaction, some may be more risky than others. Ex-Im required transactions only in the dollar until 1966 when FCIA, then implementing the credit insurance business for the United States, permitted foreign currencies for short-term coverage. The British and German systems permitted the buyer's currency or a third country currency to be used.

The three agencies had different policies with regard to any required down payment on an export transaction covered with credit insurance.[4] Before 1966, Ex-Im required a 20 percent down payment on all medium-term transactions. After that date, when FCIA began offering credit insurance, a 10 percent down payment was required for all but the riskiest of transactions, although 20 percent was still preferred. Neither the British nor the German systems published a down payment requirement. However, the British system desired to have 20 percent paid down by shipment time and 5 percent with the order. The German system in private discussions with the insured would usually require 15 percent paid down on medium- and long-term coverage. Hermes, the German ECA, required 20 percent for Soviet zone countries.

In terms of assistance for small export firms, ECGD offered plans that were designed for small business firms. The U.S. and German systems had no provisions at that time to attract new business or to cater to small export firms. In addition, another charge leveled at the U.S. system, especially after FCIA began operations, dealt with the concentration in the distribution of export market information and sales of foreign credit insurance. With the several dozen original members of the FCIA consortium, it was believed that wide distribution of information and policy sales would be the case. However, research showed that only three or four brokers processed all FCIA's policies, and one of those handled more than one-third of FCIA's business. Some of the FCIA members did not want to sell foreign credit insurance, and others were unaware of the service.[5] It may be that many of the original insurance company members of the FCIA consortium were pressured into joining the system because of the imprint of President John F. Kennedy on the concept.

On the other hand, ECGD had established a large network (of eighteen offices) in the British Isles and New York. Many insurance agencies assisted ECGD with sales of export credit insurance. The German system, centered around Hermes, had nine offices and sixteen general agencies in the major cities of Germany, which took insurance applications and furnished information and advice about foreign markets.

This analysis of the early years of the U.S. system, especially regarding foreign credit insurance, shows the United States to be at a competitive disadvantage vis-a-vis the major ECAs operating at that time. During the next thirty years, many changes were made to the U.S. system to alleviate many of these problems. With these changes, and when PEFCO's contribution to export financing was added, the U.S. system became much more competitive with the ECAs in Great Britain and Germany. A major part of the problem today is that many more ECAs have been established and the competition from these agencies has offset many of the favorable changes in the U.S. system. ECAs established by developing countries have, in many cases, become a flagship institution for their respective nation.

Finally, a nonfinancial complaint has been leveled at Ex-Im, FCIA, and other foreign ECAs. Environmentalists have accused these organizations of financing exports which, in their opinion, will harm the environment. Power plants, manufacturing facilities, and other operations have been assisted by U.S. and foreign ECAs with trade credit guarantees, insurance, or loans. It has been alleged by some critics that some of these projects will result in global warming, destroy animal habitats, or result in air or water pollution. Some ECAs do environmental analysis of the projects they assist, but others, such as Hermes in Germany, do not make any effort to determine the environmental impact of the project. Ex-Im does attempt to determine a project's impact but trade associations and export firm lobbies usually persuade Ex-Im to grant the assistance when, in fact, its impact may be questionable.

Globalization and Export Finance

Globalization was discussed in Chapter 9. A number of benefits have stemmed from globalization during the past century. However, in recent years, antiglobalization activist groups have challenged the movement. Some of this challenge has been aimed at the work of nongovernmental organizations (NGOs), including ECAs and other export trade–financing institutions and firms. The loudest complaint seems to be that export trade financing results in projects which damage the environment in some way. Some ECAs monitor the projects to insure that they are not harmful either to the global environment or the local culture. However, others are not as careful to examine their financed projects and choose only to expand the country's exports. These problems can be alleviated by regulations and supervision of such projects by organizations such as the United Nations, the General Agreement on Tariffs and Trade, the World Bank, and local governments.

One organization does exist to monitor and study the work of ECAs in these projects: the International NGO ECA Reform Campaign, known as ECA Watch, whose objective is to insure that all ECAs adopt and upgrade environmental and social policies and listen to the affected people who complain of specific harmful projects. This organized campaign includes seventy-two groups located in thirty-two countries.[6] This organizational movement seems to be biased against ECAs in general since it lists the following actions for which ECAs are responsible:[7]

1. they are one of the biggest sources of financing for harmful projects;
2. they undercut progress and violate laws;
3. they fuel a "race to the bottom";
4. they offer next to no transparency and have contempt for affected communites;
5. they promote corruption;
6. their financing results in crushing debt;
7. they are involved in arms transfers and human rights abuses;
8. their operations increase risks against which they were designed to protect;
9. they assume no responsibility.

From these charges, one could conclude that all ECAs are terrorist operations, but the analysis presented in this book would suggest otherwise. While harmful in some, isolated cases, overall ECAs have resulted in more good than harm: They have facilitated large increases in world trade, which has led to development, consumer benefits, and increases in local employment.

CHANGES IN U.S. EXPORT CREDIT INSURANCE

Since the criticism of the 1960s and 1970s over U.S. export credit insurance, a number of changes were made to make it more attractive to potential buyers.[8] First, authority was decentralized. Branch and regional managers of FCIA can now make more rapid decisions about the acceptability of credit risks. Second, the procedures for renewal have been simplified for policyholders. Third, some exporters with a good repayment record with overseas buyers now have more discretion with regard to insuring authority. Fourth, FCIA adopted a deductible, which permitted increased discretionary authority and a reduced premium. Finally, coverage was permitted that enabled the exporter to recover for loss of interest up to a predetermined maximum on a claim before it is collected. This is especially attractive for medium-term sales (six months to five years).

These changes, at the time, did not make a significant change in the percentage of U.S. exporters in the regions served being insured by FCIA policies. In fact, the percentage of U.S. exporters in the regions served being insured actually declined, from 6 percent in 1964 to only 2 percent in 1979.[9]

By 1985, criticism of U.S. export trade credit insurance, as provided by FCIA, was still quite strong. A study carried out in the early 1980s listed several criticisms in the attitudes of users of FCIA insurance.[10] The four most significant criticisms mentioned by users were: (1) foreign competitors can get more favorable credit terms than can U.S. firms; (2) approval for coverage takes too long; (3) the time to get credit reports on small foreign buyers takes too long; (4) paperwork requirements associated with FCIA insurance are too great. In addition, other complaints included the perception by users that FCIA programs favored larger U.S. firms, credit procedures had to be repeated for each new sale even to established customers, U.S. human rights restrictions eliminated some markets from approval for insurance, and ceilings on FCIA approval authority were too low.

In 1992, Ex-Im canceled its agreement with FCIA to furnish export trade credit insurance for the federal government. Ex-Im began to provide its own credit insurance at that time. It appears that the criticisms during the 1960-1990 period of FCIA insurance operations may have spurred Ex-Im to this decision. Or perhaps Ex-Im wanted to centralize all export trade finance operations—loans, guarantees, and insurance—under the management of one centralized organization.

One of the criticisms of both Ex-Im and FCIA centered on the perception that small exporters were not given the attention that large firms received from both organizations. During the 2000–2001 period, nearly 80 percent of Ex-Im's transactions were aimed at small export firms. The other side of the coin is that large firms do receive the largest absolute financial assistance from Ex-Im since small firm trade finance is still quite small if the average size of the transaction financed is considered.

In 1979, Ex-Im began a cooperative program with PEFCO. The latter organization bought existing loans from banks and nonbank financial institutions. Ex-Im guaranteed the loans and, thus, this program was especially helpful to developing countries. Ex-Im has been criticized by some who believe that some of its financial assistance is actually foreign aid. Ex-Im is not supposed to be a foreign economic assistance agency. That role is the focus of the U.S. Agency for International Development. However, Ex-Im's long-term loans made to finance, for example, commercial jet aircraft imports from the United States is, in reality, a form of economic assistance.

EVALUATION OF THE ENTIRE U.S. SYSTEM

Many of the complaints made about FCIA insurance have been remedied by changes in the organization's operations. Ex-Im has concentrated on small export firms in recent years and began to issue its own trade credit insurance policies in 1992. PEFCO has also developed a small business approach. Its short-, medium-, and long-term loans to importers of U.S. goods and services, guaranteed by Ex-Im, facilitates exports which may not be eligible for guarantees or insurance.

Effects of Government Budget Cutting

U.S. government agencies that assist exporters will be hindered in the future by federal budget cuts. These agencies include Ex-Im, the Department of Commerce, the Small Business Administration, and the Commodities Credit Corporation of the Department of Agriculture. The George W. Bush administration has already proposed a nearly 25 percent cut in appropriations for Ex-Im. Exporters will be hard pressed to obtain loan guarantees. States that offer export assistance have budget problems and will have to scale back across the board including their international trade finance operations. Small exporters may have to enter new markets on their own. However, given the tremendously wide variety of resources available from the public and private sectors examined in this book, exporters should still be able to continue their sales abroad. These sales are beneficial in many ways.

Changes in the Banking System

The banking system remains the major source of international trade finance despite the efforts of ECAs and other government agencies and their expansion into other aspects of the business. In recent years, the U.S. banking system has amended some of its previously significant methods of trade finance. For example, the banker's acceptance has been an important method of securitizing the draft written to pay for exports and passing the bank's risk on to a banker's acceptance dealer market, in which investors hold the instruments until maturity. However, the banker's acceptance has declined significantly as a means of trade finance. More and more firms use open account or cash-in-advance payment methods or else banks make loans to exporters or importers that are guaranteed or insured by organizations such as Ex-Im. More banks fund these loans using commercial paper sold in the money markets by their holding companies. Alternately, foreign banks make loans to foreign purchasers, which are funded by loans from PEFCO and guaranteed by Ex-Im when the purchases are U.S. exports.

In addition, banks have begun to utilize e-commerce to streamline international trade transactions, which are often fraught with heavy documentation. The electronic letter of credit has reduced the time and cost of preparing one by the traditional method. In fact, the entire trade transaction can be done electronically thus speeding up the transaction, lowering the cost, and reducing the risk of nonpayment.

MEETING COMPETITION FROM OTHER ECAs

Since the 1970s, Ex-Im has faced strong competition from foreign ECAs. The ECAs in Great Britain, France, and Germany have always been strong competitors. Many emerging-market countries have established ECAs. More than three dozen ECAs now operate in countries around the world. U.S. exporters often use a foreign ECA, such as the Korea Export-Import Bank, to meet their needs for export trade finance because such ECAs offer better, faster, lower cost assistance. The exporter, like foreign exchange traders, do not fly the flag of their country. They export because demand exists for their product and the sale will help their bottom line. If a foreign ECA offers trade finance assistance that is faster and less costly, with less documentation, they will use the foreign agency. Time is money.

Ex-Im can, and has, adjusted its method of operations. It has negotiated common rules for export financing under the auspices of the Organization for Economic Cooperation and Development (OECD) and it has matched credit terms offered by foreign ECAs.[11] The Institute for International Economics held a conference in 2000 to recognize Ex-Im's sixty-fifth anniversary and to examine the challenges facing Ex-Im in the coming decades. Papers presented at the conference examined Ex-Im's present environment and identified new problems and opportunities for the agency in facing a much more sophisticated trade finance system. In Chapter 9 of this book, it was pointed out that Ex-Im operations in some areas are relatively better than those offered by ECGD in Great Britain, Coface in France, and Hermes in Germany.

Significant changes have been made in some of the major foreign ECAs which furnish most of the competition against Ex-Im. A portion of ECGD's operations were sold to the private sector in 1991. These included all transactions involving credit terms of less than two years. ECGD now concentrates on credit insurance and longer-term financing arrangements. This change may make ECGD even more aggressive in competing against the U.S. system. Hermes, the German private insurer that acts as the German Government's ECA, is able to concentrate its activities on its major business of credit insurance. While Ex-Im operates in all three aspects of trade finance, Hermes can concentrate its resources on only one area, that of insuring trade credits.

ECAs in countries such as India and Korea and the multilateral ECAs discussed in Chapter 9—the African Export-Import Bank, Corporación Andina de Fomento, and the Islamic Corporation for Insurance of Investments and Export Credit— may have advantages over Ex-Im in certain areas. These agencies are more familiar with developing countries and their needs than may be the case with ECAs from the industrialized nations. And in the case of some, for example Korea, ECAs from developing countries may be able to compete favorably with Ex-Im for the export finance business of U.S. firms.

Finally, some ECAs may be able to compete favorably against Ex-Im because of their operating philosophy. For example, the Export Development Corporation of Canada (EDC) operates as though it were a private commercial entity with the aim to be financially self-sustaining. It receives little support from the Canadian government yet does not want for funds because it borrows successfully in private financial markets. On the other hand, EDC's operations are concentrated on a small number of Canadian exporters. Thus, its operations are much smaller in comparison with Ex-Im. In addition, Canada has very few banks and so EDC can concentrate its loan guarantee programs on a smaller number of banks than does Ex-Im.

CONCLUSIONS

Ex-Im has had fifty years of sustained, relatively successful operations. FCIA has operated for forty years. PEFCO also has had a long history of successful activities in operating on the import side of the equation. Large U.S. banks have been financing U.S. trade for even longer periods. More and more medium-sized banks have entered the field of international trade finance. Many U.S. banks now offer the nontraditional form of trade financing known as forfaiting, a method once dominated by European banks. Many banks and other nonbank financial intermediaries have used e-commerce methods to develop platforms that provide e-letters of credit or provide other parts of the trade process electronically. Federal and state government agencies offer guarantees for trade credits, and trade associations and other specialized entities offer education about trade and trade finance to U.S. business firms.

Thus, the U.S. system of international trade finance has become one of the most comprehensive in the world. Trade is very important to any country, and this is especially true in the United States. If government regulation of this area becomes even more liberalized and if federal and state governments continue to support the system, U.S. international trade finance should continue to compete favorably on a global basis.

NOTES

1. J. Fred Weston and Barthold Sorge, "Export Insurance: Why the U.S. Lags," *Columbia Journal of World Business* 2 (September–October 1967): 67–76.

2. Ibid., pp. 68–69.

3. Ibid., p. 69.

4. Ibid., p. 71.

5. Lee C. Nehrt, *Financing Capital Equipment Exports* (Scranton, PA: International Text Book Co., 1966), p. 114.

6. Available on-line Jnauary 15, 2003, at www.eca-watch.org, pp. 1–8.

7. Ibid., p. 1.

8. Sandra M. Huszagh and Mark R. Greene, "FCIA: Help or Hindrance to Exports?" *Journal of Risk and Insurance* 49 (June 1982): 258.

9. Ibid., pp. 258–259.

10. Sandra M. Huszagh and Mark R. Greene, "How Exporters View Credit Risk and FCIA Insurance—The Georgia Experience," *Journal of Risk and Insurance* 52 (March 1985): 127.

11. Gary Clyde Hufbauer and Rita M. Rodriguez (eds.), *The Ex-Im Bank in the 21st Century: A New Approach?* (Washington: Institute for International Economics, 2001).

Appendix 1

LEADING EXPORTERS AND IMPORTERS IN MERCHANDISE TRADE, 2001, (US$ BILLIONS AND SHARE PERCENTAGE)

Rank	Exporters	Value	Share
Exports			
1	United States	730.8	11.9
2	Germany	570.8	9.3
3	Japan	403.5	6.6
4	France	321.8	5.2
5	United Kingdom	273.1	4.4
6	China	266.2	4.3
7	Canada	259.9	4.2
8	Italy	241.1	3.9
9	Netherlands	229.5	3.7
10	Hong Kong	191.1	3.1
Imports			
1	United States	1180.2	18.3
2	Germany	492.8	7.7
3	Japan	349.1	5.4
4	United Kingdom	331.8	5.2
5	France	325.8	5.1
6	China	243.6	3.8
7	Italy	232.9	3.6
8	Canada	227.2	3.2
9	Netherlands	207.3	3.2
10	Hong Kong	202.0	3.1

Source: "International Trade Statistics," World Trade Organization, accessed at www.wto.org, February 1, 2003.

Appendix 2

OFFICIAL EXPORT CREDIT AGENCIES IN OECD MEMBER COUNTRIES

Country	Agency	Acronym
Australia	Export Finance and Insurance Corporation	EFIC
Austria	Oesterreichische Kontrollbank AG	OeKB
Belgium	Office National du Ducroire/Nationale Delcrederedienst	ONDD
Canada	Export Development Corporation	EDC
Czech Republic	Export Guarantees Development Corporation	EGAP
	Czech Export Bank	CEB
Denmark	Eksport Keredit Fonden	EKF
Finland	Finnvera Oyj	Finnvera
	FIDE Ltd.	FIDE
France	Compagnie française d'assurance pour le commerce extérieur	COFACE
	Direction des Relations Economiques Extérieures (Ministere de l'Economie)	DREE
Germany	Hermes Kreditversicherungs AG	HERMES
Greece	Export Credit Insurance Organization	ECIO

Country	Agency	Acronym
Hungary	Magyar Exporthitel Biztosito Rt.	MEHIB
Italy	Sezione Speciale per l'Assicurazione del Credito all'Esportazione	SACE
Japan	Export-Import Insurance Department	EID/MITI
	Japan Bank for International Cooperation	JBIC
Korea	Korea Export Insurance Corporation	KEIC
	The Export-Import Bank of Korea	Korea Eximbank
Mexico	Banco National de Comercio Exterior, SNC	Bancomext
Netherlands	Nederlandsche Credietverzekering Maatschappij NV	NCM
Norway	The Norwegian Guarantee Institute for Export Credits	GIEK
Poland	Korporacja Ubezpieczén Kredytow	KUKE
Portugal	Comanhia de Seguro de Créditos, SA	COSEC
Spain	Compania Española de Seguros y Reaseguros de Crédito y caucion, S.A.	CESCC
	Secretaria de Estado de Comercio (Ministerio de Economia)	SEC
Switzerland	Exportkreditnämnden	EKN
United Kingdom	Export Credits Guarantee Department	ECGD

Source: www.oecd.org/ech/act/xcred/ecas.htm, April 12, 2002, pp. 1–2.

Appendix 3

WORLD TRADE CENTERS

World Trade Center of Abidjan
World Trade Center Accra
World Trade Center Aden
Amman World Trade Center
World Trade Center Alaska/
    Anchorage
The World Trade Center
    Association of Antwerp

World Trade Center Asuncion
World Trade Center Auckland
World Trade Center Abu-Dhabi
World Trade Center Aguascalientes
World Trade Center Amsterdam
World Trade Center Ankara
World Trade Center Archamps
World Trade Center Atlanta

World Trade Center Bahrain
World Trade Center Bangalore
World Trade Center Bari
World Trade Center Basel
World Trade Center Batam
World Trade Centre Beijing
World Trade Center Beirut
World Trade Center Bergen GmbH
Brandenburg International
    Airport World Trade Center
World Trade Center Bombay
World Trade Center Boston
World Trade Center Bremen

World Trade Center Brisbane
International Club of West
    Flanders De Hanze vzw (Af)
World Trade Center Bucharest
World Trade Center Budapest
World Trade Center Baltimore
World Trade Center Bangkok
World Trade Center Barranquilla
World Trade Center Club of
    Switzerland, Basel
China World Trade Center
    (Beijing) Ltd.
World Trade Center Belgrade

World Trade Center Berlin
World Trade Center Bilbao
World Trade Center Bogota
World Trade Center Bordeaux
Sud-Quest
World Trade Center Bratislava
World Trade Center Bridgeport

World Trade Center Brno
World Trade Center Association
Brussels A.S.B.L.
World Trade Center Bucharest-Victoria
World Trade Center Buenos
Aires, S.A.

World Trade Center Co., Cairo
World Trade Center Cali
World Trade Center Wales, Cardiff
South Carolina World Trade
Center—Charleston
World Trade Center Chicago
World Trade Center Cleveland
World Trade Center Coimbatore
Stadtsparkasse Köln/Asia Pacific
Center
World Trade Center Columbus
World Trade Center Curaçao
Cyprus World Trade Center,
Nicosia

World Trade Center Calcutta
World Trade Center Caracas
Casablanca World Trade Center
World Trade Center Chattanooga
World Trade Center Club
Chengdu
World Trade Center Club
Chongging
World Trade Center Cochin
World Trade Center Köln
World Trade Center Colombo
World Trade Center Copenhagen
World Trade Center Curitiba

World Trade Center Dalian
World Trade Center Damascus
World Trade Center Dammam
World Trade Center Denver
World Trade Center Doha, Qatar
Dubai World Trade Centre
World Trade Center Düsseldorf
World Trade Center Eindhoven
World Trade Centre Martinique
World Trade Center Frankfurt
The Alliance World Trade Center
(Greater Dallas/Fort Worth)
World Trade Center Dehli-Gurgaon

World Trade Center Detroit/
Windsor
World Trade Center Dresden
World Trade Center Dublin
World Trade Center Edmonton
World Trade Center El Paso/
Juarez
World Trade Center Ft.
Lauderdale, Florida
World Trade Center Frankfurt
(Oder) GmbH

World Trade Center Gaza,
Palestine
World Trade Center Geneva

International Club of Flanders
Scandinavian World Trade Center
(Gothenburg)

World Trade Center Grenoble
World Trade Centre Club
  Guangzhou
World Trade Center Guayaquil
World Trade Center Gdynia
World Trade Center Genoa

World Trade Center Glasgow
The Greenville-Spartanburg
  World Trade Center
Guadalajara World Trade Center
World Trade Center Guatemala
  City

World Trade Center Haikou
World Trade Center Hamburg
Zhejiang World Trade Centre,
  Hangzhou
Chamber of Commerce of the
  Republic of Cuba-Havana
World Trade Trade Ho Chi Minh
  City
State of Hawaii World Trade
Center, Honolulu

Atlantic-Canada World Trade
  Center, Halifax
World Trade Center Hannover
  GmbH
Hefei world Trade Centre Club
World Trade Center Helsinki
World Trade Centre Club Hong
  Kong
Houston World Trade Association
World Trade Center Hyderabad

World Trade Center Indianapolis
World Trade Center Istanbul
World Trade Center Jakarta
World Trade Centre Johannesburg
Jonkoping World Trade Center
World Trade Center Kaohsiung
World Trade Center Katowice
Putra World Trade Centre Kuala
  Lumpur

World Trade Center Irvine
Jacksonville World Trade Center
World Trade Center Jeddah
Safto (Pty)
Greater Kansas City World Trade
  Center
World Trade Center Karachi
World Trade Center Kiel GmbH
World Trade Center Kuwait

World Trade Center La Paz
World Trade Center Canary
  Islands, S.A., Las Palmas
Le Havre World Trade Center
Kentucky World Trade Center,
  Lexington
World Trade Center Lima
World Trade Center Ljubljana
Los Angeles World Trade Center
World Trade Center Lugano
World Trade Center Lyon/
Lyon Commerce International

World Trade Center of Nigeria
  (Lagos)
Nevada World Trade Center, Las
  Vegas
World Trade Center Lausanne
World Trade Center Leipzig
World Trade Center Lille
World Trade Center Lisbon
Greater Los Angeles World Trade
  Center—Long Beach
World Trade Center Luxembourg

World Trade Center Macau SARL
World Trade Center Madrid, S.A.
World Trade Center Mallorca, S.A.
World Trade Center Manchester
World Trade Center Metro Manila
World Trade Center Maracaibo
Kyong-Nam World Trade Center,
    Masan
World Trade Center Medan
World Trade Center Medellin
World Trade Center Memphis
World Trade Center Mexico City
World Trade Center Italy S.R.L.,
    Milan
Montana World Trade Center,
    Missoula
World Trade Center Monterrey
World Trade Center Montpellier
World Trade Center Moscow
World Trade Center Muscat

World Trade Center Madras
World Trade Center Malaga
World Trade Center Managua
Manchester Chamber of
    Commerce & Industry, New
    Delhi
Mediterranean World Trade
    Center, Marseille
World Trade Center Rio Grande
    Valley at McAllen
World Trade Center Melbourne
World Trade Center Metz
World Trade Center Miami
Wisconsin World Trade Center,
    Milwaukee
World Trade Center Montevideo
    C.A.
World Trade Center Montreal
World Trade Center Munich

World Trade Centre Club Nanjing
Bahamas World Trade Center,
    Nassau
World Trade Center of New
    Orleans
World Trade Center Nice
World Trade Centre Nottingham

World Trade Center Nantes
    Atlantique
India Trade Promotion
    Organization
World Trade Center New York
World Trade Center Norfolk
World Trade Center Novosibirsk

World Trade Center Odessa
World Trade Center Osaka
World Trade Center Ottawa

World Trade Center Orlando
World Trade Center Oslo
World Trade Center Oxnard

World Trade Center Panama
World Trade Center Penang
World Trade Centre Perth Pty. Ltd.
World Trade Center Phoenix
World Trade Center Pittsburgh
World Trade Center Port Said
World Trade Center Porto
World Trade Center Poznan

World Trade Center Rhode Island,
    Greater Providence
World Trade Center Paris
World Trade Center Pernambuco
Greater Philadelphia World Trade
    Center
World Trade Center Pointe-a-Pitre
World Trade Center Portland

World Trade Center Porto Alegre
World Trade Center Prague

World Trade Center Puebla
World Trade Center Pusan

World Trade Center Qingdao
World Trade Center Quito

World Trade Center Quebec-
Canada

North Carolina World Trade
Center, Raleigh-Durham
World Trade Center Rijeka
World Trade Center Riyadh
World Trade Center Rotterdam
N.V.

World Trade Center Ramallah
World Trade Center Riga
World Trade Center Rio de Janeiro
World Trade Center Rostock
World Trade Center Ruhr Valley

World Trade Center Sacramento
World Trade Center San Antonio
World Trade Center of San
Francisco, Inc.
World trade Center San Salvador
World Trade Center Santander
American Chamber of Commerce
of the Dominican Republic
World Trade Center Seattle
Korea World Trade Center, Seoul
World Trade Center Shanghai
World Trade Centre Shenzhen
World Trade Centre Singapore
Interpre - World Trade Center
Sofia
World Trade Center Southampton
World Trade Center Split
Minnesota World Trade Center,
St. Paul
World Trade Center Strasbourg
World Trade Center Surabaya

World Trade Centre Sydney
World Trade Center Salzburg
World Trade Center San Diego
World Trade Center of San José,
Costa Rica, S.A.
World Trade Center Santiago
Sao Paulo World Trade Center
World Trade Center Schenectady-
Capital District
World Trade Center Sevilla
Shenyang Sub-Council of CCPIT
World Trade Center Shijiazhuang
World Trade Center Skopje
Bulgarian Chamber of Commerce
and Industry
World Trade Center St. Louis
World Trade Center St. Petersburg
World Trade Center Stockholm
World Trade Center GmbH
Lizenzgesellschaf Stuttgart
World Trade Center Club Szczecin

World Trade Center Tacoma
Taipei World Trade Center Co.,
Ltd.
World Trade Center Tampa Bay
World Trade Center Israel,
Tel-Aviv

World Trade Center Tianjin
World Trade Center Tokyo, Inc.
World Trade Center Toulouse
World Trade Center Tripoli
World Trade Center Turku
World Trade Center Taichung

World Trade Center Tallinn
World Trade Center Tegucigalpa
World Trade Center The Hague
World Trade Center Tijuana

World Trade Centre Toronto
World Trade Center Trinidad and
  Tobago
World Trade Center Tunis

World Trade Center Utrecht
World Trade Center Valencia, S.A.
World Trade Center Varna
World Trade Center Vancouver
World Trade Center Veracruz
World Trade Center Veronafiere
World Trade Center Vienna-
  Airport
World Trade Center Vigo
World Trade Center Vilnius
World Trade Center Warsaw
World Trade Center Washington,
  D.C.

World Trade Center Delaware,
  Inc., Wilmington
Kansas World Trade Center,
  Wichita
World Trade Center Wuhan
World Trade Center Yangon
World Trade Center Zagreb
World Trade Center Zhengzhou
World Trade Center Zurich
World Trade Center Club Xian
The Council for the United States
  and Italy

Source: Available on-line January 22, 2003, at www.iserve.wtca.org/awtc/wtcalpha.html, pp. 1–6.

Selected Bibliography

BOOKS

Aharoni, Yair. *The Foreign Investment Decision.* Boston: Harvard Business School, 1996.

August, Ray. *International Business Law: Text, Cases, and Readings.* Englewood Cliffs, NJ: Prentice Hall, 1993.

Baker, James C. *International Finance: Management, Markets, and Institutions.* Upper Saddle River, NJ: Prentice-Hall, 1998.

Ball, Donald A., and Wendell H. McCulloch, Jr. *International Business: The Challenge of Global Competition.* Chicago: Irwin, 1996.

Daniels, John D., and Lee H. Radebaugh. *International Business: Environments and Operations.* Reading, MA: Addison-Wesley, 1998.

Eaker, Mark R., Frank J. Fabozzi, and Dwight Grant. *International Corporate Finance.* Orlando, FL: Dryden Press, 1996.

Eiteman, David K., Arthur L. Stonehill, and Michael H. Moffett. *Multinational Business Finance.* Boston: Addison-Wesley, 2001.

Eng, Maximo V., Francis A. Lees, and Laurence J. Mauer. *Global Finance.* Reading, MA: Addison-Wesley, 1998.

Eun, Cheol S., and Bruce G. Resnick. *International Financial Management.* Boston: Irwin McGraw-Hill, 1998.

Export Credits Guarantee Division. *Annual Report and Resource Accounts 2000/01.* London: Her Majesty's Stationery Office, 2001.

Export-Import Bank of the United States. *Annual Report FY 2001.* Washington: Author, 2001.

Hufbauer, Gary C., and Rita M. Rodriguez, eds. *The Ex-Im Bank in the 21st Century: A New Approach?* Washington: Institute for International Economics, 2001.

Hughes, Jane E., and Scott B. MacDonald. *International Banking: Text and Cases.* Boston: Addison-Wesley, 2002.

Kim, Suk H., and Seung H. Kim. *Global Corporate Finance: Text and Cases.* Oxford, England: Blackwell, 1999.

Levi, Maurice D. *International Finance: The Markets and Financial Management of Multinational Business.* New York: McGraw-Hill, 1996.

Madura, Jeff. *International Financial Management.* Mason, OH: South-Western, 2003.

Moffett, Michael H., Arthur I. Stonehill, and David K. Eiteman. *Fundamentals of Multinational Finance.* Boston: Addison-Wesley, 2003.

Nehrt, Lee C. *Financing Capital Equipment Exports.* Scranton, PA: International Textbook Co., 1996.

Radebaugh, Lee H., and Sidney J. Gray. *International Accounting and Multinational Enterprises.* New York: John Wiley, 1997.

Shapiro, Alan C. *Multinational Financial Management.* New York: John Wiley, 2003.

Smith, Roy C. *The Global Bankers.* New York: E. P. Dutton, 1989.

U.S. Export-Import Bank. *General Overview.* Washington: U.S. Export-Import Bank, n.d.

ARTICLES

Alden, Edward. "US and Canada: Hefty Cuts Proposed in Export Finance Schemes." *The Financial Times* (London), April 10, 2001, p. 5.

A.T. Kearney, Inc., and the Carnegie Endowment for International Peace. "Measuring Globalization: Who's Up, Who's Down?" *Foreign Policy,* January/February 2003, pp. 60–72.

Baker, James C., and Raj Aggarwal. "SWIFT as an International Funds Transfer Mechanism: User Satisfaction and Challenges." In Yong H. Kim and Venkat Srinivasan (eds.), *Advances in Working Capital Management: A Research Annual.* Greenwich, CT: JAI Press, 1991.

Baker, James C., and Richard J. Wayman. "Forfaiting: A Little-Known Method of International Trade Financing," in William W. Sihler, ed., *Classics in Commercial Bank Lending.* Philadelphia: Robert Morris Associates, 1985, pp. 497–509.

Ball, Deborah. "European Union Gets Ready to Grow." *Wall Street Journal,* October 10, 2002, pp. A12–13.

Banham, Russ. "Letters of Credit Losing Favor with US Exporters: Credit Insurance Seen as More Viable Hedge." *Journal of Commerce,* February 18, 1998, p. 4A.

——. "Maiden Voyage." *CFO* 18 (November 2002): 71–76.

Barovick, Richard. "Forest Products Sector Gives Export Credit Its Due." *Journal of Commerce,* November 12, 1998, p. 10A.

——. "Most Exporters Use Brokers to Guide Them through Maze." *Journal of Commerce,* September 1, 1999, p. 9.

——. "Small Firms in Bind to Get Export Financing in China." *Journal of Commerce,* October 13, 1999, p. 9.

——. "Swiss Insurers Shine in Credit, Political Risk." *Journal of Commerce,* August 27, 1998, p. 8A.

Bell, Jonathan. "E-Trade Finance: the Race is On." *Euromoney,* December 2000, pp. 56–57.

"Boost for South Korea." *Financial Times,* June 11, 1998, p. 4.

Bowen, David. "Learning to Be Safe, Not Sorry." *Euromoney,* January 1985, pp. 133, 139.

Brown, Julie. "Exports Fly High as Government Programs Offer Financing Aid." *Corporate Cashflow* 10 (July 1989): 31–34.

"China Attracts Global Leaders." *Engineering News Record* 238 (June 9, 1997): 14.

Clement, Douglas. "Trading Places." *The Region* (Quarterly Publication of the Federal Reserve Bank of Minneapolis), 16 December 2002): 11–13, 38–41.

Daouas, Mohamed. "Africa Faces Challenges of Globalization." *Finance and Development* 38 (December 2001): 4–5.

Duncan, Robert E. "Knowledge of Financing Options Can Make U.S. Exporters More Competitive." *Business America* 118 (October 1997): 44.

Dunne, Nancy. "Earth Day Fowl Play for Green Americans." *Financial Times,* April 23, 1999, p. 7.

——. "Export Credit Agencies See Business Soar." *Financial Times,* February 4, 1999, p. 6.

Dyer, Geoff. "Agencies Sidestep the Sovereign Squeeze." *Euromoney,* May 1993, pp. 92–96.

Fidler, Stephen, and Khozem Merchant. "U.S., India Announce Deals of Dollars 4bn." *Financial Times,* March 25, 2000, p. 10.

Gilley, Bruce. "Reforming Zeal." *Far Eastern Economic Review* 162 (May 27, 1999): 50.

Guinto, Joseph. "Should Gov't Be in the Business of Subsidizing U.S. Firms Abroad?" *Investor's Business Daily,* May 16, 2001, p. A18.

Harmon, James A. "A Look at Africa and the AIDS Loan; Are African Leaders Misguided in Turning Down a U.S. Export-Import Bank Offer of Loans to Help Fight the AIDS Epidemic? Or Would the Plan Only Add to Their Economic Woes? It's Not Direct Aid, But It's What a Bank Can Offer," *Washington Post,* September 17, 2000, p. B3.

Holstein, Bill. "Congratulations, Exporter! Now about Getting Paid . . ." *Business Week,* January 17, 1994, p. 98.

Huszagh, Sandra M., and Mark R. Greene. "FCIA: Help or Hindrance to Exports." *Journal of Risk and Insurance* 49 (June 1982): 356–268.

——. "How Exporters View Credit Risk and FCIA Insurance—The Georgia Experience." *Journal of Risk & Insurance* 52 (March 1985): 117–132.

Kahn, George A. "Global Economic Integration: Opportunities and Challenges—A Summary of the Bank's 2000 Symposium." *Federal Reserve Bank of Kansas City, Economic Reviews* 85 (Fourth Quarter 2000): 5–12.

Krouse, Peter. "Ex-Im Bank Revisiting Foreign Aid for Business." *Cleveland Plain Dealer,* July 25, 2001, p. C2.

Lexis-Nexis. "Financial News." *Business Editor,* November 6, 2002.

Montagnon, Peter. "Export Finance: A Time for Ingenuity." *Financial Times,* April 20, 1988, Section 3, p. I.

Morse, Laurie. "Eximbank Backs Huge Caterpillar Deal with Russians." *Financial Times,* February 26, 1993, p. 4.

Phifer, Angela M. "Ex-Im Bank's Support for Small Business." *Business America* 118 (October 1997): 32–33.

Platt, Gordon. "Financing Trade—PEFCO Expands Export Financing Deals to Small Businesses with Success." *Journal of Commerce*, October 2, 1996, p. 9.

———. "U.S. Risk Managers Discover Export Credit Insurance." *Journal of Commerce*, April 26, 2000, p. 11.

———. "The Incredible Shrinking Letter of Credit." *Global Finance*, 16 (September 2002): 52.

———. "World's Best Trade Finance Banks 2003." *Global Finance*, 17 (February 2003): 33–38.

Platt, Gordon and Adam Rombel. "World's Best Trade Finance Banks 2002." *Global Finance* 16 (August 2002). Available on-line September 6, 2002, at www.globalf.vwh.net/content/?article_id=186, pp. 1–8.

"Raytheon Says Brazil Extends Big Contract." *Wall Street Journal*, November 28, 1995, p. B6.

Rogoff, Kenneth. "The IMF Strikes Back." *Foreign Policy*, January/February 2003, pp. 39–46.

Rudnik, David. "The Great Leap Forward." *Euromoney*, May 1991, pp. 119–122.

Sandalow, David. "Exports and the Environment." *Financial Times*, July 19, 2001, p. 17.

"Saudi Arabia Inks $1.9 Billion Plane Finance Deal." *Singapore Business Times*, November 24, 1999, p. 16.

"Saudi Mandates Chase to Arrange Largest Eximbank Financing." *Airfinance Journal* 223 (December 1999): p. 14.

"Secured Note Offering, Series L." *Business Wire*, January 23, 2001.

Seib, Gerald F. "Export Credits, a Useful Tool Abroad, Can Leave Taxpayer Holding the Bag." *The Wall Street Journal*, June 5, 1992, p. A12.

"Shin Satellite Seeks $140m Ex-Im Loan." *Bangkok Post*, May 9, 2001, p. 1.

Tavernise, Sabrina. "World Business Briefing: Europe; Russian Banking Partnerships." *New York Times*, December 6, 2000, p. W1.

"U.S. Eximbank Faces Environmental Criticism." *International Trade Finance* 206 (February 25, 1994): p. 7.

"U.S. Eximbank to Provide $1bn Trade Financing." *Financial Times*, March 17, 1998, p. 4.

Weston, J. Fred, and Barthold Sorge. "Export Insurance: Why the U.S. Lags." *Columbia Journal of World Business* 2 (September–October 1967): 67–76.

"WTO Rules against Canadian Dairy Subsidies." *Wall Street Journal*, December 23, 2002, p. A12.

Zoellick, Robert. "Bringing Down the Barriers." *Financial Times*, July 25, 2002. Available on-line December 23, 2002, at www.usconsulate.org.hk/pas /pr/2002/072901.htm, pp. 1–2.

MISCELLANEOUS PUBLICATIONS

Bank of New York. "Press Release by the Bank of New York." Available on-line December 13, 2002, at www.bankofny.com, 2002, p. 1.

Ebert, James. "International Trade Finance: The Banker's Acceptance." Unpublished paper, Kent State University College of Business Administration, August 2002.

Private Export Funding Corporation. *2001 Annual Report*. New York: Private Export Funding Corporation, 2001.

U.S. Department of Agriculture. "Commodity Credit Corporation: 7CFR Part 1493." August 1, 1997.

U.S. Department of Agriculture. "U.S. Export Credit Guarantee Programs: What Every Importer Should Know About the GSM-102 and GSM-103 Programs." November 1996.

U.S. Department of Agriculture. "Will You Get Paid For the Sale You Just Made?" September 1999.

U.S. Export-Import Bank. *Annual Report FY2001*. Washington: U.S. Export-Import Bank, 2001.

World Bank. *Economic Growth Research*. Washington: World Bank, 1997.

WEB SITES

www.afreximbank.com/docs/productinfo.aspx
www.apsu.edu/ext_ed/small_business/
www.baft.org/pages/committees.html
www.bankofny.com
www.bankofny.com/pages/ccbs_tradeservices.htm
www.berneunion.org/uk/about.html
www.business.com/directory/government_and_trade/international_trade/export_asp?query
www.bxa.doc.gov/
www.cato.org/dailys/03-19-02.html
www.census.gov
www.china.org.cn/english/30426.htm
www.coface.com/rub05_actus/pres/020916gb.htm
www.coface.com/rub05_actus/pres/021008gb.htm
www.coudert.com/practice/ecawebkorea.htm
www.credit-to-cash.com/export_import/letter_of_credit.shtml
www.customs.gov/impoexpo/imex_txt.htm
www.dfait-maeci.gc.ca/tna-nac/why-en.asp
www.ec-finance.com/site/about_lcs/letter_of_credit_process.htm
www.edc.ca/corpinfo/whoweare/index_e.htm
www.efic.gov.au/creditinsurance.asp
www.efic.gov.au/exportfinance.asp
www.epinet.org/subjectpages/trade.html
www.exim.go.th
www.exim.gov/mover.html
www.exim.gov/wcgp.html
www.exim-bank.com
www.eximbankja.com/export_factoring.html
www.eximbankindia.com

www.exportinsurance.com/company.htm
www.exportinsurance.com/insloanex.htm
www.exportmichigan.com/calendar.htm
www.factors-chain.com/b2/b2_main.html
www.factors-chain.com/b5/stats2001/fl_main.html
www.fcia.com/aboutfcia.htm
www.fcia.com/apps-info.htm
www.fcia.com/CountryUpdate4-2002.htm
www.fcia.com/exportinsurance.htm
www.fcia.com/spfininstcov.htm
www.fcia.com/whycrins.htm
www.foe.org/act/gs4pr.html
www.freetrade.org/pubs/briefs/tbp-015es.html
www.generalbank.com
www.hbs.edu/projfinportal/ecas.htm
www.hermes-kredit.com
www.hsbc.com
www.iciec.org/
www.importers-exporters.com/loan12.htm
www.ita.doc.gov/industry/otea/usfth/aggregate/h01t53.html
www.jbic.go.jp/english/profile/about/finance/A22/p08.php
www.koreaexim.go.kr/english/eximnews/20020115.htm
www.law.utk.edu/cle/letcred/1-VB.HTM
www.manateeedc.com/florida.asp
www.mdfb.org/export.htm
www.mussonfreight.com/letter.htm
www.odod.state.oh.us/itd/OEFI.htm
www.senate.gov
www.state.vt.us/labind/emplease/elloc.htm
www.un.org/reports/financing/profile.htm
www.unzco.com/basicguide/figure13.html
www.usatrade.gov/website/website.nsf
www.web.worldbank.org
www.wellsfargo.com/inatl/trade_sves/exporters.jhtml
www.winne.com/ghana/SOCS/GNPC.html
www.wto.org/english/news_e/kpres00_e/pr200_e.htm

Index

ABOUT THE AUTHOR

JAMES C. BAKER is Professor of finance and international business at Kent State University. He is the author of several books on international trade and finance, including two published by Quorum Books, a former imprint of Greenwood Publishing Group: *Foreign Direct Investment in Less Developed Countries: The Role of ICSID and MIGA* (1999) and *The Bank for International Settlements: Evolution and Evaluation* (2002).